What Do *You* Think, Mr. Ramirez?

What Do *You* Think, Mr. Ramirez?

The American Revolution in Education

GEOFFREY GALT HARPHAM

The University of Chicago Press ❋ *Chicago and London*

The University of Chicago Press, Chicago 60637
The University of Chicago Press, Ltd., London
© 2017 by The University of Chicago
Published 2017
Printed in the United States of America

26 25 24 23 22 21 20 19 18 17   1 2 3 4 5

ISBN-13: 978-0-226-48078-7 (cloth)
ISBN-13: 978-0-226-48081-7 (paper)
ISBN-13: 978-0-226-48095-4 (e-book)
DOI: 10.7208/chicago/9780226480954.001.0001

Library of Congress Cataloging-in-Publication Data

Names: Harpham, Geoffrey Galt, 1946– author.
Title: What do you think, Mr. Ramirez? : the American revolution in education / Geoffrey Galt Harpham.
Description: Chicago ; London : The University of Chicago Press, 2017. | Includes bibliographical references and index.
Identifiers: LCCN 2016050505 | ISBN 9780226480787 (cloth : alk. paper) | ISBN 9780226480817 (pbk. : alk. paper) | ISBN 9780226480954 (e-book)
Subjects: LCSH: Education, Humanistic—United States. | Education, Humanistic—United States—History. | Education, Higher—United States. | Education—United States—Philosophy. | English literature—Study and teaching (Higher)—United States. | English literature—Study and teaching (Higher)—United States—History—20th century.
Classification: LCC LC1023.H37 2017 | DDC 370.11/2—dc23 LC record available at https://lccn.loc.gov/2016050505

♾ This paper meets the requirements of ANSI/NISO Z39.48-1992 (Permanence of Paper).

To the memory of M. H. Abrams
1912–2015

Contents

Preface

The American system of education, especially higher education, is today in such disarray, with so little consensus about goals, such glaring inequalities, and such confusion about methods, that it is difficult to imagine that it was once innovative, coherent, and aspirational—that it was even a system at all. But while American education has always been decentralized, various, and resistant to central planning, there was, not long ago, a consensus on a few basic principles.

These principles informed what I am calling the "American revolution in education," which crystallized at the end of the Second World War as a national plan to prepare people for a society in which the promise of democracy would at last be fully realized. In 1945, a committee of Harvard professors produced a plan for a national system of education that would reflect national commitments, even a national identity, in the postwar era. *General Education in a Free Society*, or the Redbook as it became known, argued for a system that would serve the nation and display to the world the manner in which a democracy educated its citizens at all levels but especially at the level of higher education. Unlike any other in the world, that system was to be *universal*, *general*, and *liberal*. At the time, the determination to create such a system constituted a radical democratic event.

The twenty-five or thirty years following World War II are now often referred to as the golden age of higher education, but in recent years many aspects of that midcentury conception have been criticized. The Redbook's earnest accounts of the "whole man," "wisdom," and "moral citizenship" now seem expressions of a Cold War sensibility that we are accustomed to think of as socially complacent, arrogant, presumptuous, morally naïve, and politically defensive. And the idea of a prescribed curriculum for higher education in particular did not survive the antiauthoritarian turbulence of the 1960s. But today's clichés were yesterday's radical democratic events, the fossils of the present were the successful adaptations of the past, and throbbing beneath the surface of the Redbook's program were the ground notes of a national self-understanding that did not emerge suddenly as the war was ending but had developed over many years. We should not confuse the surface for the system, the real depth and richness of which exceeded the limited perspectives and intentions of the individuals who, for a moment, had it in their care.

This depth and richness have been recognized elsewhere. In acknowledgment of the remarkable successes of American colleges and universities in contributing not just to research but to social creativity in general, systems of higher education all over the world are now being brought into rough conformity with American premises and practices, including standardized degree programs, the adoption of new and higher enrollment goals, the reformation of teaching practices, and the introduction of curricula with two years of breadth and depth before the student chooses a major. The educational and cultural value of liberal education, and of the humanities in particular, is increasingly recognized, not only in Europe but also in many other parts of the world, including some without a history of democracy. The results have, however, been mixed because the American system grew out of American culture, and cannot be easily transplanted to other cultures and traditions, where it has often seemed foreign and inauthentic, a graft rather than a growth.

To get some sense of the differences between the American

system and others, we can compare ways of describing one of the most prominent features of American higher education, the humanities. For a sample of American discourse, consider *The Heart of the Matter: The Humanities and Social Sciences*, a 2013 report prepared by an independent panel of experts under the aegis of the American Academy of Arts and Sciences at the request of the United States Congress. "The humanities," the report says, "remind us where we have been and help us envision where we are going. Emphasizing critical perspective and imaginative response, the humanities ... foster creativity, appreciation of our commonalities and our differences, and knowledge of all kinds."[1] These are the familiar accents of a traditional American discourse on the humanities—noninstrumental, nonvocational, expansive, and open. Stressing the pleasing combination of knowledge and imagination, common values and cultural differences, broad cultural vision and individual human capabilities, the passage plainly seeks to inspire with a vision of humane cosmopolitan inclusivity. The report was submitted to the United States Congress as an affirmation of a longstanding and officially recognized connection between the humanities and democracy. As of this writing, in 2016, no consequences have ensued.

Elsewhere in the world, some of the same notes are struck, but the tone can be jarringly different. As one example standing for many others, each with its own distinctive features, take the "Vilnius Declaration: Horizons for Social Science and the Humanities."[2] Issued in English by the European Research Council in 2013, the same year as *The Heart of the Matter*, this document is part of Horizon 2020, a massive European Union program of support for research and innovation. The humanities are well provided for in Horizon 2020—but what *are* the humanities? The Vilnius boilerplate is revealing:

Europe will benefit from wise investment in research and innovation and Social Sciences and Humanities, SSH, are ready to contribute. European societies expect research and innovation to be the foundation for growth. Horizon 2020 aims to implement inter-disciplinarity and an integrated scientific approach. If research is to serve society, a resilient partnership with all relevant actors is required. A wide variety of perspectives will provide critical insights to help achieve the benefits of innovation. The effective integration of SSH requires that they are valued, researched and taught in their own right as well as in partnership with other disciplinary approaches.

Consequences have definitely ensued from this program: €80 million to be distributed between 2014 and 2020, with 17 or 18 percent customarily allocated each year to the humanities and social sciences.

But while American academics might gape in admiration and wonderment at the money flowing from this acronym-rich program, they might also feel some discomfort at the reference to an "integrated scientific approach," and a general sense of alarm at the conscription of academic disciplines in the service of "innovation" and "growth." Where, they might ask, do imaginative responses, creativity, and an interest in the past come in? Where, in short, are the humanities "in their own right"?

The answer to the first question is "nowhere." The development of individual capacities simply does not figure in Horizon 2020, which places all the emphasis on "societal challenges." The answer to the second is that they are "integrated" or "embedded": "As a cross-cutting issue of broad relevance, Social Sciences and Humanities (SSH) research is fully integrated into each of the general objectives of Horizon 2020. Embedding SSH research across Horizon 2020 is essential to maximize the returns to society from investment in science and technology."[3] It appears that while the humanities may be valued "in their own right," support from Horizon 2020 is contingent on their ability to attach themselves to, or secrete themselves in, broad-based interdisciplinary projects that try to solve big problems in "leadership in enabling and industrial technologies," "excellent science," "health, demographic change and wellbeing," "food security," "climate action," or "secure societies." In fact, all disciplines and projects are supported under Horizon 2020 only insofar as they can claim that they are addressing the specified societal challenges.[4] Universities are presumed to be research engines and state assets in direct competition with private, for-profit companies. Nothing in the Vilnius Declaration or in the rhetoric of Horizon 2020 reflects a philosophy of education as such. Indeed, the whole program seems only marginally connected to education as that term is traditionally understood in the United States.[5]

The notion that education should not merely train people for the civil service or the professions but should form people in a more holistic way as culturally versatile and self-governing citizens was developed at the beginning of the nineteenth century by Wilhelm von Humboldt and Johann Gottfried von Herder and given the name of *Bildung*. But while the German university system they theorized and helped develop—the historical antecedent and institutional model for all subsequent research universities—was organized with the needs of the nation or society at large in mind, that system never aspired to educate an entire population. It was in the vast, various, and far less systematic system of higher education that developed in the post-WWII United States that the concept of *Bildung* was applied to a national program of universal education, one that would structure the curricula of institutions ranging from community colleges to elite, private research institutions.

Even at the most prestigious science-oriented research universities, the stated goals of the undergraduate program prominently include references to the nonutilitarian virtues they seek to develop. Caltech tells prospective students, "We investigate the most challenging, fundamental problems in science and technology in a singularly collegial, interdisciplinary atmosphere, while educating outstanding students to become creative members of society"; and MIT says it seeks "to develop in each member of the MIT community the ability and passion to work wisely, creatively, and effectively for the betterment of mankind."[6] Both institutions offer a "liberal" education that reflects certain assumptions about the freedom of the individual, the purpose of education, the position of the individual in society, and the conditions of human flourishing, all of which contribute to a way of thinking about education that was once, and should still be, considered progressive and democratic.

Contemporary conversations about this way of thinking are often defensive if not defeatist, and ideas once thought innovative and even inspiring have become swaddled in clichés and banalities. The conversation can, however, be put on a new footing if we try to recall or reconstruct the historical processes by which the inspiring became the insipid. My argument is that the commitment to create a national system of general education reflected not just an immediate geopolitical context, with all the limitations and biases that inevitably reveal themselves with the passage of time, but also a national self-understanding with very deep historical and cultural roots. This understanding continues to challenge us in the most productive way.

The first section of this book undertakes a genealogy of that postwar moment and an account of the remarkably complex and fertile concept of general education, at once spacious and strangely limited, prescriptive and patrician in its mode and yet—like the Declaration of Independence—democratizing in its effects. The second section explores the distinctive position in American political life of the concept of opinion, which serves as a link between foundational principles of American civil society and specific emphases in American educational practice. It is the exceptionally high and repeatedly affirmed value placed by Americans on the right to one's own opinion that is ultimately responsible for the elevation of what became known as the humanities, as well as for the prominence of the discipline of English in the American system. The means by which this prominence was established is the subject of the third section, which traces the remarkable series of events by which English was able to advance itself at that postwar moment as the central humanistic discipline, the primary curricular instrument of democratic aspirations. In tracing these events, I am proposing a new model for understanding the history of that discipline.

My goal throughout is to recover the deep currents of commitment and aspiration that have informed an American philosophy of education. The approach is historical, but my premise is that the system of education that was formalized around the middle of the twentieth century contains precious conceptual resources that, if liberated from the defensive, moralizing, and banalized discourse that has for many years been associated with liberal education and the humanities, might, like viable genetic material immured in petrifaction, be reactivated and allowed to discover new forms in a contemporary world.

My hope, in short, is that this book might encourage the belief that the American revolution in education, like the pursuit of happiness and the search for a more perfect union, has not yet run its course.

The American Revolution in Education

Mr. Ramirez Comes to America

On a recent visit to a Midwestern university, I was approached by an elderly man who announced that he wanted to tell me his story. A half century before, he said, he was a teenaged refugee from Cuba, washed up on a Florida shore—an exemplary instance, as he put it, of "tired, poor, wretched refuse" come to this country in search of a better life. He had no money, no English, no American relatives, no friends, no papers. After a couple of years of rough living, picking up odd jobs and some English, he sought to better himself. He got a GED and enrolled in a community college where, in order to meet a requirement, he took a literature class and found himself reading, or rather staring helplessly at, the words of a Shakespeare sonnet. What did they mean? What was Shakespeare trying to say? "I always sat at the back and kept my head down," the man said. But one day, he said, the instructor came over, stood beside him, and asked, "Mr. Ramirez, what do *you* think?"

As the man I am calling Mr. Ramirez told me, "I had no thoughts at all, and nothing to say." But he made brief eye contact with his tormentor; and while the teacher's probing attention eventually found another target, the event stuck in Mr. Ramirez's mind because, as he told me, "it was the first time anybody had asked me that question. And that," he said, beaming, "is my story." He shook my hand, gave me his card, and departed. Back in the hotel, I read his card. Mr. Ramirez had apparently recovered from his embarrassment at some point, because he was now an emeritus professor of comparative literature.[1]

Humankind hungers for learning—we are, as observers of the human condition since Aristotle have said, curious creatures in every sense—and countless people all over the world living in restricted or impoverished circumstances have discovered through some chance occurrence a powerful intellectual or imaginative drive within themselves that had lain dormant and undiscovered, but which, once awakened, could not be denied. But Mr.

Ramirez's is an American story. A similar tale told by a person who had arrived by desperate chance in England, France, Brazil, South Africa, Germany, Chile, Thailand, China—or Cuba— might be considered remarkable and moving, but it would hardly inspire the blend of empathy and national pride that Professor Ramirez could count on inspiring in me. Indeed, the same story set in any other country might seem more an improbable fluke, even a kind of mistake. In America, it was the result of a deliberate policy. The presumption built into the American system that Mr. Ramirez was worth educating, an entailment of a larger hospitality to orphans of the world's storms, gives his story its peculiar force as an astonishing conjunction of individual need and national principles. The system works! A nobody, a mere atom in the human mass, comes to this country, is treated with respect in the form of an invitation wrapped in a challenge, and becomes not only a grateful and productive citizen but a man of learning.

How did this excellent result come about? What assumptions about the goals of education, the ends of human existence, and the character of American society had to be in place in order for that teacher in that classroom in that institution to point that finger at that individual and ask that fateful question? What were we thinking when we created the system that could work such wonders?

Mr. Ramirez plainly regarded his story as nothing short of miraculous, which it was, both for reasons he well understood and for many that neither he nor any other individual could have grasped. What follows is an attempt to think backward from that singular moment to the conditions that made it possible. I will not attempt a history of American educational thinking or practices, which would quickly become a chronicle of overlapping and mutating movements and countermovements, a swirling tangle of earnest experiments, utopian reforms, revanchist reactions, pragmatic concessions to the reality of scarce resources, and terminological disputes. I want rather identify the deep currents of commitment and aspiration that informed an American system of education, a system that was at one time able to produce countless versions and variants of Mr. Ramirez's story, many in the mainstream culture. (I count myself, a product of midwestern suburbia, as one of the beneficiaries of the midcentury American educational covenant.) The subject, in other words, is not how a solitary community college teacher managed to bring out the best in this one unpromising student, but rather how an American educational system was constructed, partly by intent and partly by chance, to maximize the possibility that such miracles might occur. And then, within that question, how the miracle-making role was allocated to the humanities. And finally, how the study of literature emerged as the focus of democratic aspirations.

The young Mr. Ramirez washed up on the right shore at the right moment, for at that time—the twenty-five or thirty years following WWII, a time now commonly considered the golden age in American higher education,[2] when the system enjoyed unprecedented self-confidence, success, and public support— everything was in his favor, including the fact that refugees from Cuba were far more likely to be welcomed than undocumented immigrants from other countries. And his story bears brilliantly efficient witness to many golden age premises concerning American values and aspirations. Think about it: in his account, a beneficent and bounteous America welcomes the impoverished and outcast of the world, who come to this country to repair their damaged fortunes and begin life anew. The instrument of that hospitality and the guarantor of opportunity is education. The humanities are a crucial part of the system, giving even those clinging to the lowest rung of the ladder, those whose imaginative horizons are likely to be the most restricted, an opportunity to think of themselves as the inheritors of a tradition, to acquire some sense of cultural knowledge and cultural differences, and to deploy that knowledge in forming an expanded and enriched sense of themselves and their possibilities. An abundantly gifted person, Mr. Ramirez might have made a successful life anywhere in the world, but he would not have found such premises so purposefully embraced in any other country.

To be sure, it may be an overstatement to describe as a "system" a set of practices so responsive to local initiatives, so dependent on local resources, and so vulnerable to gusts of reformist energy, lassitude, inertia, and political fashions. As Hannah Arendt pointed out in 1958, it is only in America that education is a political issue.[3] But in a sense, the disorderly interplay of all these factors actually constitutes the American system of education. From the beginning that system has charted a path very different from its European antecedents, first because of the needs of the Puritan settlements for learned clergy and for congregations that could read the Bible, and then, after the Revolution, because representative democracy forced people to govern themselves, as they would not have had to do in a country with a hereditary peerage, an established church, or an unchallenged ruling class. Even without a stable consensus about what people must know in order to govern themselves, much less how to teach it to them, the American system had, by the time Mr. Ramirez struggled ashore, come to exemplify a few distinctive propositions in that it was, throughout the land, *universal*, *general*, and *liberal*.

The system was *universal* in the sense that, by design, the overwhelming majority of students had access to publicly funded secondary and postsecondary schools whose curricula included an academic component. It was *general* in the sense that certain kinds of courses were to be required of all students on the premise that education should be organized around the purpose of creating responsible, accountable, and self-sufficient human beings. And it was *liberal* in the sense that students were exposed to different kinds of knowledge, which were studied for their own sake, without any immediate purpose or goal in mind. Further, the fact that Mr. Ramirez was brought face to uncomprehending face with Shakespeare also testifies to an assumption that some kinds of cultural knowledge carry special value and content that cannot be reduced to information—indeed, that they possess this value and this content even in the absence of full or definite understanding—and that the educational system should expose students to this kind of knowledge no matter how strange, unnecessary, or unproductive many might find the exercise to be. And finally, the fact that his teacher solicited Mr. Ramirez's opinion of Shakespeare testifies to a conviction that literary study, especially at the undergraduate level, centrally involves acts of judgment and interpretation arising from an individual's reading of a text. This was important, because, as I contend in the second section of this book, opinion has a foundational status in both literary interpretation and in American civil discourse, and beyond that, in American self-understanding.

All these premises have been contested and in some cases rejected outright since Mr. Ramirez arrived in the early 1960s. We are no longer in the golden age. And so, in explaining the remarkable success of the American educational system in this case, or class of cases, we must recall a whole series of assumptions and practices that have, over the years, been weakened, compromised, or abandoned.

Mr. Ramirez would not have had his humiliating but transformative moment if the federal government and the local community had not made a series of commitments, beginning with the promise of universal access to higher education, which entailed a system of community colleges with an academic program that included the humanities.[4] That program itself reflected a local embrace of liberal education, and a commitment to two foundational principles, the first to individual freedom and enrichment and the second to social cohesion and civic responsibility.[5]

Each of these principles was given a memorable formulation by one of the nation's founders. In a letter well known to humanists, John Adams wrote to his wife Abigail in 1780, "I must study Politicks and War that my sons may have liberty to study Mathematicks and Philosophy. My sons ought to study Mathematicks and Philosophy, Geography, natural History, Naval Architecture, navigation, Commerce and Agriculture, in order to give their Children a right to study Painting, Poetry, Musick, Architecture, Statuary, Tapestry and Porcelaine."[6] In the dreamy vision evoked by this passage, people once freed from the burdens of want and oppression will become increasingly refined and subtilized, eventually settling into a state of aesthetic bliss. More pragmatic, Thomas Jefferson saw the diffusion of knowledge as a necessary condition of democracy. If knowledge were concentrated in a single class, he thought, the result would be a reconstituted and potentially despotic aristocracy—the progeny of people like Adams and himself perpetuating their privilege forever by obtaining a monopoly on knowledge. "Every government," Jefferson wrote in *Notes on the State of Virginia* (1781–83), "degenerates when trusted to the rulers of the people alone."[7] Governments and the people they govern would, Jefferson thought, flourish only if significant numbers of people were proficient in such subjects as mathematics, the sciences, languages, anatomy, medicine, moral philosophy, and law, thus qualifying themselves for leadership in society. Democracy's viability, he concluded, hangs on the success of a "crusade against ignorance."[8]

Both Adams and Jefferson saw education as the solution to a problem specific to democracy, and even as the very core of democracy itself, the essence of the American experiment. For Adams, the problem was how the nation's most privileged citizens could occupy the unused time and energy created by the elimination of external threats and immediate needs. For Jefferson, the issue was how to improve the moral and intellectual character of the population so they could govern themselves. Neither man could be called a populist, or even a supporter of direct democracy. Adams's vision of successive generations evolving (or devolving) from warriors into dilettantes was, at least in this passage, specifically restricted to his distinguished lineage and their peers; he did not contemplate an entire population of farmers, shopkeepers, tradesmen, and peasants spending their days admiring tapestry and porcelain.[9] For Jefferson, the educational system would have a sifting function, identifying the most talented and ambitious students, who would be recruited into leadership positions—a process, as he told Adams in a phrase that has become famous, of "pure selection of these natural aristoi into the offices of government."[10]

The Founding Father rhetoric with which Jefferson articulated his vision for education has been much admired. Among other worthy goals, Jefferson wished "to develop the reasoning faculties of our youth, enlarge their minds, cultivate their morals, and instill into them the precepts of virtue and order; to enlighten them with mathematical and physical sciences, which advance the arts and administer to the health, the subsistence and comforts of human life; and, generally, to form them to habits of reflection and correct action, rendering them examples of virtue to others and of happiness within themselves."[11] Jefferson's understanding of both human nature and the needs of a civil society led him to argue that what we would today call a liberal education was a public good, as much a necessity as a virtue in a democratic society in which people were expected to work to improve their conditions and manage their own affairs. His convictions about the intimate connection between a democratic polis and a multidimensional education embracing languages, mathematics, mechanics, chemistry, "fluxions," pneumatics, law, grammar, ethics, and belles lettres have been cited countless times in efforts to promote the liberal arts. Less often noted, and then rarely with approval, is his equally heartfelt belief that humankind was in effect self-sorted through "natural" inequalities that would be exposed and then aggravated by the educational system.

Some of the opinions of the omnidirectional genius of Monticello would place him on the right edge of today's political spectrum. The passage quoted above on the role of education in preventing the rise of a permanent ruling class occurs in the section of *Notes on the State of Virginia* devoted to laws and the administration of justice, a section that includes lists of crimes punishable by death and dismemberment and prescribes gibbeting for initiators of duels. The same section contains Jefferson's most pungent deliverances on "the real distinctions which nature has made" between the races, which are said to include, in addition to profound differences in powers of reasoning and imagination, other differences pertaining to beauty and general physiognomic suitability. The ability of whites to blush, for example, compares favorably to "that eternal monotony, which reigns in the countenances, that immoveable veil of black which covers all the emotions of that other race" (264–65).[12] Jefferson brought his formidable knowledge of biology to bear on the issue of racial difference. "They secrete less by the kidneys," he noted; they have a "greater degree of transpiration" perhaps owing to "a difference of structure in the pulmonary apparatus," "they seem to require less sleep," "they are more ardent after their female" but appear to be incapable of the "delicate mixture of sentiment and sensation" characteristic of love. And, their lesser need of sleep notwithstanding, they demonstrate when not working a puzzling "disposition to sleep" (265). For Jefferson, "that other race" is strange, tragic, and uneducable, almost a distinct species.

"Natural" differences also play a decisive role among whites. Under Jefferson's plan, many children might receive basic schooling ("reading, writing, and arithmetic"), but only one in each school would be chosen to attend one of the twenty grammar schools in the country, where he would be taught Greek, Latin, geography, and mathematics. Once in grammar school, a high-stakes test would produce a winner, "the best genius of the whole." "By this means," Jefferson wrote, "twenty of the best geniuses will be raked from the rubbish annually," and "the residue dismissed" (*Notes on the State of Virginia*, 272). Of these twenty, half would become grammar school teachers and the triumphant ten remaining would go to college. A meritocracy, in short, but not a democracy of opportunity.

Despite these pronounced limitations in their democratic vistas, both Adams and Jefferson understood that education would play a different and more central role in the progress of the new nation than in other nations. Jefferson in particular grasped the key fact, that the overarching point and purpose of education was to produce self-governing citizens, not scholars, and that, as a consequence, educational policy and practice should be driven by the needs and principles of democracy rather than by those of the academy or the professions. Most important, both men identified with great prescience the abiding concerns and main

lines of force that would come to dominate American thinking on education. The line descending from Adams, or at least
from the sentiment to which he gave voice in this brief passage
in a letter to his wife, was essentially humanist, with fortunate
individuals freed from immediate wants or threats looking to
artifacts of the cultural past for refined pleasures, edification, and
instruction; the line descending from Jefferson was pragmatic,
future directed, and focused on problem solving and the needs
of the community.

Teaching the Intangibles: General Education in Postwar America

In time, "general education"—a curriculum that included either
core courses required of all students or a set of distribution requirements all students must fulfill, a more purposeful and directed version of liberal education—emerged as the name for
the kind of crusade against ignorance that a democracy must
wage. In what has been described as "a remarkable paroxysm
that swept through the postsecondary system" in the 1920s and
1930s, at least thirty independent general education programs
were established, with the most prominent being at Columbia
University and the University of Chicago.[13] At first, most such
programs arose in institutions that were necessarily exclusive,
unembarrassed about their Jeffersonian mission of educating a
leadership class. Some educational theorists, like the influential
Harvard literary scholar Irving Babbitt, were explicit about their
commitment to training the few rather than uplifting the many;
others, such as University of Chicago president Robert Maynard
Hutchins, defended the Great Books program at his university
on the grounds that it was democratic in a particular way, serving
the larger interests of society by providing its future leaders with
a critical perspective on industrial and professional society.[14] For
many observers, the connection between a high-minded program
at an elite university and democracy throughout the nation must

have seemed tenuous, since only a tiny number of men—and no women, African Americans, or poor people, and a limited number of Jews—would ever be exposed to it.[15]

How, then, did Mr. Ramirez, who was at the time certainly not Ivy League material, ever encounter general education? The answer is that general education gradually assumed a more "Jacksonian" form, dedicating itself to the task of educating not just the natural aristoi but the population at large—and not just in anatomy, moral philosophy, and fluxions, but in a range of subjects. Elite postsecondary institutions may have attracted the most public attention, but larger numbers of students were being exposed to more worldly versions of the program devised by such figures as Horace Mann, John Dewey, and Alexander Mieklejohn, all of whom described their educational philosophies in terms that suggested a wider applicability beyond the institutions they led, to the nation as a whole.

The crucial moment in the democratization of general education was the publication in 1945 of *General Education in a Free Society*—the Redbook, as it became known, after the color of its cover.[16] This book was the brainchild of Harvard president James Bryant Conant, who, in 1943, with the outcome of the war still very much in doubt, convened a group of Harvard administrators and scholars, gave them the unthinkable sum of $60,000, and instructed them to come up with a new master plan for the nation's educational system at the high school and college levels. The resulting volume, published when the lava of war had barely begun to cool, became extraordinarily influential—"the bible," as the Columbia sociologist Daniel Bell put it, "of general education," as well as "the national symbol of renewal" after the war.[17] The Redbook represents the fullest and most authoritative expression of the principle of general education, but like the Bible itself, it also gave voice to tensions, contradictions, and impasses around which schismatic movements subsequently formed. Indeed, it may have been the multiauthored equivocality of the Redbook that made it so broadly appealing and fertile in its effects. There were probably very few people who read the entire book with sufficient attention to be greatly disturbed by its internal tensions, but there were many who read enough to confirm the views they already had.

The committee's charge began with more local issues. The elective system introduced (at Harvard) in the late nineteenth century to replace the highly restricted classical curriculum had increased student freedom of choice but had done so at the cost of curricular coherence.[18] The fragmentation and increasing specialization of knowledge were registered in both the growth of powerful departments—then as now a development much lamented by administrators—and in a curricular jungle in which four hundred courses, none of them required, were offered to Harvard undergraduates. Conant wanted to restore order to the curriculum so that a Harvard degree would mean something definite beyond the brute fact of prestige. While some forms of disorder lay beyond the committee's comprehension (including two problems for which no ready solution presented itself, "the elephantine growth of athletics" and "the strange flourishing of fraternities"), the committee made an effort to address the issue of incoherence by devising a hybrid system (Redbook, 33, 34). Some courses—six of the sixteen required to graduate, with required courses in the sciences, the social sciences, and the humanities—would be designated as general education, representing knowledge that the committee deemed essential for any educated person, while the rest would be considered "specialized education." While, as John Guillory notes, the basic premises of general education were "already rather stale" by the time the committee was formed, it was also true that there was no other model for education with anything like comparable support, and Louis Menand reminds us that general education is "a twentieth-century phenomenon . . . in some respects, the most modern part of the modern university."[19] Determined not only that the Harvard curriculum should be reformed but that the new system should serve as a pattern for educational institutions across the postwar nation, Conant demanded in addition to suggestions and guidelines a fully worked-out rationale, a national philosophy of education that could be adopted by colleges, universities, and high schools all over the country in the confidence that they were doing the work of democracy.

A new philosophy was needed in part because of the radical change about to come to the educational system as a consequence of the Servicemen's Readjustment Act of 1944, better known as the GI Bill, which encouraged immense numbers of returning soldiers to pursue postsecondary education. Because of the GI Bill, higher education was about to become mass education. Like general education itself, this arrangement was decisively American. The connection between democratic citizenship and higher education established by the GI bill would have been inconceivable even in prewar Europe, where secondary education was in many countries optional, and postsecondary education was available only to those seeking to enter professions. But in postwar America it seemed logical, even imperative, that the opportunity to improve one's condition through education should be made part of the democratic compact.[20] A private citizen and head of the most exclusive institution in the country (which he was trying to make even more selective, or at least differently selective, through the innovative use of standardized testing), Conant seized the opportunity to take advantage of a war-forged spirit of national unity by proposing that the nation's colleges and universities, as well as its secondary schools, assert their own commitment to the fundamental principles of the American polity by providing people instruction in "the general art of the free man and the citizen" (Redbook, 54). "War," the Redbook notes, "is the great educator"; among its lessons was the kind of education required of a democracy (276).

The postwar college as envisioned by the Redbook was to be in effect a national security institution, advertising to the world American values of openness, freedom, equality, and opportunity. With a startling candor, the Redbook announces the arrival of an exultant new superpower, hungry for the future, eager to show the world what an affluent society, to anticipate the phrase used by John Kenneth Galbraith, was capable of.[21] It begins with an epigraph, a passage from Pericles's funeral oration as recorded by Thucydides: "We need no Homer to praise us. Rather, we have opened the whole earth and sea to our enterprise and raised everywhere living memorials to our fortune" (3). Indeed, the Redbook is Homer's Homer, praising the Greeks and the rest of the "Western tradition" as the fountainhead of freedom and liberty, a bright stream of enlightenment to which Americans now had privileged access as a consequence of their military preeminence, inclusive history, commitment to democracy, and present prosperity. For the authors of the Redbook, the imminent Allied victory would mark the moment when the United States would be able to realize the commitments to individual freedom made in the Declaration of Independence and to the search for "a more perfect union" mentioned in the Preamble to the Constitution.

Both commitments receive their due in the Redbook, which often seems in the reading to slalom between the principles of individual self-realization and civic virtue. At many points, civic virtue seems to prevail. Stressing "common discipline," a "common spirit," "common culture," "common purposes," "common beliefs," a "common fate," "common standards," and a "common view of life," and insisting at every opportunity on the need for consolidation, protection, and unity, the Redbook reads in places like a manifesto for community and even conformity. But overall, the vision of the American community of the future that emerges from the Redbook is that of a polity in which the commitment to individual self-determination in a meritocratic society is the most deeply held of the common values by which the nation was defined. Communicating that bipolar vision, and providing the intellectual equipment that would enable people to realize it, was to be the task of education at the secondary and postsecondary levels. Education would become a laboratory of democracy, and schools sites of individual betterment for all, including both native-born Americans and people such as Mr. Ramirez, who came to the country from the dark places of the earth in search of a better life. "Our purpose," Conant wrote in his charge to the committee, "is to cultivate in the largest possible number of our future citizens an appreciation of both the responsibilities and the benefits which come to them because they are Americans and are free" (Redbook, xiv–xv).

The phrase "laboratory of democracy" evokes one of the first and most widely noticed general education programs, the Laboratory School founded in 1896 by John Dewey at the University of Chicago. So great was Dewey's influence through his writings as well as through this school itself that no general education program that followed could ignore his example. Antitheoretical, anti-idealistic—even, some felt, antiacademic—Dewey saw the world, not the classroom, as the primary setting for education, with each school representing "an embryonic community life."[22] Throughout his career Dewey argued for an underlying unity between the experiences made available through art and those encountered in everyday life, but at the heart of his theories about education was an insistence on a "progressive" model of general education based on problem solving and practical skills, an orientation that led naturally to an emphasis on the sciences, with their respect for evidence, objectivity, and rationality.

For Dewey, the connection between the growth of democracy and the development of the experimental method in science was clear and compelling. Science, he argued, is the very instrument of modernity. If education could implant in students the essentials of the scientific method, a generally diffused democratic habit of mind would result. As he somewhat inelegantly put it, "The problem of an educational use of science is then to create an intelligence pregnant with belief in the possibility of the direction of human affairs by itself. The method of science engrained through education in habit means emancipation from rule of thumb and from the routine generated by rule of thumb procedure" (*Democracy and Education*, 263). At a time (1900) when, by his calculation, half of all children left school after the fifth year of elementary school, 5 percent went on to high school, and 1 percent attended college, the reformation of education to "appeal to those whose dominant interest is to do and make" had political as well as educational consequences (*School and Society*, 28).

Dewey was in many respects a powerfully original thinker, but his faith in the connection between science and democracy was a conventional prejudice. This connection, as Andrew Jewett has recently demonstrated, had been firmly established in the decades following the Civil War, when science was widely viewed as a source of intellectual authority especially well suited to democracy in that it was committed to free and open curiosity and to a teachable practice leading to repeatable results. No respecter of persons, titles, or credentials, science provided a rationalist and democratizing counter to inequalities in the broader culture, where status was attached to wealth, genealogy, or patterns of sensibility and responsiveness that could only be mysterious and oppressive to those who did not have them. Science, as Jewett puts it, was thought by many to embody and encourage "a set of personal virtues, skills, beliefs, and values that could ground a modern, democratic public culture."[23] As colleges and universities began, in the second half of the nineteenth century, to detach themselves from the religious organizations that had originally sponsored or supported them, many of them found ways to retain the idea that knowledge might ultimately constitute a unified field with a definite moral purpose. In a postreligious environment, science was able to step into the place of moral privilege formerly held by the church.

From the vantage point of the present, we can see more clearly the limitations of "scientific democracy," including epistemological naïveté, insensitivity to the effects of corporate capitalism, and plain confusion or misprision; but for Dewey and others, it was self-evidently clear that science represented empiricism, pragmatism, and democracy, while the humanities did not. This identification of science and democracy lasted up to the middle of the twentieth century.

But not beyond. By midcentury, the general perception of the character of scientific inquiry had been greatly altered by two factors: the rise of the idea of value-neutral research, which had the effect of disambiguating knowledge and morality, and the dominance of instrumental rationales for science. These do not necessarily go together, but they were often invoked as a pair, as in the extraordinarily influential report by Vannevar Bush, director of the Office of Scientific Research and Development, which appeared in July 1945 with the title *Science, the Endless Frontier*.[24] Solicited by President Roosevelt and submitted to President Truman, this report established the terms of scientific progress after the war. In it, Bush declared that only the government could ensure that science was funded on a scale adequate to the challenges of the day, and only colleges and universities were capable of carrying out the necessary work. Translated into national policy to be executed by the National Institutes for Health (1948) and the National Science Foundation (1950), this pronouncement would effectively alter the character of higher education by elevating the role of research in universities. In the new environment, universities were forced to compete with one another for government funding (including the innovative revenue stream of contract overhead), which became an increasingly dominant measure of prestige and value by which all disciplines would come to be judged.

Henceforth, science would be a government project, but one that was to be performed, in Bush's account, by altogether unregulated individuals. As the pursuit of an "endless frontier," science, according to Bush, is characterized by a "freedom of inquiry and that healthy competitive scientific spirit so necessary for expansion of the frontiers of scientific knowledge"; progress results from "the free play of free intellects, working on subjects of their own choice, in the manner dictated by their curiosity for exploration of the unknown" (*Science*, 12). But this depiction of harmless idlers dreaming their way through reason's mazes, undisturbed by or even unaware of the uses to which others might put their work, applied only to individual scientists. In describing the cumulative result of this collective dreamwork, Bush was aggressively instrumentalist, citing, in addition to progress in the fight against diseases and strengthening of the economy, the contribution science could make to the defense of the country through the development of "new and improved weapons" and "the strengthening of our Armed Forces" (5, 12). So while Bush could speak in charmingly antiquated terms about the unmonitored meandering of the individual scientific brain, the fully intended effect of his report was to make science into a government project that would be justified by its results.[25] Science became both apolitical in its conduct and geopolitical in its effects. This new rationale, as Jewett puts it with understated efficiency, "blunted the critical edge of scientific democracy" (*Science*, 16).

Nobody understood the consequences of this development better than Conant. A brilliant chemist and fierce defender of Harvard's independence, he opposed classified contracts for universities because they had the inevitable effect of entangling the university in the state apparatus, compromising the independence not only of the university but of science itself. As the head of a powerful research institution, Conant was committed to assisting the government in its work, but he was acutely aware of the fact that many government jobs were, as he noted on one occasion, "neither entirely peaceful nor pleasant," including "the grisly business of military armament."[26] But such scruples could not withstand the force of government contracts. As the Cold War deepened and the government funding for science increased, university-based science became increasingly dependent on federal as well as corporate funding, less able to set its own agenda, and altogether unable to claim with a straight face that it was committed to free inquiry and open-ended curiosity. Further, government contracts, flowing primarily to universities that already had leading scientists and robust infrastructure, effectively increased the competitive advantage of the elite institutions. With the political and ethical credentials of science compromised by privilege, profit, and war, the chain that linked science to democracy was effectively broken.

The eclipse of scientific democracy imperiled the entire project of general education. But the Redbook committee discovered an ingenious work-around for this difficulty, recalibrating the relationship between the disciplines, beginning with a description of a diminished science that bore no traces of any connection to abstract principles or values. In their sharply circumscribed account, science is "primarily a distinct type of intellectual enterprise, involving highly restricted aspects of reality"; it is "distinguished by a persistent effort toward precision," and "measures whatever can be measured" (Redbook, 150–51). Oh—and it does some useful things as well, contributing to "greater convenience, technical efficiency, military power, or economic advantage, for example" (150). Every phrase speaks not of an endless frontier but of constraints, limitations, and specifics. In the Redbook's account, science does not even have a claim to producing hard knowledge, since, as the committee points out, the data can always be enlarged or conclusions combined with other conclusions to produce different knowledge from the same material. In the chapter titled "Heritage and Change," science is associated with the latter, and the humanities with the former. This is all to the advantage of the humanities, since heritage is the central concept in the Redbook's idea of general education.

What, the Redbook asks, is education if not a transmission of heritage? How can democracy be secured if the educational system does not impart a vivid sense of the Western cultural and intellectual tradition, with its distinctive emphasis on the dignity of man, on "the view of man as free and not as slave, an end in himself and not a means" (46)? The Redbook advances the humanities as the heart and soul of the general education project, the one branch of academic work that can transmit and fortify the "intangibles of the American spirit" (41). The difference in altitude between the accounts of the humanities and those of science—the domain of the all-too-tangible—is striking.

Scientists could not have failed to notice that their work was effectively relegated by the Redbook to an ancillary role in the advance of humanistic civilization, its "medical and technological applications" helping "foster the spiritual values of humanism" and implement "the humanism which classicism and Christianity have proclaimed" (50). They may well have been alarmed by the kind of generalist courses recommended by the Redbook, the harbingers of the "Physics for Poets" courses that arose in later years. But humanists must also have been disoriented. Still a relatively new administrative category within higher education—the first Program in the Humanities was instituted at Princeton in 1930—the humanities were now being called on to secure both ends of the general education program, ministering to people both "because they are Americans" (civic virtues) and "are free" (individual self-realization). Neither had been central to the mission of the humanistic disciplines prior to that moment. While forms of "humanism" had always been part of American education, the concept of heritage had traditionally been associated with cultural and intellectual conservatism. The Harvard-centered New Humanism of the first decades of the twentieth century had been tradition based, antipopulist, unapologetically patrician, and barely postreligious. Harkening back to Matthew Arnold's invocation of "imaginative wholeness" and "rounded human nature," New Humanists such as Irving Babbitt, Paul Elmer More, and Norman Foerster declared themselves in vigorous opposition to science, determinism, individualism, Rousseauistic sentimentality, the heresies of John Dewey and other modern laxities, and strenuously in favor of discipline, duty, Christian morality, and the monuments of high culture.[27] For the New Humanists, an overvaluation of science, including what they saw as soulless social science, led to moral and cognitive rot—the worship of wealth, rampant materialism, social engineering, naturalism, and industrialization—which could only be countered by a reunification of knowledge, spiritual discipline, and morality.

This immense reclamation project, the New Humanists agreed, should be placed under the careful supervision of the English department, which would teach fundamental lessons about life through the great books. This was heritage with a vengeance, and not necessarily an American, or even a democratic heritage; and it is against the background of this determined rear guard movement that we can measure the boldness required of the Redbook committee to represent the humanities not as their Harvard New Humanist colleagues would have wished, but as a source of national identity linked to egalitarian democracy and modernity. For the modern humanities to flourish, the New Humanism had to go.

In short, the Redbook committee implicitly but effectively reformatted the then-prevalent notion of general education, reducing the role of science and redefining the humanities in order to produce a comprehensive program that included social, cultural, and historical knowledge at its educational, political, and moral core. At the same time, the enlarged role for the humanities in the national curriculum entailed a certain disciplinary toughening up in the humanistic disciplines. As David Hollinger puts it, "The academic humanities in the United States after World War II were a major institutional apparatus for bringing evidence and reasoning to domains where the rules of evidence are strongly contested and the power of reason often doubted."[28] In the new dispensation envisioned by the Redbook, the humanities disciplines bore immense responsibility for realizing the cultural goals of the entire educational system, including the management of what Hollinger calls "the dynamics of inclusion," the processes by which the nation made good on its promises of equal opportunity, equal access, equal protection, and equal rights.

Confident, comprehensive, and progressive, the Redbook commanded the attention of many thoughtful people. But its program would have remained a kind of thought experiment for the thoughtful had it not been taken up and translated into public policy in the 1947–48 Truman Report. A six-volume tome issued with the general title *Higher Education for American Democracy*, the Truman Report linked higher education to economic development, set the educational agenda for the next generation, and laid the groundwork for a massive expansion of the entire system of higher education.[29] Although just two years separated the Redbook from the Truman Report, the world had changed in the interval. Within two months after Conant signed the introduction to the Redbook in June 1945, Hiroshima was bombed and North Korea was occupied by the Soviets. With the rapid consolidation of Soviet power over the nations of Eastern

Europe, the Cold War had begun. The Truman Report speaks to the new circumstances, in which the War Department had become the Department of Defense, enemies or shadows of enemies were appearing both over the horizon and within our midst, and science fiction fantasies about the destruction of the world seemed suddenly realistic. Indeed, the first volume opens with a section on the "world-wide crisis of mankind" brought about by the appearance, at virtually the same moment as the publication of the Redbook, of atomic weaponry (1:6).

With the stakes of democracy so abruptly and dramatically raised, the Truman Report's commitment to the outlines and aspirations of general education and the liberal arts is impressively steadfast. The point of education, the report insisted, was the kind of "fuller realization of democracy" that would back up American claims for moral leadership in a devastated and dangerous world (1:8). The educational system required was "a unified general education for American youth," with general education defined clearly as a "nonspecialized and nonvocational learning which should be the common experience of all educated men and women" (1:49). A remarkably liberal document—especially considering the "world-wide crisis of mankind"—the report is unapologetic in its promotion of the humanities. "It can scarcely be necessary," the authors say, with an assurance that humanists today can only dream about, "to urge the importance of literature in the program of general education" (1:54). Most emphatically, the authors denounce all forms of discrimination and exclusion, including the quotas on Jews and Negroes that had restricted access to the well-intentioned but exclusive institutions that had first sponsored general education. The most fundamental, and fundamentally Jeffersonian, conviction communicated by the report is that knowledge is power and the concentration of knowledge constitutes an abuse of power. "General education," the report asserts, is henceforth to be understood as "liberal education with its matter and method shifted from its original aristocratic intent to the service of democracy," which, for its part, is to be regarded not as a heritage to be simply preserved and transmit-

ted but as "unfinished business" (1:49, 13). Most astonishingly,
the authors include a prescient warning about "anti-feminism in
higher education" (2:39–30).[30]

The Truman Report was most fervent, and most effective,
in calling for *"free and universal access to education"* as a democratic imperative (1:36). In large part as a consequence of this
call, the community college system was dramatically expanded
and oriented toward the educational needs of the community,
with many institutions offering courses that could be accepted as
part of a college degree at a four-year institution. A distinctively
American invention, two-year community colleges appeared at
the end of the nineteenth century in large part as a response to
the rapid growth of economic inequality, which was threatening the American dream of achieving success through hard work
and merit.[31] Two-year colleges manifested a commitment to the
belief that the way to address economic inequality was through
the extension to a wide population of the benefits of a general
education.[32] The two-year college played a crucial role in increasing access to higher education during the period from 1890 to
1920 when the American system of education was assuming its
modern form. But it was to play a far greater role after midcentury when, fueled by massive increases in federal funding, it was
charged with the task of serving as a gateway to higher education
for millions of students, including minority, immigrant, or culturally marginal students who were unprepared to enter a four-year
college upon leaving secondary school—including, eventually,
Mr. Ramirez.

Limitations of the Whole Man

The general education movement, which included among its intended effects the dramatic growth of community colleges and
huge increases in funding for education across the board, clearly
succeeded in many ways. As a consequence of policies growing
out of the national commitment to general education, millions
of young men and women acquired postsecondary education.

Disciplines flourished, faculties grew, and universities expanded in order to meet the demand. And yet today the movement is widely considered to have been a wrong turn, a misguided product of a more naïve era; the subtitle of John Guillory's important 2006 retrospective is "The Failure of General Education." Even a committee of the Harvard faculty in 2013 disdained the efforts of its predecessors. In a document titled "The Teaching of the Arts and Humanities at Harvard College: Mapping the Future," a committee of professors cast only a brief and condescending glance back at the history of the humanities at Harvard, and particularly at postwar general education. By the end of the 1960s, they say, the rhetoric of general education had come to sound "preachy and unsubstantiated"; indeed, "it seemed to undermine the sense of free inquiry that was supposed to be central to an education in the humanities, and it seemed to claim a unity and authority about who we should be as a people that was at odds with the thought that our sense of identity and purpose might be to some extent up to us to discover." "Mapping the Future" concludes with a casually dismissive minilecture to its predecessor committee, saying that "fundamental sources of value are neither necessary nor universal; they change over time" (a point on which the Redbook authors had in fact insisted).[33]

The question, then, is not, Why did general education fail? but, Why does it now seem like a failure? or, Why it is necessary to assert that it failed?

Several possibilities arise. First, with a greater sensitivity to markers of privilege and power, even Harvard professors are today more inclined to denounce any attempt by Harvard professors to set the course for the entire nation. Second, the theory of general education was never realized in practice. Harvard faculty resistance stymied the efforts of the Redbook committee to revamp the curriculum even at their own university, where the program was subjected to what one historian calls "an almost satiric distortion of its objectives."[34] At Harvard and elsewhere the high rhetoric of general education was translated into minor curricular alterations, mostly taking the form of distribution requirements. In practice, as Guillory notes, the burden of general education typically devolved onto the humanities alone—a sign, he argues, of the project's failure.[35]

A third reason to think general education a failure is that our opinion of the entire milieu has changed. We are, today, likely to look back on the Cold War not as the time when democracy outfaced its totalitarian enemies, but as the time when the combination of real and imagined threats brought out the worst in the American character: conformism, standardization, and intolerance, all cloaked in a tactical rhetoric of unity. "National life," as the Truman Report said at the outset, is best conceived as "a dynamic unity . . . a democratic reconciliation . . . one continuous process of interpersonal, intervocational, and intercultural cooperation" (1:2). Such anodyne formulae gave comforting expression to the sense that democracy was not to be considered an abstract preference for freedom or government by the people, but rather an institution or a regime to be defended. As one historian has commented, the focus of attention during the Cold War years was "not on the creation of citizens able to shape a democracy, but on citizens to recognize their *responsibilities*."[36] Today, with the sense of a worldwide crisis not abated but rather rendered numbingly chronic, and with wars fought in distant places by volunteer armies, proxy forces, and technology, the value placed on individual sacrifice for the common good has sharply diminished. Indeed, with dramatically increased forms and degrees of cultural diversity, along with radicalized inequality, the very notion of a common good arising from common values and common heritage no longer seems as compelling a principle, or as realistic a description, as it once did. Conant himself wrote in his autobiography that he eventually decided that a "unified, coherent culture" was not a viable aspiration in a democratic and pluralistic culture.[37] And so, the fundamental rationale for general education now seems to many to be antiquated, delusional, and oppressive—one among many Cold War embarrassments.[38]

And, too, there are complaints about the core of the Redbook's program, the proposed required courses and particularly the required humanities course, "Great Texts of Literature," with a suggested reading list that, as the committee put it, "might include Homer, one or two of the Greek tragedies, Plato, the Bible, Virgil, Dante, Shakespeare, Milton, Tolstoy" (207). Patching together a synthetic "tradition" out of wildly various texts from ancient Greece, the ancient Middle East, medieval Florence, the English Renaissance, Puritan culture of the seventeenth century, and nineteenth-century Russia, this list has been criticized on several grounds: first, for its "Western" and "traditional" orientation; second, for the presumption that a ginned-up list of this kind could be called "Western"; third, that it constituted a coherent "tradition" of any kind; fourth, for its assumption that anyone, and especially Americans, could claim such a heritage as their own; fifth, that culture had ever been or ever could be so contained and homogeneous that it could be reliably transmitted by pedagogy; and sixth, for the cultural arrogance required to prescribe such a list at all.[39]

But perhaps the most exposed, avoidable, and, in retrospect, regrettable aspect of the Redbook is its much-derided evocation of the "whole man," a well-nigh allegorical figure whose full development is said to be nothing less than "the aim of liberal education" (74). This iconic figure, the human face of general education, is described in considerable detail, as "full-blooded," "alert and aggressive," possessed of "an inner integration, poise, and firmness," grounded in and curious about the world—an altogether "gregarious animal" (75, 74, 77, viii). To some, the whole man represents nothing more or other than a midcentury middle-class dream of fully assimilated sociality, an exemplary cipher-citizen of an imaginary homogeneous polis whose entire robust being could be comprehended within the bounds of acceptability, with no disorderly passions, peculiar abilities, dangerous eccentricities, or indeed individuating marks of any kind—a small unit of interpersonal, intervocational, and intercultural cooperation.

Whatever else he may be, however, the whole man is not a shallow or simple figure. He may appear to be unreflective and ahistorical, but the whole man is in fact a multilayered composite, drawn not from actually existing models of exceptionally well adjusted individuals living in a modern society, but from several traditions, all alien, foreign, and antidemocratic.

The idea of a nonspecialized, uniformly perfected personality was, as the great German philologist Erich Auerbach points out, inherited from antiquity by the Renaissance humanists, who contributed to this tradition the late feudal notion of the perfect courtier, a member of a class composed partly of noblemen and partly of the urban bourgeoisie, men who required not specialized knowledge but "a non-professional, strongly social and even fashionable form of general knowledge." The class of the educated consisted, in the sixteenth century, of socially influential people to whom "good breeding and conduct in the fashionable sense, amiability in social intercourse, aptitude for human contact, and presence of mind meant more than any specialized competence . . . [education was] an ornament indispensable for the man destined to the most general life and to political leadership." The most brilliant—so brilliant, indeed, as to be altogether unrepresentative and atypical—example of this kind of learning is Montaigne, who describes himself as an *homme suffisant*, which Auerbach translates as "whole man."[40] Deep in the genealogy of the earnest, progressive, sunny figure of the midcentury whole man of the Redbook is the Renaissance courtier.

The patrilineal line of the whole man also includes other, much less worldly ancestors. The Redbook committee may have been familiar with Samuel Eliot Morison's recent book, *The Founding of Harvard College* (1935), where the Renaissance conception of schooling, on which the early leaders of Harvard drew, is described as oriented toward the development of "the whole man—his body and soul as well as his intellect."[41] Members of the committee might also have been aware of the association of the term with notions of sanctification and religious enthusiasm, since John Henry Newman, author of *The Idea of a University*, drew on this tradition in his *Apologia pro vita sua* (1864), where he described his decision to embrace the Catholic faith by contrasting "paper logic" with the more profound transformation in which "the whole man moves."[42] And at least one committee member, I. A. Richards, a Coleridge scholar who will come to figure more prominently in the third section of this book, was fully aware of Samuel Taylor Coleridge's use of the term to describe the ideal unity of intellect and understanding, combined with a zeal for the right.[43]

With a family tree populated by such remote and regressive figures, the whole man—seen today as more sanctimonious than sanctified, more ideological than ideal—stands as a multiplex impediment to a sympathetic contemporary reading of the Redbook or a receptive hearing for general education. Organized around the whole man's *suffisance*, the entire concept of general education seems, for many today, irredeemably tainted by the preferences and prejudices of an earlier, less progressive or enlightened time, a regressive ethos damningly signaled by the conventional, but by no means merely rhetorical, use of the masculine.

But if general education had been no more than a Cold War artifact, a way of coercing citizens to march to the same funkless drummer, Mr. Ramirez would have been spared his embarrassment, and his career. He was not a whole man, and an educational program dedicated to serving the interests of gregarious animals who comported themselves with poise and firmness would have taken little interest in him. Lucky for him and millions of others, the general education program outlined in the Redbook and translated into national policy by the Truman Report was not so restrictive: it managed to preserve within itself the germ of a vision that, while limited by the constraints of its intellectual and cultural contexts, retained elements of a more spacious, humane, and aspirational conception of life in a democratic society. With its heavy stress on social and cultural knowledge, this conception was responsible for the centrality of the humanities in the secondary and postsecondary curricula that followed the general education model, and was responsible, too, for placing in the path of Mr. Ramirez the formidable obstacle of Shakespeare.

Breaking the Stranglehold of the Present

Why Shakespeare? Why, in a system designed to produce social cohesion and civic virtue, was Mr. Ramirez forced to break his head against the indecipherable and culturally remote bard? How did Shakespeare manage to get into a curriculum that claimed to foster democracy? And why does his work continue to be taught and sometimes even required in the liberal arts programs even of many community colleges today? Does his dominance suggest that general education is in reality a program for John Adams's grandchildren, giving them something to admire between the porcelain and the tapestry? Or might there be some other, more Jacksonian rationale for requiring Shakespeare?

Clearly, Shakespeare's inclusion reflects his unchallenged position in, or rather atop, the canon of world literature. To a greater degree than any other single author, Shakespeare has come to represent the institution of literature, at once the essence and apogee of literariness as such. Any college or university that claims to introduce its students to the humanities can require its students to read Shakespeare with confidence that the choice will be uncontested, no matter how little enthusiasm or comprehension its students bring to the challenge. The inclusion of Shakespeare in a curriculum marks even a community college as an academically serious institution.

In a deeper sense, however, the value of Shakespeare's work is precisely that it forces students to confront an alien cultural sensibility, with its peculiar modes of thought, feeling, and expression. In one of those single-authored moments that punctuate the Harvard committee style that characterizes much of the text, the Redbook asserts that "one of the aims of education is to break the stranglehold of the present on the mind" (70). The experience of reading Shakespeare can do that—more radically, perhaps, the farther one gets from Harvard, where the past is so present and the study of the cultural monuments of the past such a commonplace. But the most profound reason for any educational institution to require its students to read Shakespeare is that Shakespearean discourse, given voice by a vast range of characters drawn from all spheres of life, operates in an emotional and intellectual register that, for most people, remains otherwise inaccessible. Breaking the stranglehold of the present also entails breaking out of the flattened discourse of the everyday into a more passionate, deeply felt, vividly imagined, and, most importantly, hyperarticulate world, the world in which Shakespearean characters live.

What makes Shakespeare so transhistorically and transculturally compelling is that his characters—even the humbler ones, ensnared in the often ludicrous, poignant, or pathetic little tangles of their lives—invariably labor to articulate the essential character of their circumstances, reflecting on their experience in terms that detach from particularity and reach out toward a more generalized dimension of experience, achieving what Coleridge described as the "concrete universal," a "union and interpenetration of the universal and the particular."[44] A Shakespearean gravedigger, assassin, lady-in-waiting, despised king, reflective prince, barroom raconteur, Jewish moneylender, suspected wife, teenager in love, or regicide stands for all time as a model for those who find themselves in similar, even distantly similar, situations. This is why Shakespeare's plays can be set in any location, with *Much Ado about Nothing* set in American suburbia, *Macbeth* in 1920s Chicago, or *King Lear* in nineteenth-century Japan.[45] One constantly encounters in Shakespeare characters whose self-understanding takes them both deep into and far beyond themselves. Readers or audiences of Shakespeare are invited to do the same, to hear echoes of their own perhaps fragmentary or half-formed thoughts or intuitions in the words of these characters, distant, extreme, and impossibly fluent as they are. Doing so—if they can—they are awakened to two liberating possibilities: first, that all human experience might be generalizable, shareable, translatable; and second, that there are aspects of ourselves that exist beyond or beneath our comprehension, rarely rising to the level of direct expression—that in short we contain more than we know and are more than we think.

We are invited, not compelled, to make this discovery. As the literary theorist Jonathan Culler has written, a literary text about a fictional character "presents itself as exemplary but simultaneously declines to define the range or scope of that exemplarity."[46] We *may* discover ourselves, or some facet of ourselves, in Coriolanus, Desdemona, Goneril, Falstaff, Puck, or Cleopatra, or in all of them, but need not do so; we retain a measure of volition in the matter. By soliciting a self-recognition that may be fleeting, provisional, or exploratory, literature—and preeminently Shakespeare, with his singularly vast range of characters—enlarges our sense of our own capacities.[47]

Such deepened and expanded self-understanding does not necessarily encourage social cohesion, and might not even qualify as cultural knowledge, but it is one of the things that education can and, in the view of the Redbook, ought to do: "the chief reason for [a required course in the humanities] . . . is that too many students today have too little contact with thoughts which are beyond them . . . and that many are in fact passionately if inarticulately hungry for greatness in the common cares of man" (207). The required course in the humanities—that blunt Cold War instrument, that authoritarian holdover from a less enlightened era, that deferential homage to the cultural peerage—was the means by which Mr. Ramirez and his classmates were exposed to intensities of thought and feeling, and therefore to dimensions of their own experience, that would otherwise have remained unsuspected and disregarded. Perhaps very few—perhaps none—of the people in that class would have chosen to take such a course or read such a work, much less to answer questions about it in public. Perhaps only one retained a vital memory of the experience. But if they had had their way, taking a curriculum that conformed to their preferences or immediate needs, they might well have left college with no exposure at all to "thoughts which [were] beyond them" when they entered.

A curriculum constructed as a response to a "hunger for greatness" will lead in directions that cannot be reduced to civic virtues, and may disrupt the inner integration of the whole man.

But the exercise of imaginative or intellectual freedom cannot be restricted to the field of the already known, the already imagined, the already desired. Such freedom requires, in the first instance, the capacity to imagine something different from what one has learned in the course of one's limited experience. As the German-born philosopher Ernst Cassirer wrote in *An Essay on Man*, which appeared the year before the Redbook, "The great mission ... is to make room for the possible as opposed to a passive acquiescence in the present actual state of affairs. It is symbolic thought which overcomes the natural inertia of man and endows him with a new ability, the ability constantly to reshape his human universe."[48] Shakespeare, Cassirer says, represents an exceptionally pure, powerful, and focused instance of such thought. It may be authoritarian to require students to do something they would not choose to do, but to offer them an education that avoided any encounter with the unfamiliar or unimagined would be to deny them one of the indispensable sources of the freedom from necessity or circumstance that one is claiming to promote by educating them in the first place. In their own ways, Jefferson and Adams understood this paradox perfectly, and so, eventually, did Mr. Ramirez.

The kind of "reshaping" Cassirer is thinking of takes place on a different plane from the kind of problem solving that preoccupied Dewey and other pragmatists. But Cassirer, who had come to the United States very late in a distinguished career, was not merely voicing a haughty European skepticism about the limits of the American cult of know-how and ingenuity. In the first of his books to be written in English and on American soil (published when he was teaching at Columbia), Cassirer gives a newly emphatic voice to the progressive dimension of the Enlightenment tradition to which he had devoted a life of study.

Having fled Germany when the Nazis came to power, Cassirer spent his last years insisting once again, in an entirely new context, on the ability of man to achieve through symbolic thought a "progressive self-liberation" (*Essay on Man*, 228). His last, posthumously published book, *The Myth of the State* (1946),[49] describes from the vantage point of the exile the regression of mankind through a tragically passive acquiescence to the forces of "myth," by which he means the tendency exemplified by Germany in the 1930s to see life in mystified, irrational, origin-obsessed, individual-suppressing terms. While he had devoted an appreciative volume to the subject of myth early in his career,[50] stressing its vital holistic creativity, he now saw myth in a new light as a primitive thought-form haunting the present, with devastating consequences. It is, Cassirer argues, mythic thought that undergirds the concept of the state, acquiring a hypertrophic salience in the fascist or totalitarian state. The background of his now-devastated homelands—both Silesia where he was born and Germany where he began his professional life—gives an unarticulated force and poignancy to Cassirer's reflections on art, which are wide-ranging and various but return again and again to Shakespeare, whose work, he says, liberates us from "the hard pressure, the compulsion of our emotions" (*Essay on Man*, 148).

Reading Shakespeare, Cassirer says, we become able to "envisage a new reality," attain a new and masterful perspective on our own lives, and experience an "inner freedom which cannot be attained in any other way" (*Essay on Man*, 146, 149). This discovery within ourselves of a principle of freedom is, Cassirer argues, the ultimate mission of art. It is surely significant that this "American" book contains Cassirer's most extended and impassioned reflections on art, which had, in his previous work, figured as a repository of instances of symbolic thought but never as a subject in itself. Indeed, it is tempting to speculate that Cassirer was stimulated by the concept of the humanities being articulated in his new homeland, in which his own field of philosophy was bundled with literature and the other arts, along with narrative forms of history, rather than having to share conceptual space with law, theology, and economics as in the German *Geisteswissenschaften*.[51] He may have found particularly fruitful the connection being drawn between the humanities and individual self-realization in a democratic society, a connection that enabled a radical extension of, and a new rationale for, the arguments he had made in his previous work about the need for intellectual and imaginative sympathy in historical understanding. In *Essay on Man*, this prerequisite of the professional historian becomes moralized and democratized by being identified with literary understanding, which is available to anyone. The "aim of historical knowledge," he writes, is not merely the determination of the truth of the past, but "a form of self-knowledge" leading to the "enrichment and enlargement, not the effacement, of the self, of our knowing and feeling ego" (191). The aim, he almost says, is to foster the development of the whole man.

As depicted in the Redbook, the whole man seems to lack the kind of depth or psychic complexity required to achieve the inner freedom Cassirer speaks of. But when Cassirer describes how Shakespeare "discloses a new breadth and depth of life," and enables us—all of us—to sense "vaguely and dimly, the infinite potentialities of life, which silently await the moment when they are to be called forth from dormancy into the clear and intense light of consciousness," he seems to be approaching from a different angle the Redbook's "hunger for greatness" (*Essay on Man*, 147–48). Indeed, Cassirer's American work, carried out in wartime and composed in English by a Jewish émigré-refugee, is instinct with a vision of human fulfillment achieved through art and humanistic reflection on art that is, if anything, more "American" than the fervent expressions of patriotic belligerence that were ubiquitous during the wartime years.

We can also see the extraordinary suggestive power of this relatively unstressed dimension of general education on non-Americans in the thinking of another German-Jewish émigré-philosopher, Hannah Arendt. Immensely impressed by America's political and social system, with its stability, its checks and balances, its hospitality to dissent enabled by its "modern" conception of authority, Arendt was less enthusiastic about the American system of education. In "The Crisis in Education" (1958), Arendt registers an old-world disdain for the "astounding hodgepodge of sense and nonsense" reflected in that system (174–75). Nearly everything about American education seems to her misguided, beginning with the presumption, grounded in a distinctively American "pathos of the new," that a new world order is always within reach (174). Bewitched by this illusion, she argues, the American system deprives children of what they really need: actual knowledge imparted by people who know what they are talking about. "The function of the school," she writes, "is to teach children what the world is like and not to instruct them in the art of living" (192).[52] Deriving educational practice from political premises, American policy makers have gotten badly off track, convincing themselves that education is to be considered "one of the inalienable civil rights," and—something unthinkable in Europe, where secondary education was traditionally reserved for the preprofessional few—that the entire school system should be devoted to the production of citizens (176). The consequence of this blunder is a cascading series of disasters: the authority of the teacher is eroded because teachers are not professionals in a field but self-authorizing moral guides, knowledge is reduced to a skill, gifted students suffer by being given the same education as the average and below-average students, and everyone—teachers, students, and parents—is indoctrinated in progressive fantasies.

Harsh criticisms from one of the most distinguished philosophers of her time. But Arendt's critique is leveled only against what she considered the dominant ideas and practices. The hodgepodge she chastises includes, mixed in with the "nonsense," a modicum of "sense," even brilliance. Like Cassirer, Arendt rediscovers America at the point when she begins to articulate the basic principles that should, in her view, ground educational practice, proposals that turn out to conform to the humanities-centered model of general education.

The fundamental difference between the old world and the new, for Arendt, is that the new world is more created than given. While the prospect of a wholesale world renovation is merely a dream, that dream is, she acknowledges, an "illusion stronger than reality" for those who have had the "basic American experience" of immigration ("Crisis in Education," 174). Arendt is deeply impressed, even thrilled, by the role played in the national self-understanding of America by immigrants, who bear massive witness to the possibility of founding a new world that, unlike other utopias, was not shut off from the outside world, but open to those who wished to come, a refuge for "all the poor and en-slaved of the earth." She cites with warm approval "the words spoken by John Adams in 1765—that is, before the Declaration of Independence—'I always consider the settlement of America as the opening of a grand scheme and design in Providence for the illumination and emancipation of the slavish part of mankind all over the earth'" (172).[53]

The image of waves of immigrants, arriving "slavish"—curiously, neither Adams nor Arendt seems to be thinking of actual slaves—but educated in freedom, elicits from Arendt a spontaneous and almost defiantly unworldly expression of respect for the specifically new-world concept of the dignity of the individual, and admiration for the world that might be founded on that concept. Education, she insists, ought to assume responsibility for "the free development of characteristic qualities and talents . . . the uniqueness that distinguishes every human being from every other, the quality by virtue of which he is not only a stranger in the world but something that has never been here before" ("Crisis in Education," 185). Thinking about education in these terms leads Arendt to introduce a concept that plays a central role in *The Human Condition*,[54] published the same year as this essay, of "natality," which refers to the fact that everyone is born into a "pre-existing world, constructed by the living and the dead" ("Crisis in Education," 174). Suggesting both the inertial resistance of the world to innovation and the constant fact of newness, natality sets the agenda and the parameters for education, and has a political dimension Arendt is unafraid to name: "Exactly for the sake of what is new and revolutionary in every child, education must be conservative; it must preserve this new-ness and introduce it as a new thing into an old world" (189).

Preserving newness in an old world, insisting on the revo-lutionary potential of the newly arrived stranger—such phrases not only describe an educational imperative but also evoke the desperate project of the immigrant, who must, to recall Cassirer's terms, find a way to make room for the possible in order "to reshape his human universe." In Arendt's discourse, the educable child aligns with the immigrant, united by a common commitment to the belief that, as she says, the world can be "set right anew" ("Crisis in Education," 192). Denouncing contemporary American practice, and the American tendency to derive educational philosophy from political commitments, Arendt in fact prescribes a philosophy of education that is ultra-American, grounded in the redemptive promise of a new world in which individuals realize their potential, and where talent and dedication are justly rewarded.

In "The Crisis in Education" Arendt herself is undergoing a kind of negative crisis. Halfway between *The Origins of Totalitarianism* (1951), her massive, even obsessive exhumation of the roots of the unprecedented and distinctly twentieth-century form of evil by which her own life had been so profoundly marked, and *On Revolution* (1963), in which she celebrates the Mayflower Compact as the first instance in human history where people voluntarily committed themselves to a "Civil Body Politick," Arendt is here beginning to discover in American political history a nontotalitarian solution to the problem of modernity. Thrilled by the Polish and Czech uprisings against Soviet occupation, Arendt found in the American experience a worldly precedent for a different form of political modernity, a form, precisely, of politics, in which people enter into voluntary compacts and agreements in pursuit of common ends. Arendt's insistence on the political was undoubtedly determined by her own experience. After eighteen years as a stateless person following her emigration from Germany in 1933, Arendt became an American citizen, and, like millions of immigrants before her, began a new life. Unlike most others, she forged from that experience, and from her deeply sympathetic reading of the experiments in micropolitics of the first settlers of the New World, a positive theory of politics to set against the monstrous world-slaughtering example of totalitarianism.[55]

To sophisticated twenty-first-century minds—like those be-longing to the Harvard faculty of 2013—the thinking behind the Redbook may seem simplistic, jingoistic, and reactionary, an untroubled expression of the most uncritical form of what has become known as American exceptionalism.[56] To the same eyes, Cassirer and especially Arendt figure among the mighty cosmo-politan intellects of the twentieth century. But on the subject of the fundamental purpose of education, the Redbook committee and the sages are in substantive agreement, the primary differ-ence being that the sages are more starry-eyed than the commit-tee about the prospects for the world renovation in an American setting.

James B. Conant, American Radical

General education is today rightly evaluated more on the basis of its actual results than on the unrealized possibilities or aspira-tions to which the Redbook gave voice. This evaluation has been harsh, and even some of the aspirations have come in for criti-cism. The grand claims made in the Redbook and the Truman Report about democracy, society, values, and human nature, "al-ready rather stale" in 1945 and by now unmistakably moldy, have not aged well. But in pronouncing general education a failure, we may be holding it to a standard that no program of universal education could measure up to, and missing its real contribution.

The forms assumed by general education in schools and col-leges across the country represented Cold War reductions or ad-aptations of the full and various energies of the Redbook into a set of operational routines that reflected local compromises between idealistic visions and a number of uninspiring reali-ties on the ground, including faculty willingness to buy into the program. In fact, as Louis Menand says, general education, by which he means a thoroughgoing program of required nonspe-cialist courses directed toward the ends of liberal education and not simply the addition of a few distribution requirements, "has seldom been tried, even in the 'great books' format" (*American Studies*, 107). (One program adopted without compromise was the system General Douglas MacArthur imposed "as an essential requirement of education for democracy" on the Japanese after WWII.)[57] Judging the entirety as if it were a program rather than a movement or a set of principles misses the point. It is more appropriate to consider general education as a statement of postwar American self-understanding cast in the form of a plan for an educational system. If we substitute the appealing and empathetic (if perhaps semifictionalized) figure of Mr. Ramirez for the now discredited (and altogether fictional) figure of the Harvardian whole man, then we can more readily grasp the value of the perhaps quixotic but fundamentally noble attempt to realize through education the promise of democracy. Internally conflicted, limited, and naïve though it was, the program of universal liberal education to which the Redbook gave form and force was the most socially productive contribution to educational and indeed social theory that the United States has made since the founding of the Republic. As we consider this legacy today, the task is the same as the one Jefferson assigned to the educational system as a whole: to rake from the rubbish the genius ideas—and dismiss the residue.

Many of the problems encountered by general education were consequences of massification. With vast numbers of new students entering the educational system after the war, it was becoming increasingly difficult—and in the view of some, decreasingly desirable—to try to impart common values, a common heritage, or a common view of life. To a diverse and divided population, any heritage, and especially one that revolved around the distant sun of Shakespeare, was likely to seem unmoored from experience. And given the manifest failure of high schools to instill an adequate understanding of the cultural past, attempts to impart a sense of heritage at the postsecondary level necessarily involved a discouraging amount of remediation. In order to deliver on its promises for the college population, general education had to focus on secondary as well as postsecondary education. Indeed, many felt that the entire project of general education was more appropriately directed at the high school curriculum.

James Bryant Conant himself might have made that argument. He published his first essay on high schools in 1940, and ended his long career by writing a series of books about secondary education, with the last appearing in 1967. During his lifetime, the American high school had been transformed twice, from an elite college preparatory institution to an institution of mass secondary education, and then, in the decade after WWII, to a universal secondary institution and a mass college preparatory institution.[58] Conant endorsed general education because he thought it was the best response to the problems associated with the dramatically increased scale of the nation's educational system. A key figure in the conceptualization of the postwar community college system, Conant was even more influential in the growth of the "comprehensive" high school during the 1950s.[59] This institution was widely criticized as a top-down initiative prescribed by Harvard grandees, with Conant—the most prominent instance of the midcentury technocrat/intellectual convinced that he was possessed of the knowledge needed to put society right—being the grandest. This charge is not altogether unfair, but it is not the impression one gets from a reading of Conant's writing on high schools, which includes a number of striking passages that reflect the depth of his commitment to ideas that, today, would seem nothing short of radical.

Conant is remembered today with mixed feelings, with due respect for his extraordinary, even visionary scientific accomplishments, his wartime role as chair of the National Defense Research Council that supervised the Manhattan Project, his long and transformative Harvard presidency (1933–52), and his service as United States high commissioner to West Germany and subsequently the first ambassador to West Germany—all this weighing against a persistent feeling, shared even by his biographer, that he was emotionally distant, mild where he should have been strong, inconstant in defense of tolerance, more Jeffersonian than Jacksonian in his instincts, sometimes a defender of the status quo against those who saw more clearly and fearlessly, overly given to consensus and committees, an occasional Cold

Warrior himself, a key figure in the decision to use the atomic bomb not just on Hiroshima but also on Nagasaki, and, most damningly, passively supportive of Hitlerian anti-Semitism.[60] He was a man of significant imaginative and dispositional limitations who nevertheless cast an inordinately long shadow over many areas of American life. Conant's public record is extensive, offering many items to be judged: so crowded was his life that James G. Hershberg's biography, nearly a thousand pages long, does not include a single mention of his initiative in producing the Redbook. Conant operated on a large stage—Hershberg's book is titled *James B. Conant: Harvard to Hiroshima and the Making of the Nuclear Age*—and his interest in secondary education may seem a very minor strand in a fabulous tapestry. But it is precisely in his thinking about this relatively small subject that Conant unfurls the full dimensions of his thinking about education, which is to say his thinking about America.

Like many others, Conant believed that universal general education was a principle deeply inwoven with the American national character, that general education and democracy existed in a dialectical relationship, each implying and affirming the other. After the Cold War had set in, he described general education as an effective "instrument of national policy," a native herb that could be applied as an antidote to "European radical doctrines of the nineteenth-century based on the notion of class struggle" (*Education in a Divided World*, 5, 108). But these were not his first thoughts on the subject, nor did he always strike the nationalistic or anti-Marxist note. Readers of the *Atlantic Monthly* must have been surprised by the titles of two of Conant's early articles on secondary education, which denounced inherited wealth and privilege and advocated for universal education as an effective leveler: "Education for a Classless Society" (1940) and "Wanted: American Radicals" (1943).[61] In these articles, he traced a line of indigenous political thought that ran through Jefferson, Jackson, Emerson, Thoreau, and Whitman, and actually brushed up against Marx, Engels, and Lenin, for whom Conant recommended "respect" if not enthusiasm. The authentic "American radical," Conant wrote, "believes in equality of opportunity, not equality of rewards; but, on the other hand, he will be lusty in wielding the axe against the root of inherited privilege. To prevent the growth of a caste system, which he abhors, he will be resolute in his demand to confiscate (by constitutional methods) all property once a generation. He will demand really effective inheritance and gift taxes and the breaking up of trust funds and estates. And this point cannot lightly [be] pushed aside, for it is the kernel of his radical philosophy" ("Wanted," 43). The key to such a utopian but emphatically American project is one that Conant himself endorsed wholeheartedly: "truly universal educational opportunity at every level" (43). While the University of Chicago's president Robert Maynard Hutchins was worrying that the GI Bill would result in colleges and universities being inundated by unprepared students, turning them into "educational hobo jungles,"[62] Conant was pushing for a vast expansion of opportunity.

Conant extracted such ideas directly from his reading of American history. If more Americans than Europeans went to high school, he said, the reason was that enlightened child labor laws in the United States prevented young people from working; and if American schools differed from one another in so many ways that there simply was no "American high school," the reason, he argued, was that American society, formed in large part by the frontier experience, always resisted centralized authority and prized local control. But the deepest determinant of American education, according to Conant, was the enduring love of liberty described by Tocqueville, who noted the "most extraordinary phenomenon," that people in America are "seen on a greater equality in point of fortune and intellect, or in other words, more equal in their strength, than in any other country of the world, or in any age of which history has preserved the remembrance."[63]

Unimpressed by Jefferson's plan for culling a natural aristoi from the mass and educating them at public expense, Conant offered a more sweepingly democratic argument to the effect that it was more consistent with the character of the nation to afford not just a few people but all people the opportunity for education, even higher education. "If," he wrote, "you combine a belief in equality with a belief in the desirability of a full-time education leading to a collegiate degree for all who can afford it, the American pattern of education is the logical outcome." This belief led to his unwavering support for a distinctively American innovation, the "comprehensive" high schools that had arisen in great numbers beginning in the late nineteenth century, in which all children in a given community were educated in a single large institution that combined remedial, vocational, and college preparation courses, with about half the school's curriculum to be required of all students. Providing general education at the secondary school level, the comprehensive high school served, Conant argued, as a "great engine of democracy" providing "ladders of opportunity" for everyone. He regarded any proposal that would strengthen private schools at the expense of public schools as viciously un-American: "To use taxpayers' money to assist private schools," he wrote, "is to suggest that American society use its own hands to destroy itself."[64]

Conant presented these views as if they were axiomatic, constructing his arguments as if-then propositions in which conclusions follow directly from basic principles:

> If one accepts the ideal of a democratic, fluid society with a minimum of class distinction, the maximum of fluidity, the maximum of understanding between different vocational groups, then the ideal secondary school is a comprehensive public high school. . . . If one wished generation after generation to perpetuate class distinction based on hereditary status in a given society, one would certainly demand a dual system of schools [with vocational training separated from college preparation]; . . . a dual system [like those in European countries] serves and helps to maintain group cleavages, the absence of a dual system does the reverse. (*Education and Liberty*, 81–82)

Not himself an immigrant—while middle class, he was descended from the family that founded Salem, Massachusetts, which predates Boston—Conant, like his near contemporary Arendt, understood that immigration was both the fundamental fact of the nation and the problem to which education had to be the solution. One of the appeals of the comprehensive school to Conant was that it was particularly effective at minimizing or moderating distinctions of birth, and served better than any other kind of school as a counter to the paranoia and defensiveness of nativism by "assimilating many strains of migrations" (62).

With anxieties fueled by the 1957 Soviet launch of Sputnik (after which, in the words of one historian, "a shocked and humbled nation embarked on a bitter orgy of pedagogical soul-searching"[65]), the comprehensive high school, and Conant's defense of it, came under attack. From the Right, Conant was criticized by those who argued that such an institution was simply too democratic, too committed to social mobility and to the equitable distribution of resources and opportunities to serve the interests of a nation that urgently needed scientists and engineers in order to combat the Communist threat. With critics blasting all forms of progressive education as "red-ucation," defenders of the comprehensive high school had a difficult time defending its patriotic credentials.[66] On the Left, the attacks on Conant came from those who felt that his practical suggestions did not live up to his egalitarian rhetoric. They charged that his support for "differentiated" curricula that would respect variances in ability and aspiration meant that he was supporting the notion of training women for housekeeping (or "domestic science") and secretarial work, while minorities would inevitably become hewers of wood and drawers of water.[67] Conant's skepticism (later retracted) about the effectiveness of busing, and, consequently, his reluctant endorsement of segregated schools, was to some unforgivable. His conclusion that the prevailing system needed only minor tweaking disappointed those who felt bolder measures were required. In Dianne Ravitch's account, Conant's *The American High School Today* (1959) was "the whitewash the educational establishment had been hoping for."[68]

Hammered from both sides and sustained only, it seemed, by the support of the now-elderly Conant and various professional organizations, the comprehensive high school, which had stood for much of the twentieth century as the educational embodiment of the American dream—"democracy's high school," in the title of one book—lost its way, and in a development described somewhat melodramatically by Ravitch as "the great meltdown," collapsed in some cases into outright anti-intellectualism, with "progressive" schools featuring a "life adjustment" curriculum that included such subjects as home budgeting, taxation, and how to buy insurance, while excluding up to 60 percent of students from academic courses.[69]

This is not an inspiring story, but the devolution of the progressive spirit into home budgeting and tax filing was not a necessary or inevitable outcome of the general education movement, any more than was the co-optation of general education for Cold War purposes. I would argue to the contrary that the ideas behind general education were victims rather than expressions of a nationalistic, homogenizing, anti-intellectual Cold War sensibility, and suffered particularly from the shift noted earlier from thinking of democracy in terms of individual freedom and civic responsibility to thinking of democracy as an institution or regime to be strengthened and defended.

By the end of the 1950s, the pendulum was beginning its long arc toward a more instrumental or managerial view of education as a means to the end of scientific and technological supremacy. In this new context, the Redbook's emphases on the humanities, on individual freedom, and on cultural knowledge—not to mention the "hunger for greatness"—seemed increasingly like archaic remnants from a premodern era. The book's repeated mentions of "art" ("the general art of the free man and the citizen" [54]; "living is an art" [75]; "reading . . . is an art" [118]; "the translation from theory to practice involves an art all its own" [70]) were seen in the following decade as signs that the visionaries of that postwar moment were oblivious to the real character of the challenges the nation actually faced. The humanities were particularly vulnerable to grave warnings from Cold War "realists." The first of what would become many publications with the title *Crisis in the Humanities* appeared in 1964 with essays by many hands, including Ernest Gellner's defiant but defensive description of humanists as "the artisanate of cognition" making a last stand against the overwhelming forces of the machine, the system, the mass.[70] Across the country, "heritage" was reduced to bleached and heroic accounts of American history presented in textbooks that had been carefully vetted by state boards of education, many of which were not composed of scholars, much less artisans of cognition. The words "crisis" and "the humanities" were effectively joined into a single concept.

The general education movement began as a prescriptive program centered in elite institutions. It became a Cold War shuttlecock; then, undermined by faculty resistance, attacks from the outside, and failures of imagination or sympathy embedded within the program itself, it withered away, lingering on primarily in the ghostly form of distribution requirements, often centered in the humanistic disciplines, a form of curricular diversity Menand describes as "mandatory smattering" (*American Studies*, 107). The connection between the educational system and a never-realized but often reaffirmed national commitment to equalizing opportunities for success as part of the pursuit of a more perfect union was broken. But while it can be said to have failed in many respects, the general education movement gave voice and form to certain beliefs about the connection between education and American democracy that continue to challenge us today. These include the following:

Education is a way of giving people the opportunity to improve, advance, and fulfill themselves in whatever way they might choose.
The education best suited to this purpose is "liberal," that is, various and holistic rather than vocational or professional.
Local control and the vast diversity of the nation notwithstanding, all citizens should be given a formally comparable education through the secondary level, as well as the opportunity to pursue postsecondary education.

Education should contribute to fostering social cohesion and a commitment to common values, including the value of diversity.[71]

The humanities are equal in educational importance to mathematics, science, and social science, and are directly instrumental in helping education realize the promise of democracy.

The study of the humanities cannot be reduced to the acquisition of information, nor can humanistic knowledge be expressed in quantitative terms.

Education should extend one's intellectual horizons, enrich one's stock of cultural knowledge, and deepen one's sympathies and understanding.

Never fully translated into practice, these principles have found fewer adherents in recent years. They reflect an expansive confidence no longer in fashion. But they have proven difficult to eradicate because they have a long American pedigree, a deep rootedness in traditional American self-understanding and aspirations.

And so, in the early 1960s, when Mr. Ramirez, seeking to improve his lot, entered a community college, he found himself not just in a small and uninspiring classroom with impossible reading, an irritating teacher, and no air conditioning, but entangled in a dense mesh of convictions and commitments reaching all the way up and back to the windy abstractions voiced at the founding of the nation and animated by the spirit of welcome extended to huddled masses yearning to be free. The program at his community college may have had a vocational dimension; it certainly had a remedial component for those who needed it. But it also had academic courses that invited him to acquaint himself with the capacious "tradition" claimed by the West—and then to insert himself into it by forming an opinion.

II

Rights of the Pryvat Spyrit:
From Dissent to Interpretation

Nothing is more surprising to those, who consider human affairs with a philosophical eye, than to see the easiness with which the many are governed by the few.... When we enquire by what means this wonder is brought about, we shall find, that as Force is always on the side of the governed, the governors have nothing to support them but opinion. 'Tis therefore, on opinion only that government is founded; and this maxim extends to the most despotic and most military governments, as well as to the most free and most popular.
« DAVID HUME, "Of the First Principles of Government" »

From Separation to Society

So now we have constructed, or reconstructed, the American system of education that emerged at the end of the Second World War: a system of universal, general, and liberal education explicitly designed to meet the needs of a democratic society rather than the more restricted and specific needs of the professions or the workplace generally. We have built the community college system that could serve those unprepared to enter a four-year college; we have given community colleges an academic program structured on a general education model, with required courses in a range of disciplines; we have included in that program a humanities course informed by the principle that all people should be introduced to social or cultural knowledge and given some sense of a tradition; we have assigned literature a place of privilege in that tradition; and we have included Shakespeare in that curriculum on the grounds of his singular historical centrality, and in the belief that everyone should be considered worthy of exposure to this pinnacle of culture. We have created all the conditions for Mr. Ramirez's humiliation.

What remains to be explained is how this humiliation was transformed into triumph. The crucial event, in Mr. Ramirez's account, is the question posed to him by his teacher: "What do *you* think?" What was the teacher himself thinking at this moment? Why was it important to ask such a poorly prepared and culturally disadvantaged person for his opinion about the meaning of a literary work? The search for the answer to this question takes us in two directions, one of them concerning the American context, and the other concerning the academic approach to literature, two vectors that crossed in a particularly fruitful way in that fertile Florida moment. Mr. Ramirez's English course also reflected the serendipitous intersection of design and chance: the overall system of education emerging from the postwar years was fully intentional, and the connection between American citizenship and textual interpretation was, as I will argue, deep and longstanding. But the distinctive conventions and assumptions of academic literary study that enabled it to serve as the cornerstone of the educational edifice at that moment have to be accounted as historical contingencies.

This American story begins at the very beginning, with a founding commitment to individual reading and understanding, a populist practice driven by a religious imperative. The Puritans were so fiercely committed to this practice that they left their homeland for the wilderness of the New World rather than compromise it. Like Protestants generally, the Puritans and other dissenters believed that Bible reading was the surest and most essential way for people to form a direct relationship with God. The fact that the Bible was written in Hebrew and Greek, and the Vulgate in Latin, had been an insuperable barrier to such a relationship for ordinary people, who were by necessity dependent on a learned clerisy to relay the Word to them. Martin Luther's translation of the New Testament into vernacular German in 1522, quickly followed in 1525–26 by William Tyndale's English translation, made it possible for lay readers to realize the promise of the Reformation by contemplating the Bible in private. Luther was vilified by Rome, which was outraged at his assumption of private authority; Tyndale, living in a Protestant country, nevertheless made an enemy of the Crown, which retained control of the Church of England. He was apprehended, strangled, and burned at the stake. But as printed Bibles became more common, individual Bible reading was seen by an increasing number of Protestants as the surest path to salvation, and universal literacy as the only protection against the reassertion of ecclesiastical authority. By the end of the sixteenth century in England, the whole dissenting movement had become intolerable to both church and state, which saw in it a dangerously subversive force as well as an implicit accusation that the English Reformation remained an incomplete project.

The interdenominational dispute between the dissenters and the established church turned on crucial subtleties, like those that came into play during a dramatic 1590 conversation between the imprisoned Henry Barrow, a leading member of the Brethren of the Separation, a radical group that argued for a clean break with the Church of England, and Lancelot Andrewes, a powerful cleric who eventually became the bishop of Winchester and the leading figure in the new translation of the Bible authorized by King James.[1] Andrewes's goal in this conversation was to elicit from Barrow, through cunning insinuation, some manifestly culpable utterance. Contemporary portraits of Andrewes show a man fully equal to the task: pale, subtle, inward, tenacious. As Adam Nicolson says, there is in these portraits "a certain distance in the eyes, as if the person had withdrawn an inch or two below the surface of the skin."[2] Andrewes approached indirectly, by way of a discussion of the general principles of interpretation:

ANDREWES: All men cannot judge, who then shal judge of the word?
BARROW: The word, and let every one that judgeth take hede that he judge aright therby. "Wisdom is justified of her children."[3]

In its simplicity, Barrow's assertion is a subtle reply. Each person is to read and comprehend the Bible for him- or herself, but the reading was not to be considered a personal one. Indeed, a merely personal or idiosyncratic interpretation would represent a corruption of the plain sense of the text, a human invention superimposed on the Word of God. It is the duty of the righteous reader to divine the meaning contained in the Word through an act of obedient recognition. "The word" is to judge itself, as it were, and each person must be careful to judge "aright." Such a judgment could not be credited to the wit, probity, learning, or virtue of the individual, but only to that person's success in permitting, through a perfect and pious passivity, the meaning of the text to reveal itself. Such readings had the authority not of the reader but of Scripture itself. Both Andrewes and Barrow would have agreed on the authority of Scripture itself over human interpretations. They differed on the question of how to determine the meaning of Scripture. Andrewes believed that the church establishment, operating through assemblies of learned divines, had the authority to determine what the plain sense of Scripture was; Barrow and the Separatists placed the responsibility with each reader.

And so, in the phrase "every one that judgeth," Andrewes found what he was looking for, the implication that judgment was a task to be undertaken by unbound individuals. "This," he announced to the now-doomed Barrow, "savoreth of a pryvat spyrit." No orderly Christian society, Andrewes believed, could tolerate the arrogance of a sect—in his view a libertine cult—seeking only a personal salvation, to be obtained not through the ceremony of the church but through individual illumination. Andrewes won the battle—Barrow was executed at Tyburn three years after this exchange—but Barrow could be said to have won the war, because the prosecution of Separatists, Puritans, and others of a like mind produced a consensus on all sides that a break was required: Andrewes wanted them gone so their practices could not corrupt the faith of others or compromise the authority of the Crown, and the dissenters wanted to leave so they could cultivate the private spirit without hindrance. The Separatists, seeking to create a church without blemish that conformed to the Augustinian concept of the "invisible" church, the church in the eyes of God, believed that the "visible" Church of England was corrupt beyond possibility of reform. The 102 Pilgrims who embarked on the *Mayflower* in 1620 were mostly Separatists; they, and the Puritans who began to arrive in 1629, sought to found in the wilderness of America a New Jerusalem where each person could seek an individual salvation by grappling with the meaning of the translated and printed Word of God.

The subsequent history of the Puritan settlements suggests that Andrewes may have been right in his suspicions about the effects of the principle of separation on civic life. Having renounced the comforts of their homeland to pursue the Separatist principle, the Puritans found that principle impossible to contain or regulate. Although the harsh conditions of the New World demanded a far greater degree of rigidity, hierarchy, and discipline than had been required in England, the Puritan congregations suffered constant defections, with Gortonites, Baptists,

Anabaptists, Quakers, and others shearing off from the more theologically moderate leadership, each group interpreting the Bible in its own way, each denying in its own way the necessity of church authority even of the antiauthoritarian Puritan kind, and each suffering at the hands of that authority such punishments as banishment, whipping, fining, and even hanging. None of these measures proved to be an effective deterrent to further deviations, however, since deviation was the founding and, as it were, the unifying principle of the entire movement.

The principle of separation was a solution, but it was also a problem, for it created permanent tensions between autonomy and solidarity, unity and schism. These tensions were a constant feature of new-world Puritan society, on display even in the very services of worship—four-hour marathons beginning with readings from the Geneva Bible followed by lengthy analyses by the minister, which would in turn be followed by impromptu interpretations offered by members of the congregation. Nor was the excited suspicion of hidden meanings lurking in the surfaces of things confined to the reading of texts. In a religious community committed to the idea of predestination, the search for "signs of grace"—visible marks of God's favor—was relentless.[4] Still, the most eminently interpretable of all God's works was, for the Puritans, always the Bible, and Bible reading was an imperative for every individual. Indeed, it could be said that one truly became an individual only by reading the Bible, thereby establishing an identity in the eyes of God.

Interpretive facility was a prerequisite for the ministry. Harvard College, formed on European models, chiefly Cambridge University, assumed responsibility for educating those who would guide their congregations in the right direction. The teaching responsibilities of the Puritan minister were spelled out more explicitly than in other religions, and ministers were expected not only to be well informed about the texts they preached from but to devote themselves to spreading literacy. "Dreading to leave an illiterate Ministry to the Churches, when our present Ministers shall lie in the Dust," an early chronicler of the college wrote, "it pleased

God to stir up the heart of one Mr. Harvard," and the result was the founding of a college devoted to literate religiosity.[5] The college was also devoted in its own way to the principle of separation. The first president, Henry Dunster, broke with the church over the issue of infant baptism, thus threatening the authority of the Puritan leadership of the Massachusetts Bay Colony. Dunster was not whipped or fined, but he was strongly encouraged to leave his position. His forced resignation inaugurated a long struggle between Puritan orthodoxy and dissenting voices, a struggle that may have divided the religious communities in the colonies but reaffirmed the primacy of the Separatist principle.

In fact, Harvard was separated from itself. Its primary and original mission was the training of ministers, but only half the early graduates of Harvard entered the clergy, and they had to wait until they had completed their undergraduate degrees before they could take specialized courses in theology. The object of a Harvard education, as one account of the origins of the college puts it, was the cultivation of that figure who would reappear with such full-gathered force in the Redbook, the "whole man," the exemplary moral citizen who would assume leadership responsibilities in the civic life of the community. Toward the end of the seventeenth century, as Puritan dominance faded and the ferocious Puritan concentration on salvation was complemented and necessarily diluted by commercial, cultural, and political interests, learning was put to other uses. The Greek and Latin needed to read the Bible were found to be helpful in inculcating qualities needed in a secular protorepublic; the study of Isocrates, Plato, Homer, Cicero, and Demosthenes could, as one writer put it, "breed statesmanship, nobility, *virtus*."[6]

The enduring Puritan legacy in the New England colonies of the eighteenth century was not directly theological but broadly social and political: widespread literacy, greatly enriched by the increasingly powerful secular print culture of the eighteenth century in which books and the popular press circulated a rich mix of information and opinion. The popular press in particular embraced the spirit of political opposition, which was born in

England but came to maturity in the American colonies. As Michael Warner writes in *The Letters of the Republic: Publication and the Public Sphere in Eighteenth-Century America* (1990), the political development of the colonies depended on the growth of a public for which reading and writing were habitual.[7] The medium was the message, for, as Warner argues, people who read are perhaps dimly but necessarily aware of a public sphere composed of all those who are reading the same thing. And since many of the publications in circulation did not issue from the state but rather from some private, often unnamed source, readers were invited to form their own opinions in response to what they read, so that individual interpretation and evaluation were intrinsic parts of the social process of reading.

The proliferation of print in the last half of the eighteenth century made an immense, even decisive contribution to the emergence of what Christopher Grasso has called "the republican public sphere," "the usually anonymous writing that contributed to a public forum distinct from the mechanisms of the state and from the concerns of private life."[8] The leading revolutionists, many of whom were first-generation gentlemen, were men of letters, and many were college men who had received the eighteenth-century version of a liberal education. Unlike the French revolutionists, or the revolutionists of the nineteenth and twentieth centuries in Europe, they were not desperate men driven by passion but enlightened men animated by a desire for liberty in the form of a new state. They sought, as one writer has put it, to make "a revolution in favor of government."[9] The trigger for the French Revolution was widespread suffering, humiliation, and deprivation; for the American Revolution, it was the desire to create a political order in conformity with reason, nature, and the public good, notions that had been disseminated by print. The connection between democratic legitimacy and a reading public was felt throughout the colonies, nowhere more strongly than at Harvard, a center of revolutionary enthusiasm where the sons of the leading colonial families received an education that prepared them for insurrection.

From Faith to Fiction

When the Founders looked back on their Puritan past, they saw not an embattled congeries of sects incapable of organizing themselves, much less a cult of zealots who burned women and children as witches. They saw a group battling against all odds to cultivate the habits of mind—including a stern rejection of luxury, vice, corruption, and sedimented distinctions of rank and prestige—that were necessary for egalitarian democratic self-governance. This, at least, is the story told by the twenty-nine-year-old John Adams in his "A Dissertation on the Canon and the Feudal Law" (1765), where he argues that the Puritan movement constituted a heroic resistance to the two "great systems of tyranny," the established church (most particularly the Roman Catholic Church) and the system of hereditary nobility.[10] The Puritans had to flee England, Adams argues, not because their religious beliefs were schismatic but because the authorities were infuriated by the Puritans' determination to become, in defiance of established hierarchies, "intelligent in general": "This people had been so vexed, and tortured by the powers of those days, for no other crime than their knowledge, and their freedom of inquiry and examination, and they had so much reason to despair of deliverance from those miseries, on that side the ocean; that they at last resolved to fly to the *wilderness* for refuge from the temporal and spiritual principalities and powers, and plagues and scourges, of their *native* country" (114). The battle for freedom of inquiry and examination was never-ending, for even in the wilderness a force of reaction tended always to reinstate a "dark ribaldry" of privilege and power that would, if unchecked, reduce the citizenry to a condition of "Sordid Ignorance and staring Timidity," ending in "a blind, implicit obedience" (117, 109, 110). Only a resolute Puritan commitment to "knowledge diffused generally through the whole body of the people," Adams insists, had prevented the emergence of a recrudescent tyranny (118).

Even in his own time, Adams notes, there was resistance to the diffusion of knowledge, coming not from descendants of the first settlers, but from a few recently arrived

high churchmen and high statesmen . . . who affect to censure this
provision for the education of our youth as a needless expence, and
an imposition upon the rich in favour of the poor—and as an institution productive of idleness and vain speculation among the people,
whose time and attention it is said ought to be devoted to labour,
and not to public affairs or to examination into the conduct of their
superiours. And certain officers of the crown, and certain other mis-
sionaries of ignorance, foppery, servility and slavery, have been most
inclined to countenance and increase the same party. ("Dissertation," 120)

It is striking how explicitly and vehemently Adams denounces
the vocationalist argument as a proxy for imperial power and
privilege, a dark force opposing the real interests of the colonial settlers, which included the ceaseless and skeptical examination of the conduct of the ruling class.[11] Equally striking is
the manifest pride with which he describes the Puritan practice
of levying penalties on towns that did not support a grammar
school at public expense, and the general respect in the early
settlements for knowledge, such that even poor people were, he
reports, proud to contribute to the colleges. In Adams's account,
the connections between learning and liberty were self-evident:
a humanistically informed populace that had studied history,
philosophy, religion, and politics is a populace prepared for self-
governance. Increase Mather would have been horrified by the
thought that the Puritan settlements had been merely a bridge to
enlightened republicanism, civic humanism, and nascent nation-
alism, but in Adams's account, this is what they were.

The strength and clarity of the genealogical line leading from
the Puritan separation to colonial revolutionary fervor was also
recognized on the other side of the ocean. In his 1775 address
to the House of Commons, "On Conciliation with America,"
Edmund Burke traced the extraordinary, even violent devotion
to the concept of freedom among the colonials to their peculiar
form of religion which, he said, was not merely Protestant but
Protestant "of that kind which is the most adverse to all implicit
submission of mind and opinion" and therefore implicitly hostile
to government.[12] This hostility set American Protestantism apart

from both Roman Catholicism, which had always been on easy terms with state power, and the Church of England, which "was formed from her creadle under the nursing care of regular government." The "dissenting interests," by contrast, "have sprung up in direct opposition to all the ordinary powers of the world; and could justify that opposition only on a strong claim to natural liberty. . . . All protestantism, even the most cold and passive, is a kind of dissent. But the religion most prevalent in our northern colonies is a refinement on the principle of resistance; it is the dissidence of dissent; and the protestantism of the protestant religion" (121–22). Although many of the most influential colonial leaders were more deistic than theistic, the revolutionary principles they were proclaiming represented, according to Burke, a distilled form of the already highly distilled form of American Protestantism, a political continuation of the Puritan principle of separation.

The revolutionary freedom sought by the French thirteen years later was, by contrast, explicitly antireligious. The French revolutionaries issued no pronouncements on religious freedom, but rather, as Burke put it in *Reflections on the Revolution in France* (1790), enlisted the aid of a "literary cabal" to undermine the Christian religion "through the medium of opinion," dedicating themselves to the task with such zeal that that "their whole conversation, which otherwise would have been pleasing and instructive, [was] perfectly disgusting."[13] Customarily, Burke noted, major changes in government are attended by greater exactness in religious practices; but the French, in the name of equality, had "doubled the license of a ferocious dissoluteness in manners and of an insolent irreligion in opinions and practice" (125). They reaped what they sowed, and revolutionary France, flouting its atheism and independence from the past, degenerated into an ungovernable chaos.

Many of Burke's contemporaries were mystified by the difference between the stances he took toward the two epochal revolutions of the age. How could Burke so warmly approve the cause of freedom for the Americans (as well as colonial subjects in

South Asia) from British authority and influence and yet condemn their counterparts in France? William Hazlitt asserted that the two versions of Burke on display in these debates "are not the same person, but opposite persons—not opposite persons only, but deadly enemies."[14] Recent scholarship has been more inclined to devise ingenious ways of seeing points of connection or a deeper compatibility between the two Burkes, but the manifest opposition between the two arguments represents a conundrum that all Burke scholars must struggle to comprehend. The question is best left to specialists, but perhaps the problem will not seem so intractable if we understand the real issue for Burke to be not revolution or democracy as such, but the effectiveness with which a society manages the immense and potentially destructive force of opinion.

Burke understood that there was a great gulf fixed between opinions that were respectful of, and regulated by, reason, religion, and tradition—for example, his own *Reflections*, which he described as "opinions" formed by "long observation and much impartiality"—and those that were not (*Reflections*, 376). He understood, too, however, that this gulf, or channel, was alarmingly easy to cross, and that opinion was eminently corruptible, especially during turbulent times when, in the absence of stable authority, issues of great consequence might be decided by sudden gusts of popular sentiment. In the American case, Burke saw the right kind of opinion—the English kind. England, he pointed out, had in effect exported the spirit of opposition and dissent to the colonies, which had become "not only devoted to liberty, but to liberty according to English ideas, and on English principles" ("Conciliation," 120).[15] If English soldiers were to take arms against the revolutionaries, they would, Burke argued, be opposing their own heritage, denying their own deepest commitments.

The English were forensically outmaneuvered before they were engaged on the battlefield. Having purchased as many copies of Blackstone's *Commentaries* as had been sold in all of Britain, the Americans understood the English Constitution every bit as well as the English; they fully grasped, for example, the specific injustice of taxation without representation. Not merely intelligent in general, the Americans were sophisticated about the law. "Permit me," Burke said to his fellow MPs,

> to add another circumstance in our Colonies, which contributes no mean part toward the growth and effect of this untractable spirit—I mean their education. In no country perhaps in the world is the law so general a study.... The greater number of the Deputies sent to Congress were Lawyers.... This study renders men acute, inquisitive, dexterous, prompt in attack, ready in defence, full of resources. In other countries, the people, more simple and of a less mercurial cast, judge of an ill principle in government only by an actual grievance; here they anticipate the evil, and judge of the pressure of the grievance by the badness of the principle. They augur misgovernment at a distance, and snuff the approach of tyranny in every tainted breeze. ("Conciliation," 123–24)

The colonial educational system had produced a lawyered-up population (a trend that has continued: the United States is among the world leaders in the number of lawyers per capita, with three times as many as Britain). Building on bedrock religious principle, and deeply informed by English law and customs, the American revolutionaries had constructed not a New Jerusalem but a New England in the New World; and given the vast ocean that stretched between the Crown and its recalcitrant colonies, and defended as these colonies were by their well-regulated arms-bearing militias, any attempt at applying force majeure was doomed. Conciliation, for Burke, was the only course.

Burke lost the argument, and the vote. As it turned out, he had been speaking in dissent. By the time news of his three-hour oration reached the colonies, the battles of Lexington and Concord had been fought and the course of revolution set.

That this was a war fought over the legitimacy of dissenting opinion had been clear from July 4, 1776, when the Continental Congress issued what has become known as the Declaration of Independence, announcing its determination to establish the "separate and equal station" to which they believed the "Laws of Nature and of Nature's God" entitled them. The Puritans would have found preposterous and even horrifying the idea of submitting themselves to the "laws of Nature," but if they had been able to look into the future and read the Declaration, they might have recognized a certain continuity between their insistence on individual Bible reading and the idea of a community defined by its commitment to individual rights: life, liberty, and the pursuit of happiness, to be sure, but beginning with and grounded in the right to one's own view. Indeed, they may even have been sensible of an affinity between their own insistence on the radical reformation of the church and the revolutionary premise that the English Constitution, once the glory of the nation, had become, as one politically engaged minister put it in 1775, "*rotten* to the very core."[16] While the distance between the Separatists and what the signers of the Declaration called "our Separation" was considerable, the cord connecting them was strong.[17]

The Declaration echoed around the world, inspiring well over a hundred variations that adapted its basic form to local circumstances, homages that included the 1848 Seneca Falls Declaration of Sentiments on women's rights signed by Elizabeth Cady Stanton, Lucretia Mott, and Frederick Douglass, among others.[18] What all these declaring groups had in common was a set of strong opinions about the rights to which they were entitled. And what appealed to them about the Declaration was the document's insistence on the fundamental, and indeed "natural," right to such opinions. This right is in fact the real issue engaged by the Declaration. The document we now call the Declaration of Independence was not the actual declaration, which had been voted on by the Continental Congress two days earlier. The point of the July 4 document was, Carl L. Becker writes, "not to declare independence, but to proclaim to the world the reasons for declaring independence"—in other words, to attempt to influence world opinion.[19] Becker finds the appeal to natural law voiced in the Declaration sadly lacking in depth and substance, and somewhat beside the main point, which he locates in the inconspicuous phrase near the end of the very first sentence that explains why a declaration was needed. When in the course of human events one people seeks to break the political bonds that have bound them to another, "a decent respect to the Opinions of mankind requires that they should declare the causes which impel them to the separation."

An unaltered inheritance from the first English settlers, the silent premise of these words is that opinions are to be respected because they represent a particularly pure and foundational instance of the principle of separation itself, the right of each person to his or her own thoughts. This right is the basis of what Hannah Arendt describes as modern political authority, which is founded, as she memorably puts it in *The Origins of Totalitarianism* (1951), on "the right to have rights."[20] The revolutionists understood what the Protestant Separatists had not, that this bedrock of minimal human dignity could only be secured by a legal and political structure. The poor, bare, forked human animal who stands altogether beyond the boundaries of a political community is, Arendt says, more utterly dispossessed of humanity than a slave, who still has a place, however degraded, in society. (In fact, she points out, the slave or stateless person who commits a crime actually rises in stature because the law suddenly takes notice, and the person acquires the rights of the accused.) The American Revolution was fought not on behalf of a maximal separation, an absolute individual freedom, but rather in pursuit of a political and legal system that would provide people with both freedom and a measure of security, justice, and order.

Arendt's "right to have rights" is often cited; less often noted is the sentence that follows this phrase, in which she develops a very particular conception of opinion as an indicator of rights in general. People who lack rights, she says, "are deprived . . . not of the right to think whatever they please, but of the right to opinion" (*Origins of Totalitarianism*, 296). The distinction suggests that opinion, for Arendt, is not simply an unformalized inner conviction but the public form of that conviction, not just a thought but an expression, not just a belief but an argument. "Opinions," she says in *On Revolution*, her comparative study of the French and American Revolutions written twelve years later, "never belong to groups but exclusively to individuals ... no multitude, be it the multitude of a part or of the whole society, will ever be capable of forming an opinion." And yet— the crucial point—opinions are not to be hoarded or kept in secret, but shared: "Opinions will rise wherever men communicate freely with one another and have the right to make their views public. ... Opinions are formed and tested in a process of exchange of opinion against opinion."[21] Politically speaking, the opinionated private spirit realizes itself in public conversation in a civil society.

Like Burke, Arendt praised the American and excoriated the French Revolution. For both, the point of distinction was the status of opinion. The mighty force of opinion in the modern political order, she writes, "was discovered by both the French and the American Revolutions, but only the latter—and this shows once more the high rank of its political creativity—knew how to build a lasting institution for the formation of public views into the very structure of the republic" (*On Revolution*, 220). While the French Revolution sank into a "chaos of unrepresented and unpurified opinions" as the people waited for a strong leader to mold the nation into a single unanimous "public opinion" (a unanimity that would absorb and nullify all individual convictions), the Americans sought ways to preserve and enhance the integrity of uncoerced individual opinions, on which, they recognized, the legitimacy of the government would depend. Thus, for Arendt, the "greatness" of the Declaration, and indeed of the Revolution itself, lies in the appeal to what the Declaration calls "the tribunal of the world," a phrase that marks the entry of a new political form into the world (120).

Asserting the privileged status of opinion is thus the real project of the Declaration, which addresses itself to a vast cosmopolitan community of those sensible of their own freedom to think and to argue. Submitting their case to the opinions of mankind, and implying that these opinions deserved respect precisely because they were opinions and therefore the product of free thinking, the revolutionists made their argument not by presenting a list of (now largely forgotten) "abuses and usurpations" committed by the Crown and Parliament, but rather by the mere act of addressing a universal humanity whose defining feature was a respect for independent opinion.[22]

The magisterial solemnity of the Declaration obscures the delicacy with which it finesses two very different kinds of statement, the first an appeal to freedom signaled by the phrase "we hold"—that is, we freely choose to believe—and second an appeal to transcendent necessity in the affirmation of "self-evident" truths from which no dissent is possible. On moral and political grounds, Arendt deplores the "self-evident" as a weakness and praises the "we hold" for its admirably modern emphasis on accountability, mutuality, and reciprocity. But Jefferson may have been thinking more pragmatically.[23] Since the revolution was to be undertaken in the service of freedom, he may have felt that act of separation had to be represented as one of solidarity and volition; hence "we hold." But given the inevitable sacrifices of the coming war, he may have thought that the impelling causes had to be represented as incontestable. People had to feel that they had an obligation to rebel; hence "self-evident."

The Declaration was not Jefferson's last word on the rights of opinion. The text now known as the Bill for Establishing Religious Freedom in Virginia, drafted in 1777 and finally enacted into law in 1786, extended the domain of opinion to religion, describing faith not as obligatory reverence but as a set of "opinions and modes of thinking" that people might choose to adopt.[24] In a theologically nimble turn of argument, Jefferson derives the capacity and the right to make such a choice directly from God, who "hath created the mind free"—so free that any elevation of one religion over another, or of religion over agnosticism or atheism, would represent a state-sponsored violation of the divinely ordained condition of human existence. Any governmental regulation of opinion, Jefferson warns, could lead directly to general hypocrisy and tyranny. "Be it enacted," therefore, the statute says, that "no man shall be compelled to frequent or support any religious worship, place, or ministry whatsoever, nor shall be enforced, restrained, molested, or burdened in his body or goods, nor shall otherwise suffer on account of his religious opinions or belief; but that all men shall be free to profess, and by argument to maintain, their opinions in matters of religion, and that the same shall in nowise diminish, enlarge, or affect their civil capacities" (546). The rights of religious freedom, the statute concludes, are numbered among "the natural rights of mankind" (546–47).

In Jefferson's view, the classification of religious belief as a species of opinion was crucial because it provided a prima facie case for freedom. In a phrase deleted from the original document by the more cautious and conservative Virginia Senate, Jefferson had stated that "the opinions of men are not the object of civil government, nor under its jurisdiction" (546). The manifest impossibility of the state regulating opinion provided a pragmatic and "natural" justification for religious freedom, just as the appeal to the opinions of mankind had by itself made the case for the Declaration of Independence.

Opinions may have been private, but, for Jefferson, they provided the very substance of public discourse. They were, that is, not merely to be held, but shared: all men should be free to profess *and by argument to maintain* their views. Jefferson recognized not just a personal right to one's opinions, but also a right and even an implied responsibility to enter into public discussion to advocate for or defend those opinions. The mark of a democratic society, in Jefferson's rapidly crystallizing view, was a culture of open public debate turning on differences of opinion. This concept of a culture of public argumentation represents, according to Arendt, a democratic departure from a monarchical model in which the sovereign sought, at least in times of peace and prosperity, to ensure the private happiness of his subjects. In the new model, private happiness gives way to "public liberty" or "public happiness," in which citizens find their deepest fulfillment in the public realm, engaging with their fellow citizens in argumentation, disputation, persuasion, and public discourse generally.[25]

In exploring the conceptual and political resources of opinion, Jefferson and his co-revolutionists were groping their way toward a radical reinvention of the English concept of popular sovereignty. As Edmund S. Morgan argues in *Inventing the People* (1988), the consent of the people on which popular sovereignty depends is "sustained by opinions,"[26] a term to which he, like Arendt, gives a very particular meaning. An opinion, for Morgan, is a belief that stands at a certain remove from fact. The king is God's vice-regent on earth; our representatives are citizens like ourselves, not part of the ruling class; all men are created equal; all power rests ultimately with the people; the founding of the Republic conformed to natural law and had a religious sanction; a militia composed of virtuous yeomen will easily defeat the hired minions of a professional army; free-market capitalism is the best possible economic system—all these propositions would qualify, in Morgan's account, as opinions of the sort that might sustain a government, a ruling class, a national self-understanding. They have this stabilizing function not because they are incontestable, but because they are doubtful. A proposition, for Morgan, is only an opinion—and therefore capable of bearing the load of a democratic government—if there is evidence both for and against it. If the emperor is manifestly a degenerate scoundrel, then consent will be withdrawn and the government will fall. But if, on the other hand, the king is truly divine, consent will be rendered irrelevant by reverence, with the same catastrophic consequences for popular sovereignty.

Why should the survival of the state depend on the precise calibration of the distance between opinions and the truth? Morgan does not say as much, but the most plausible explanation is that what he calls opinion is one name for the permanently unstable compromise between the freely given consent signaled by "we hold" and the rational necessity announced by "self-evident." A free people can choose their opinions and change them when they wish. But if the change is seen as arbitrary, whimsical, or merely opportunistic, then their opinions will count for little, and authority itself will suffer. The new opinion, like the old, must be seen to have some evidentiary basis so that those who make the change can plausibly claim to have been persuaded by the facts.[27] But the new view must not be so self-evident that no judgment is required to embrace it, for in that case the adoption of the new view would testify not to freedom but to necessity.

The entire delicate dance of conviction and doubt, freedom and necessity, resembles nothing so much as a reader's engagement in a fictional narrative, in which credence is granted on the condition that it not be tested beyond its limits. Morgan appropriates a phrase from Samuel Taylor Coleridge in noting that "government requires make-believe . . . a willing suspension of disbelief" (*Inventing the People*, 13). Coleridge was referring, in the *Biographia Literaria*, to the peculiar magic of a fantastic or supernatural tale that manages to enlist the reader's "poetic faith" despite its manifest implausibility. An analogy between political consent and a reader's voluntary submission to a fictional text runs throughout Morgan's thinking. For Morgan, fiction is the answer to the many paradoxes and mysteries of popular sovereignty, beginning with the most thoroughly mysterious and indeed fictional concept of all, "the people." "Before we ascribe sovereignty to the people," Morgan says, "we have to imagine that there is such a thing, something we personify as though it were a single body, capable of thinking, of acting, of making decisions and carrying them out, something quite apart from government, superior to government, and able to alter or remove a government at will" (*Inventing the People*, 153). The people must be conceived before they can be born.

Who is responsible for the work of conceiving, or, as Morgan would have it, inventing? In the English case, it was Parliament itself. When, in England in the 1640s, the members of the House of Commons invoked "the people" as a mystical body in whose name they rose up in defiance of the king, they "invented the sovereignty of the people in order to claim it for themselves. . . . In the name of *the* people they became all-powerful in government" (*Inventing the People*, 49–50). In the American instance, "the people" were in effect "invented" by the Declaration—and then, as we will see, reinvented by the Constitution.

Morgan is a highly original and sometimes iconoclastic thinker, but his title, *Inventing the People*, is now a cliché, shared by a number of other books, essays, courses, and seminars, along with numerous other works that discuss the "invention" of American history, American reality, the American presidency, American broadcasting, American fashion—and, of course, a comparable number of works that describe the "reinvention" of some or all of America.[28] The term "invention" has technical-mechanical associations that invoke the shades of Benjamin Franklin, Thomas Edison, Alexander Graham Bell, Henry Ford, and the tradition of American pragmatism and know-how; but given the highly rhetorical and even fabulistic dimensions of the founding of the American nation, the invention in question is actually closer in spirit to the act of literary creation. The founding of the Republic was a creative act undertaken on a different scale and in a different medium but of the same ex nihilo kind as the writing of, say, a novel: the long-sought Great American Novel is—America.[29]

From Origin to Originalism

Those living in the colonies may have had to represent themselves, or consent to be represented, as "one people" in order to win their independence. But the war having been won, the overriding question was how to create a system that could accommodate both the desire for freedom and the necessity of law. In order to build such a system, the fable of the unitary populace united in its fervent desire for independence had to be, as it were, unwritten or overwritten, and the temporary and strategic unity disambiguated, so the "will of the people" would not constitute itself as what Adams called a "dark ribaldry" of homegrown oppression. This was a real fear. As Burke had said, Americans "augur misgovernment at a distance, and snuff the approach of tyranny in every tainted breeze," even when the breeze was coming not from England but from their own land. During the years before the adoption of the Constitution, with proposals of all kinds, including the eighty-five Federalist Papers, proliferating in the public press, any ambiguity in a given proposal was thought, especially by the anti-Federalists, to harbor a potential for oppression, or to provide a foothold for luxury, corruption, or ambition.[30] How to preserve the rights of the private spirit in a society of laws? How to create a republic that would also be a democracy? How to protect against the dangerous fantasy that "the people" was "one"?[31]

In addition to the Bill of Rights, which the political theorist Michael Walzer has described as a list of "entitlements to nonconformity and dissidents," three other constitutional "inventions" provided sanctuaries for the dissenting private opinion.[32] The first was broad and structural: the construction of a system that distributed authority in a new way through a "mixed" or "compounded" governmental structure. The system included at the federal level an executive and a legislature, both popularly elected; and then a further division within the legislature between one body that was more populist and another that was less so; and an appointed judiciary—and then, as a check on the power of the federal system as a whole, the entire structure was replicated at the state level, with the addition of judicial elections. As Bernard Bailyn notes, the Framers of the Constitution were focused on "the fear of centralized power" and motivated by "the belief that free states are fragile and degenerate easily into tyrannies unless vigilantly protected by a free, knowledgeable, and uncorrupted electorate working through institutions that balance and distribute rather than concentrate power" (*Ideological Origins*, 323). Reflecting a "kinetic theory of politics," the checks and balances created by the Constitution were, Gordon Wood says, designed to create "such a crumbling of political and social interests, such an atomization of authority, such a parceling of power . . . such a multiplicity and a scattering of designs and passions, so many checks, that no combination of parts could hold, no group of evil interests could long cohere" (*Creation of the American Republic*, 605). Even with all the checks and balances, Patrick Henry felt that the Constitution contained, as John Quincy Adams was to recall, "an awful squinting towards a monarchy."[33]

The second means of ensuring protections for the dissenting individual was through an adaptation of the English principle of representative government. Clearly, the English model, in which suffrage was far from universal and most people never saw (or had even heard of) their representatives, was inappropriate for a representative democracy. Nor was the presumption of a British MP that he represented not a borough or a county but rather the nation as a whole the right approach in a nation in which separation, and therefore local difference, was a founding principle.[34] The American people demanded a closer and more responsive relationship with their elected officials. Individuals wanted to feel a direct connection to the authority that exercised the power that the people theoretically possessed, and this could only be achieved through a more direct and accountable form of representation.

But what did a representative really represent? And how was he to go about representing it? What *was* a representative—what is representation?

Morgan offers a definition: "Representation is itself a fiction." Indeed, he says, it is "our fiction" in the sense that a willing suspension of disbelief in representation defines and stabilizes the American system of government (*Inventing the People*, 23, 38). Representation has become such a familiar concept to us that it is now difficult to recover the strangeness, the deep improbability of a system in which "the people" are held to be the sole legitimate source of power even as they are compelled by law to submit to the power of their governors. Just as fictional, in Morgan's sense, as the "power of the people" is the popular belief that representation involves a merely political relationship centering on public issues and calculable interests, when in fact it involves profoundly subjective and intersubjective judgments. Those whose votes are solicited must assess not only the stated views and documented accomplishments of the candidate, but also his character, capacities, and inclinations; and then, once in office, the representative has to speculate about the true wishes, deeper interests, shifting priorities, and general understanding of those he represents. Deep, probing, and continuous speculation about the mental states of others is required of all parties, with no certainty possible. How does it all work? Somehow, it does. As Morgan says, representation is "the central enigma of popular sovereignty" (39); or as Arendt puts it, representation is "one of those dilemmas which permit of no solution" (*On Revolution*, 228–29).[35]

The third accommodation for the private spirit is not "in" the Constitution; it is the Constitution itself. Composed in the simplest and sparest possible language by a tiny group of influential men, the Constitution represents an audacious and paradoxical act of self-founding, in which liberty granted itself power (as opposed, for example, to the Magna Carta, through which authority granted liberty). Itself unconstitutional in that it preceded its own adoption and therefore lacked constitutional warrant, the Constitution serves as a law of laws, a fundamental law standing above or behind all the actions of government. Unlike statutory law, the Constitution does not legislate; it legitimates, decreeing the forms and processes by which legislation is written and adopted. The bootstrapping result of years of ideological, intellectual, and political dispute, the document simply absorbs and annuls the confusions and compromises that preceded the inscription of its pristine sentences. "It is," Arendt comments, "in the very nature of a beginning to carry with itself a measure of complete arbitrariness" (*On Revolution*, 199). *Let there be law!*

One of the battles fought during the drafting concerned the status of the Constitution itself. More committed than many of his co-revolutionists to the principle of revolution, Jefferson thought that constitutional conventions ought to be held on a regular basis; Madison, on the other hand, felt that such periodic revisitations of basic principles would convey an "implication of defect in the government," and "would in great measure deprive the government of that veneration, which time bestows on every thing, and without which perhaps the wisest and freest governments would not possess the requisite stability."[36] Madison prevailed, and Americans have venerated their founding documents, if not their governments, ever since. The Constitution in particular has been, as one writer put it at the time, considered to be "*sacred and inviolate,*" something that "no Legislature ought to presume to alter or amend."[37] Most consequentially, the sacral view of the Constitution has had adherents on the Supreme Court, exemplified by Justice Hugo Black (raised in the Primitive Baptist church in Clay County, Alabama), who argued his case in a book called *A Constitutional Faith.*[38] The venerable Constitution anchors what some have called America's "civil religion," and serves as the focal point for what Sanford Levinson describes as the "faith community" devoted to its interpretation.[39]

In keeping with the Separatist tradition, this faith community is both unified in its devotion to the Constitution and fragmented by it, divided on the question of whether the document is a fixed repository of timeless wisdom or a historical artifact produced by people no wiser than we. This division corresponds to what Levinson characterizes as a "Protestant" camp that insists on the words of the text itself (*Sola scriptura!*) and a "Catholic" camp that accepts the legitimacy of subsequent judicial interpretations, especially those by the Supreme Court. Each camp contains sectarian subdivisions, with the entirety, according to Levinson, comprehensible only in religious terms. He cites one scholar who notes that America, having prohibited the establishment of a state religion, got one anyway: "The very habits of mind begotten by an authoritarian Bible and a religion of submission to a higher power have been carried over to an authoritarian Constitution and a philosophy of submission to a 'higher law.'"[40]

Would that it were so simple. The Constitution is not sacred, but quasi-sacred, ambivalently secular and religious. Nothing in the document is untouched by this ambivalence, not even the most basic question of all: does the Constitution guarantee rights that people already have (and if so, are these natural or divine in origin?), or does it grant rights as a consequence of a political agreement struck at a particular time and place?

Issuing from fully visible public and political processes but strongly implying transcendent authority, the Constitution invites debate at every level, and thus solicits both veneration and interminable doctrinal controversies. These controversies, arising from the documentary, textual character of the Constitution, have been extraordinarily effective in securing the rights of people to their own opinion. The Framers apparently wanted to produce a simple, transparent statement of grounding principles, a text whose meaning could be comprehended by any citizen without specialized learning or refined interpretive skills. They deliberately rejected the complexities and subtleties of English law as organic products of the long and tumultuous history of another land, and therefore inappropriate as a model for the new nation. Quirks, intricacies, contradictions, controversies—all these were strenuously rejected by Jefferson, who wrote that "the great principles of right and wrong are legible to every reader: to pursue them requires not the aid of many counsellors."[41]

The Framers may have sought transparency, but the effect of their efforts was to create extraordinary occasions for dispute, controversy, and legalistic pettifoggery. Simplicity does not guarantee clarity. In fact, Wood points out, the very lucidity of the Constitution's language "demanded an increase, not a lessening, of judicial interpretation and discretion" (*Creation of the American Republic*, 303). As a Connecticut minister said in 1781 of the new system then coming into focus, "Much will depend upon the wisdom and integrity of the judges."[42]

Contemporary legal conservatives sometimes equate interpretation with "judicial activism," and prefer to think of the judiciary on the model of baseball umpires calling, as Chief Justice John Roberts put it in his 2005 Senate confirmation hearing, "balls and strikes" as each case whizzes by.[43] Thinkers of this persuasion often say that the Constitution is a plain and pristine statement of unambiguous principles whose meaning was fixed at the time of enactment, and that the document itself, rather than anyone's interpretation of it, should command our allegiance. This distrust of interpretation underlies the "originalist" positions taken by Supreme Court justice Clarence Thomas and his former colleague Antonin Scalia, who have argued that any difficulties that arise in the interpretation of the Constitution should be settled not by referring to judicial precedent or custom, but by adhering as closely as possible to what is often called the original public meaning of the text.[44] A related but even more restrictive formulation holds that the meaning of the Constitution was fixed by the original understanding of the Framers, the first intentions that informed the text.

It would be logical to assume that those who hold originalist views are referring, and deferring, to the intentions of people like James Madison, the "Father of the Constitution." But Madison never intended his intentions to be given special authority, or even to be considered at all. Recalling in an 1821 letter the Constitutional Convention of 1787, Madison said that he believed at the time that the meaning of the Constitution ought to be "derived from the text itself," but experience had shown him that the text is unclear in places, and its application to real situations often uncertain. In some cases, he said, a "key" seems to be required. That key, he proposed, was to be found in the intentionality behind the text. This seems like the original originalism, but it is not, for by intention Madison meant the general theme or spirit of the document, and not the subjective states of the Framers, which he regarded bluntly as irrelevant.[45] The only intentions Madison would even consider admitting were not his or those of his fellow Framers and Founders, but rather those of a large number of people whose identities he did not even know. The full passage in that 1821 letter reads: ". . . derived from the text itself, or if a key is to be sought elsewhere, it must be not in the opinions or intentions of the Body which planned and proposed the Constitution, but in the sense attached to it by the people in their respective State Conventions where it recd. all the authority which it possesses."[46] By this means, Madison meant to draw a bright line not just between public meaning and private intention, but also between the Framers and the legitimate source of authority, "the people."

Madison believed that while the Framers, at least some of them, may have known what they intended, they were merely authors—indeed, most of them were merely signatories—and the document that left their hands was not yet the law of the land. The Constitution only became law when it was ratified by the states, which is to say, by "the people in their respective State Conventions." By "the people," Madison clearly intended to designate not the individual citizens of the states, but rather the collective populations whose general will was expressed by representatives. Nor were those representatives to be considered as real historical individuals. Madison certainly did not intend to lodge the final authority for the law of the land in the hearts of men who, for all we know, were pressured, uninformed, indifferent, confused, drunk, or bribed. Nor did he intend to efface the memory of the robust debate that ended with ratification. (In the crucial state of Virginia, the vote was eighty-nine in favor, seventy-nine opposed.) The representatives, in Madison's view, were to be taken in the loose aggregate as the rough instrument of a plural citizenry, also taken in the aggregate.

Madison's equivocal originalism has two consequences: first, it affirms that the meaning of the Constitution can be determined even in hard cases through the application of an interpretive key based on intention; but second, it casts profound doubt over the likelihood of ever determining with any precision the "sense attached" (whatever that could mean) to the document by "the people" (whoever they may be).

The textuality of the Constitution ensures an endless quest for definitive meaning, a quest that will last as long as the Republic itself. So dependent is the text on the interpretive activity of the people, so incomplete is the unalterable inscription without a continuous collective reinvestment in the founding moment, that many legal scholars have felt that in order to be workable at all, the Constitution requires the stabilizing supplement of a vast "unwritten Constitution" composed of Supreme Court opinions, congressional statutes, political norms, important presidential speeches, and accepted legislative practices.[47] The mass of such material approaches the condition of the British Common Law, an uncodified mass of binding judicial precedents that has sustained the British legal system since the Middle Ages. An admirable system in many respects, common law lacks, however, the democratizing feature of being equally accessible to any citizen. Professional training is required in order to master the vast array of possible precedents that might bear on any given case, and a learned clerisy, marked by extravagances of dress and speech, is interposed between the people and the law that governs them. By contrast, an unalterable constitutional text written in plain English whose meaning is held to be a function of the intentions animating it provides a sanctuary for the individual interpretive determinations of the private spirit.

Ensuring perpetual disagreement and contention, the Constitution seems to some theorists a "tragic" betrayal of the revolutionary solidarity of the Declaration. Others read the Constitution as a prescription for an "agonistic" politics oriented toward the increase of freedom through regulated conflict.[48] One could argue whether either of these is an intended outcome, but what is unarguable is that while the Declaration speaks of "one people" united in revolutionary assurance and solidarity, the Constitution speaks in the name of "we the people," a plural form that suggests a mass of individuals struggling collectively toward a "more perfect union" than the one they currently have. As Arendt says, the French Revolution sought to identify the "unanimous" or "General Will" of the people, while the Americans sought precisely to avoid any sense of unanimity, and to erect a permanent law that ensured that the public would remain plural and heterogeneous, with generous provision made for dissenting opinion.[49] In the American system, popular struggle lies within the mandate of the law; indeed, one of the perennial forms of that struggle is a continuous conversation about the law itself.

From Eloquence to Abolition

Anachronism is inevitable when describing periods of transition: we give the name of the achieved form to an emergent energy that entered public conversation under a different title, cloaked in the reassuring guise of a traditional idea. A particularly striking example is provided by John Quincy Adams's *Lectures on Rhetoric and Oratory*, delivered in the first decade of the nineteenth century to Harvard undergraduates.[50] The son of the second president of the United States, the Boylston Professor of Rhetoric and Oratory at Harvard, and a senator from Massachusetts, Adams argued not on behalf of the print culture that drove the Revolutionary movement, but on behalf of a much older concept, the dialectical opposite of print, "eloquence."[51]

The immediate object of Adams's lectures was to put the scions of the ruling class in mind of the classical tradition to which their status and education gave them privileged access. To his audience, the man who would become known in his later years as "Old Man Eloquent" may have seemed a voice of reaction, praising classical virtues in a postclassical era. But it is possible to read Adams's lectures another way, as attempts to explain to those likely to be in positions of influence the deep rules of the new game of democracy. At a moment when American culture was being transformed from the Enlightenment-based republican model most in evidence during the Revolutionary and immediately post-Revolutionary years to the more egalitarian, tumultuous, ambitious, and—Adams felt—vulgar and disorderly democratic society of the early nineteenth century, Adams sought to represent the rhetorical tradition of Demosthenes and Cicero as an invaluable resource for American public culture, the noblest form of that humble democratic phenomenon, persuasion.[52] To do so, he had to wrest classical eloquence free from two antidemocratic associations—the culture of privilege, and the mob passions of the French Revolution—and to hold out the possibility of a contemporary discourse that was both democratic and worthy of its predecessors. An American eloquence based not on irrational mystification or the "Babylonish dialect of the schools" but rather on reason would, Adams argued, preserve the republican ethos of the nation's origins even as the nation was abandoning classical republican virtues (*Lectures*, 1:55). Eloquence properly considered, Adams told his young listeners, is essentially and inherently democratic and emancipatory, "grappled, as with hooks of steel, to the soul of liberty" (1:71). Thus "the only birth place of eloquence therefore must be a free state. . . . Eloquence is the child of liberty, and can descend from no other stock" (1:68–69).

Adams was trying to get his audience of Harvard undergraduates to understand that the responsibility for preserving the integrity and autonomy of the private spirit, and thus the character of the nation, had been passed from the Puritans to them—or, to be more comprehensive and precise, from God to Moses and the prophets, to the heroes of classical rhetoric, through the Puritans, and then to the Founders such as himself, before finally coming, hopefully, to rest on the young men he was addressing as "Sons of Harvard!" (*Lectures*, 1:29). Adams was eloquent in the service of eloquence: "Let then the frosty rigor of the logician tell you, that eloquence is an insidious appeal to the passions of men. Let the ghastly form of despotism groan from his hollow lungs and bloodless heart, that eloquence is the instrument of turbulence and the weapon of faction. . . . Answer; silence them forever, by recurring to this great and overpowering truth. Say, that by the eternal constitution of things it was ordained, that liberty should be the parent of eloquence; that eloquence should be the last stay and support of liberty; that with her she is ever destined to live, to flourish, and to die" (1:71–72). One can imagine the response of today's undergraduates to repeated (thirty-six!) harangues in this vein by a figure who so fully exemplified both lofty eloquence and "frosty rigor." Adams's students, according to the volume's preface, unanimously demanded that his lectures be published so they could be cherished in perpetuity.

The term "eloquence" no longer strikes the democratic note, and Adams's lectures now seem, like many subsequent proclamations to undergraduates, less like plausible advice for future conduct and more like an elegy for the rotundities of the past. The tide was with Andrew Jackson, who ended Adams's presidency after a single term, trouncing him in the 1828 presidential race. But one of the new, even revolutionary thoughts Adams was laboring to express in the almost quixotically antiquated terms most natural to him represents a political discovery the importance of which was, at the time, far from self-evident: that a democratic society is knit together by a collective commitment to argumentation and persuasion, activities centered in the numerous deliberative bodies that constitute a democratic citizenry, but ideally distributed throughout the society. For Adams, the connection between democracy and articulated opinion was clear and urgent: "Under governments purely republican"—Adams does not distinguish between "republican" and "democratic"—"where every citizen has a deep interest in the affairs of the nation, and, in some form of public assembly or other, has the means and opportunity of delivering his opinions . . . the voice of eloquence will not be heard in vain" (*Lectures*, 1:30–31).

The circumstance of Adams's lectures powerfully suggested stability, hierarchy, culture, and privilege. But the image of the polis that gradually materializes over the course of Adams's extended speechifying is that of a conflictual but self-correcting social organism—not a mass of isolated, self-sufficient individuals seeking only their own security or advantage, but a heterogeneous collectivity in constant exchange, each with all. In Adams's lectures, we can see coming slowly into focus an emergent national self-understanding grounded in the idea—derived far more directly from the Declaration than from the Constitution[53]—of a civil society composed of self-reliant and independent-minded citizens committed to a general conversation in which anyone might undertake to convince anyone of anything.

The greatest exponent of American eloquence entered Harvard in 1814, too late to hear Adams speak. But in time, the lectures and essays of Ralph Waldo Emerson—impressionistic, unsystematic, inventive, brilliant, optimistic—came to be considered not just as instances of extraordinary speechifying but as a compendium of American virtues and qualities. Sui generis, Emerson was nevertheless claimed by several movements eager to be associated with him. He was assimilated into the tradition of American pragmatism because his thinking seemed to deploy whatever materials were ready to hand and gave the impression of being not just unsystematic but improvisational and experimental—a prose equivalent of Whitney, Bell, Fulton, or Edison. At the same time, however, Emerson was embraced by a literary culture that appreciated his deep responsiveness to dreams, thought experiments, mystical experiences, and the various extravagances of creative genius, a tendency so pronounced that George Santayana said, "Imagination, indeed, is his single theme."[54] And last, Emerson was taken to be the authentic voice of the American polity, "the Philosopher of Democracy," as John Dewey put it, "the prophet and herald of any system which democracy may henceforth construct."[55]

Emerson was American and democratic above all in the kind of individualism he propounded. To many readers, the Emersonian individual is an atom of self-reliance. Supporting evidence for this view is not hard to find. In a single essay, "The American Scholar" (1837), we are told that "in self-trust, all the virtues are comprehended," that the genius of the age consists in "the new importance given to the single person," that "the world is nothing, the man is all," that "in yourself is the law of all nature," and that the "chief disgrace in the world" is "not to be an unit—not to be reckoned one character."[56] At such moments Emerson seems to have sprung directly from the Bill of Rights, with its uncompromising promotion of the individual. But in the same essay we also read, "I run eagerly into this resounding tumult. I grasp the hands of those next me, and take my place in the ring to suffer and to work" (61). A comprehensive view of the Emersonian individual would recognize a larger truth than Emerson, committed to vivid and angular formulations, expresses at any given moment, that the atomistic unit is necessarily part of a larger whole, defined and justified not by personal excellence alone but also by his benign effect on his fellow citizens, the model of personhood he presents to them.

Developing and exemplifying this model is for Emerson the function of the American scholar. Scorned by the world for his failure to subscribe to the prevailing moods and mores, the American scholar, in Emerson's account, must seek consolation in "exercising the highest functions of human nature. He is one, who raises himself from private considerations, and breathes and lives on public and illustrious thoughts. He is the world's eye. He is the world's heart" ("American Scholar," 64). These very unworldly sentences still invoke the world, and make the discursive point that the real value of the "heroic mind" of the scholar can only be realized in the less heroic minds that surround him (61).

While Emerson's praise of great men can seem unbounded, he is also insistently democratic, if mannered and even somewhat histrionic, in his embrace of the ordinary, the low, the common, the familiar, the outcast, the unimportant. "The literature of the poor, the feelings of the child, the philosophy of the street, the meaning of household life" seems to Emerson a "great stride" and a sign of "new vigor" ("American Scholar," 67). And pragmatic though he may have been in some respects, he turned to literature as the instrument of personal enrichment and the fulfillment of the promise of democracy. Poets were to him "liberating gods" who open the door to the unrecognized, the unthought, the unrealized. "Therefore we love the poet," he wrote, "the inventor, who in any form, whether in an ode or in an action . . . has yielded us a new thought. He unlocks our chains, and admits us to a new scene."[57]

When he wrote these words, Emerson seemed to be thinking in conventionally post-Romantic terms of the role of literature in expanding and stimulating the imagination and investing the familiar objects of life with new significance. But he was also reflecting in a manner more peculiar to himself and virtually without precedent in his nation on the paradoxical way in which literature fostered a kind of self-recognition and self-realization that was not merely personal or interior, but intersubjective, effected through an imagined exchange with other minds. His most important essay, "Self-Reliance" (1841), suggests how this process might work. The essay begins with the recollection that he had recently read "some verses written by an eminent painter which were original and not conventional."[58] The originality of the lines had provoked Emerson to an appreciation of genius, a term to which he gives an unusual definition as the capacity "to believe that what is true for you in your private heart is true for all men" (121). The Emersonian genius is the man convinced that his own thoughts, sensations, or beliefs echo in the larger world, making other minds vibrate at a new frequency. We read the work of such people in order to discover some form or degree of their extraordinary capacities in ourselves. "In every work of genius," Emerson writes, "we recognize our own rejected thoughts: they come back to us with a certain alienated majesty. Great works of art . . . teach us to abide by our spontaneous impression with good-humored inflexibility then most when the whole cry of voices is on the other side. Else, to-morrow a stranger will say with masterly good sense precisely what we have thought and felt all the time, and we shall be forced to take with shame our own opinion from another" (121). The force of this characteristically taut passage is that a reading practice that responds honestly and courageously to the originality of the author calls forth and fortifies the reader's own inner resources; that real independence must be discovered in dialogue, mind to mind; that one can discover oneself as a kind of overtone in the words of another; and that self-reliance is elicited by the sympathetic apprehension of the same quality in others through the reading of their texts.

As it did with John Quincy Adams, the novel implications of democracy announce themselves through what would seem to be conventional thoughts, in this case not about classical oratory but about great works of art produced by geniuses. George Kateb has argued that Emerson's thinking was not just unsystematic, inconsistent, or antidogmatic, but fundamentally paradoxical, with each strong statement seeming to call forth its own negation.[59] The famous aphorism "Trust thyself: every heart vibrates to that iron string" is glossed by the statement that "great men" have always "confided themselves childlike to the genius of their age." "Insist on yourself; never imitate"—but do so by reading. "Traveling is a fool's paradise"—but knowledge of distant places and cultures is indispensable to the imagination. Emerson prescribed this complicated program not for all humankind but only for his American audiences, who were, he felt, in danger of failing to understand their singular, unprecedented, and in fact paradoxical circumstance of being a nation that had founded itself, a people who had freely given themselves the law. Such a founding, Emerson thought, imposed on all Americans a challenge of self-invention that could easily become a crushing burden, a source of bewilderment and despair, unless some way could be discovered of anchoring oneself in precedent. This is the task, at once private and social, imaginative and pragmatic, that Emerson assigns to the reading of literature, a project he described in "The American Scholar" as "the right way of reading," or, more suggestively, "creative reading" (60).

At the same time Emerson was delivering his lectures in Boston in the latter part of the 1830s, a young man who would become the greatest example of self-fashioning through creative reading was escaping, with the aid of disguises, borrowed papers, and bravado, from slavery in Maryland and finding his way to New Bedford, Massachusetts, where he took the name of Frederick Douglass in order to confound pursuers. Having learned to read through a combination of determined application and kindly assistance given by those who ran considerable risk to give it, the young Douglass had discovered *The Columbian Orator*, a publication that the young Abraham Lincoln also read eagerly, an anthology of patriotic and republican materials that was widely used in classrooms in the early years of the nineteenth century. The experience of reading in *The Columbian Orator* speeches uttered by slaves in opposition to slavery, Douglass writes in the first of his autobiographies, "gave tongue to interesting thoughts of my own soul, which had frequently flashed through my mind, and died away for want of utterance."[60]

An extraordinary and singular individual, Douglass was gifted in his ability to discover himself in the words of others. In 1844, only twenty-six but already well known, Douglass had the extraordinary experience of hearing Emerson lecture in Concord on "the emancipation of the Negroes in the British West Indies," a speech that called for the emergence of "the Anti-Slave," the black man who could speak for himself as a free man, "clothed and in [his] own form."[61] The author of "Self-Reliance" would become one of the most profound influences on Douglass, who went on to a career as a public speaker and author and became the most compelling voice in the abolitionist movement, a figure of international renown, and the most determinedly creative reader of the Constitution of his century.

As a young man, Douglass had been deeply impressed by William Lloyd Garrison, who had argued that abolitionist commitments dictated a repudiation of the Constitution. Judging the Framers and Founders as tolerant of and even sympathetic to slaveholders, Garrison had concluded that the document they composed was intended to countenance chattel slavery, and declared that he could not swear allegiance to it—or vote, or hold office, or participate in any process legitimated by the Constitution. At first, Douglass agreed. In 1849, he wrote a letter subsequently published under the title "The Constitution and Slavery," stating his belief that the "original intent and meaning of the Constitution (the one given to it by the men who framed it, those who adopted, and the one given to it by the Supreme Court of the United States) makes it a pro-slavery instrument—such an one as I cannot bring myself to vote under, or swear to support."[62]

The history of chattel slavery presented a formidable challenge for any abolitionist who wished to venerate the Constitution. Nearly half the delegates to the Constitutional Convention owned slaves. Twelve of the first fifteen presidents owned slaves, eight while in office. The last slave-owning president would be

Ulysses S. Grant, who acquired them two years after Douglass's speech. It would seem that any argument about the meaning of the Constitution would have to recognize certain brute facts about the nation's tolerance of slavery. But as Douglass soon realized, while a defiant rejection of the Constitution may have been bracing, it made it impossible for him to argue for the abolition of slavery without also arguing for the abolition of the Constitution. He was abrogating his citizen's right to interpret the Constitution—and perhaps to claim its protections—out of deference to the wicked intent of the Framers. He began to explore a different approach.

In a letter written in 1851, Douglass agreed that slaveholders were undoubtedly justified in seeking support in the personal views and practices of the Framers of the Constitution, but wondered whether some other account of their purpose could also be maintained by construing their intentions differently. He questioned whether "we may avail ourselves of legal rules which enable us to defeat even the wicked intentions of our Constitution makers. . . . Is it good morality to take advantage of a legal flaw and put a meaning upon a legal instrument the very opposite of what we have good reason to believe was the intention of the men who framed it?"[63]

He decided that it was very good morality. On July 5, 1852, Douglass rose before the Rochester Ladies' Anti-Slavery Sewing Society to deliver an address that has taken its place among the great instances of American rhetoric and oratory, a landmark in the history of opinion in the United States. Douglass began the speech that has become known as "What to the Slave Is the Fourth of July?" by inviting his audience to reflect on the meaning of Independence Day at a moment when, as Douglass noted, 14 percent of all Americans were enslaved. He recalled to them the sentiments of their Revolutionary forebears, who "presumed to differ from the home government" in finding their situation "unjust, unreasonable, and oppressive, and altogether such as ought not to be quietly submitted to," adding, "I scarcely need say, fellow-citizens, that my opinion of those measures fully

accords with that of your fathers." Warming to the case, he posed
the question directly:

> What, to the American slave, is your 4th of July? I answer; a day that
> reveals to him, more than all other days in the year, the gross injustice
> and cruelty to which he is the constant victim. To him, your celebra-
> tion is a sham; your boasted liberty, an unholy license; your national
> greatness, swelling vanity; . . . your prayers and hymns, your sermons
> and thanksgivings, with all your religious parade, and solemnity, are,
> to Him, mere bombast, fraud, deception, impiety, and hypocrisy—a
> thin veil to cover up crimes which would disgrace a nation of savages.
> There is not a nation on the earth guilty of practices, more shocking
> and bloody, than are the people of these United States, at this very
> hour. . . .
> . . . Oh! be warned! be warned! a horrible reptile is coiled up in
> your nation's bosom; the venomous creature is nursing at the tender
> breast of your youthful republic; for the love of God, tear away, and
> fling from you the hideous monster, and let the weight of twenty
> millions, crush and destroy it forever![64]

It is easy to miss, in this astonishing and celebrated passage, the
presumption that informs it, that any citizen, even a former slave,
has the right to dissent from the social consensus; in fact, he can
use the occasion of a patriotic public holiday to tell his socially
prominent, well intentioned, sympathetic—and white—listeners
that in his eyes they were hypocritical, criminally complicit, de-
luded, and, their advanced views notwithstanding, headed toward
a justly hideous demise. It is hard to imagine a more aggressively
offensive exercise of free speech.

Offensive it was, but it was not entirely denunciatory, for the
silent core of his argument concerned the interpretation of the
Constitution. We think of Douglass as a man inflamed by righteous fury over injustice, but he was for several decades obsessed
with the theoretical question of interpretation. Omitting any
mention of his own very recent conversion from the Garrisonian
position, Douglass noted that while some of the Framers had
countenanced slavery, a proper reading of the document yielded
a different picture. Such a reading had to take into account not

just the words in the text but also the words not in the text, which speak just as eloquently and forcefully in their absence: "Interpreted as it ought to be interpreted, the Constitution is a glorious liberty document. Read its preamble, consider its purposes. Is slavery among them? Is it at the gateway? or is it in the temple? It is neither. While I do not intend to argue this question on the present occasion, let me ask, if it be not somewhat singular that, if the Constitution were intended to be, by its framers and adopters, a slave-holding instrument, why neither slavery, slaveholding, nor slave can anywhere be found in it?" ("What to the Slave," 2:202).

Reading the words not present was certainly an innovation, but Douglass insisted that he was merely following accepted principles. In a passage that, rhetorically, is so anticlimactic, peripheral, and deflated in tone compared to the thunderous declamations that dominate the text that it is commonly omitted when the speech is reprinted, Douglass offers a discourse on method, referring his listeners to

certain rules of interpretation, for the proper understanding of all legal instruments. These rules are well established. They are plain, common-sense rules, such as you and I, and all of us, can understand and apply, without having passed years in the study of law. . . . I hold that every American citizen has a right to form an opinion of the Constitution, and to propagate that opinion, and to use all honorable means to make his opinion the prevailing one. . . . The Constitution, in its words, is plain and intelligible, and is meant for the home-bred, unsophisticated understandings of our fellow-citizens. . . . I take it, therefore, that it is not presumption in a private citizen to form an opinion of that instrument. (2:202)

His reading may have been unconventional, but, he assured his listeners, he, like they, had every right to offer it: the very plainness of the Constitution was evidence that the Framers intended people to read the document for themselves.

Douglass's own private opinion clashed most directly with that of the established powers in the infamous Dred Scott case of 1857, in which Chief Justice Roger Taney, in what has been called "one of the first self-consciously 'originalist' opinions from the Supreme Court," determined that the Constitution countenanced slavery in the slaveholding states, and that Negroes were not, at the time of the founding of the nation, "acknowledged as a part of the people, nor intended to be included in the general words used in that memorable instrument."[65] Grotesquely, Taney supported this opinion by noting that the Framers were "great men—high in literary acquirements, high in their sense of honor and incapable of asserting principles inconsistent with those on which they were acting" (Dred Scott, 407).[66]

Douglass disagreed with the decision but not with the rationale—that the Founders were men of transcendent gifts for whom inconsistency was inconceivable—and replied with an originalism of his own, one based on a different understanding of intention. In a speech later on that same year, Douglass agreed with Taney that the meaning of the text was rightly determined by referring to the intentions of the Framers, but insisted that these intentions were precisely the opposite of the ones generally ascribed to them. The relevant intentions, Douglass argued, were of a different order altogether—not the private views of high-achieving individuals, but rather a broader intentionality that could be inferred from "the nature of the American Government, the Constitution, the tendencies of the age, and the character of the American people," all of which, Douglass said, pointed to the conclusion that the Constitution did not intend to legitimate slavery.[67]

In this account of the Framers' intentions, Douglass was placing himself in opposition not just to slavery or to the dominant interpretation of the Constitution, but also to the then-current understanding of intention. As H. Jefferson Powell has demonstrated, the meaning of intention had been shifting since the beginning of the century from an older, Madisonian meaning of intention as public or popular meaning to what Powell calls "the modern, subjective use of the word" to mean "the historical intentions of *someone*."[68] The newer sense of the term had advocates in the North and in the South, but was exploited particularly by Southern states' rights advocates who thought the Framers' views, especially on the subject of slavery, were more in keeping with their own than the lofty rhetoric about human equality in the Declaration or the Constitution would suggest. Powell cites Jefferson Davis, who claimed that the Confederate Constitution differed from the "Constitution formed by our fathers" only "insofar as it is explanatory of their well-known intent."[69]

Douglass rejected this more recent understanding of intention. But he did not simply insist on the older account. Rather, he combined the two, arguing in the spirit of Madison that the Framers had intended to produce a document that would stand alone, sufficient unto itself. The tense complexity and power of Douglass's mature reasoning was unfurled in a majestic speech in Glasgow, in March 1860, in which he described the Constitution as "a written instrument full and complete in itself," a document to which "no Court in America, no Congress, no President, can add a single word thereto, or take a single word therefrom." The "mere text and only the text" is, he said, the only legitimate authority, not any "commentaries or creeds written by those who wished to give the text a meaning apart from its plain reading." "I am," he said, audaciously appropriating the term then commonly used by states' rights advocates, "for strict construction."[70]

In "What to the Slave Is the Fourth of July?" Douglass had read the silences of the text, but here he reads the words on the page, and construes them in the most literal and indeed simple-minded way possible, treating them as if they meant exactly what they seemed to, challenging his listeners and readers to invent any other meaning. In this, he claims, he is relying on a different but entirely legitimate concept of intent. The fact that the deliberations leading to the final text had been conducted behind closed doors, with no notes or transcripts published, strongly suggested, Douglass argues, that the Framers did not want their merely personal views to be confused with the fundamental law of the land, which registered in the clearest possible terms the convictions and sentiments of the people at large: "It would be the wildest of absurdities, and lead to endless confusion and mischiefs, if, instead of looking to the written paper itself, for its meaning, it were attempted to make us search it out, in the secret motives, and dishonest intentions, of some of the men who took part in writing it" ("Constitution," 2:469). To treat the Constitution as the work of the Framers' hands alone, as if they had been unable to transcend their own circumstances or limitations would, Douglass suggests, be an act of insulting disrespect to them and a disservice to the nation. The Framers were men of genius who fully intended to produce a document that would guide and inspire a nation, and it could only do so if their own limited mentalities were effectively annulled.

Douglass is sometimes regarded as personally forceful, even ferocious, but intellectually conventional. As the author of *The Mind of Frederick Douglass* says, "Insightfulness and complexity, rather than originality, characterized Douglass's mind. . . . In their historical context . . . his ideas were more often representative than novel."[71] But reading the words not in the Constitution was not the ordinary way of proceeding, and his insistence on the depthless transparency and simplicity of the Constitution represents subtle and strategic thinking of a high order. His most dramatic departure from conventional thinking was, however, in his understanding of the fundamental meaning of the text. In the 1850s, very few people even in the abolitionist movement saw the Constitution as a "glorious liberty document." Indeed, subsequent history would demonstrate that whatever promise of liberty that document held had to be redeemed through a war of unimaginable destructiveness, which had itself to be followed by Reconstruction and then by the contentious and protracted process of ratifying the Thirteenth, Fourteenth, and Fifteenth Amendments. Taney's opinion in the Dred Scott decision had stated outright what most people had assumed, that the Framers of the Constitution proclaimed liberty not for all men but only for nonslaves, and that if they did not say as much, it was only to avoid tonal incongruities. (There were obvious real incongruities, of course, that were obscured by the Constitution's lofty tone. Samuel Johnson asked, "How is it that we hear the loudest yelps for liberty among the drivers of negroes?"[72]) Insisting on the most literal meaning inscribed on the surface of the parchment, Douglass calls the Framers' bluff, adopting what Charles W. Mills refers to as "the straightface/blackface literal-mindedness that, with a sophisticated 'naïveté,' refused to see any exclusionary racial subtext in its moral guarantees, thereby enabling him to ask, in deadpan puzzlement, what had happened—if indeed all men were created equal—to the rights of black citizens. ('But Massa, dis-here paper says I'se created equal . . . ?')."[73] Douglass seizes on the assertion of universal equality and, to the silent, gnashing outrage of those who knew perfectly well that equality was a fiction, heartily congratulates the Framers on their enlightened views.

It is difficult to imagine the astonishment many must have felt on hearing a former slave thundering at them from the podium, raining down threats of a righteous conflagration even as he was recommending careful textual study according to commonsense rules of interpretation, commanding attention not just as a moral force but as an authority on the law of the land. The question of how he managed to discover within himself the kind of authority the task required must remain in the domain of wonderment, but the narrower question of the radical alteration in his reading of the Constitution can be approached through Emerson's formulation: "the possibility of interpretation lies in the identity of the observer with the observed."[74] Somehow, by sheer force of imaginative will, Douglass managed to discover in the Constitution, as he had once discovered in the speeches by slaves printed in *The Columbian Orator* and in Emerson's essays, a kindred spirit whose ghostly presence in the text enabled him to read it as a statement of his own convictions.

Once he found himself in the Constitution, Douglass was able to possess, and to conceive of himself as the inheritor of, the revolutionary story behind it. Douglass's mature understanding of constitutional interpretation compresses and focuses a rich national history of reflection, recapitulating the past and launching the future. He holds the Constitution to be a quasi-sacred document that stands outside of history, "full and complete in itself," the only authority on its own meaning. Mere personal views on the meaning of the document are rejected on the principle that the truth can only be corrupted by interpretation. The word, to recall the Separatist Henry Barrow's formulation, judges itself. At the same time, Douglass insists, again like Barrow, that every person can judge the word and must try to "judge aright." But Douglass is not entirely Separatist in his sympathies. Sensitive to a potential for anarchy if everyone was empowered to determine the law according to his or her own lights, Douglass accepts the authority of the Supreme Court, whose decisions he is seeking to influence. This is the secular and legal version of the council of learned divines who had the power to decide theological or doctrinal questions in Lancelot Andrewes's England. Not only did Douglass blend the two positions whose opposition was so fateful in determining the beginning of the nation, but he added another element as well: the citizen's right "to form an opinion of the constitution, and to propagate that opinion, and to use all honorable means to make his opinion the prevailing one." With this addition, an all-but-theological dispute about who gets to decide the meaning of the quasi-sacred text is translated into the terms of a civil society based on disputation and dissent in which all citizens may engage in the project of determining and arguing for the true meaning of the fundamental law of the land.

Douglass's approach is originalist in that it is premised on a recovery of original intent, but his example suggests that originalism is not the straitjacket it is sometimes represented as being. It is illuminating in this context to compare Douglass's approach to that of Abraham Lincoln, who delivered his Cooper Union speech—the speech, he later said, that made him president—in New York City within days of Douglass's speech in Glasgow.[75] The broad issue in both speeches is the view of the Constitution on slavery. Both argue that the Constitution is hostile to slavery, and both base their arguments on the intentions of the "fathers who framed the government," a phrase repeated a dozen times in the course of Lincoln's speech. But where Douglass refers to deeper and more impersonal intentions that might be inferred from the character of the nation, Lincoln combs over the historical record of the words and deeds of the Father-Framers, naming names including George Washington's, and drawing his conclusions about their intentions on that basis. Historically, the Cooper Union speech is celebrated primarily for a passage at the end, in which Lincoln addresses "the Southern people" directly. But that brief passage is preceded by and predicated on a series of painstakingly historical and legalistic accounts in which he argues that the meaning of the Constitution must be inferred from the intentions of the Founders, and that discussions about the meaning of the law must therefore take the form of historical narrative combined with psychological speculation. In search of original intent, Douglass turns away from the Framers as individuals, while Lincoln probes their personal conduct for clues.

Today, originalism is often regarded as a conservative, even reactionary approach to constitutional interpretation, binding the present to the ossified past, locking in the privileges of the formerly privileged, serving as a deceptively neutral shield for political reaction. Progressives and liberals often maintain that the evolving social consensus, as reflected both in social practice and in the history of prior court decisions, represents a more appropriate and reliable guide to the law, the kind of guide most needed by a forward-looking nation. But consider the examples of Douglass and Lincoln. Both men argued for an originalist recuperation of intention, and both sought *by that means* to wrench the Constitution free from the historically most-plausible understandings of the actual views of the Framers. In their hands, originalism opened up rather than restricted the question of meaning, creating rather than eliminating the domain of interpretive choice and judgment, and, in this case, expanding rather than limiting the scope of human freedom and rights.[76]

There is, in short, more to originalism than many of today's originalists, and anti-originalists, suspect. Originalists can, like

Douglass, construct an account of a collective intentionality that animated the Framers regardless of their personal views; or, like Lincoln, they can choose to study the writings and acts of the Framers as an index of their innermost and perhaps unexpressed thoughts, which might have been at variance with their public utterances or actions; or they can set both these options aside and mine the text for the meaning most useful in the contemporary context or suited to their present purposes, claiming that the Framers themselves intended that their successors should be as creatively attentive to present needs and circumstances as they had been. None of these meta-interpretive options by itself would determine any particular decision; speculation is entailed and judgment required by all of them. One originalist (Taney) could write, and others (Douglass and Lincoln) could denounce, the Dred Scott decision.

In a sense, all readings of the Constitution are originalist because they all realize the manifest "intention" of written language—that it should be read by those who try to understand it, including, in the American instance, all citizens. As we have seen, the Framers endorsed this intention on democratic principles. Originalism and historicism represent two versions of a citizen's right that is so deep-laid in American self-understanding that contradiction of it is almost unimaginable: the right to read and interpret foundational texts such as the Constitution and the Declaration of Independence—two origins, not quite in synchrony—and, as Douglass insisted, to argue for one's interpretations in court and in public. This right has, if anything, an even more sacrosanct status than the (amendable) Constitution itself. Across the spectrum of ideological commitment, people believe that the Constitution is legible to all, not just to a small priesthood of lawyers and judges. Even the often-voiced disdain for "activist" readings of the Constitution is undergirded by a reading of the Constitution.

Paradoxically, it is the quasi-sacred status of the Constitution that secures democratic participation in the nation's legal system and civil society. The document is unalterable, the law is the law—but the Constitution is revered in large part because it was the hard-won issue of heroic historical events, and a substantial part of its authority, as Arendt writes, "resides in its inherent capacity to be amended and augmented" (*On Revolution*, 194). When the Constitution is amended—and, in a weaker sense, whenever the question of the meaning or import of the Constitution is questioned or contested—citizens revisit the act of founding itself. Progress is made only through a ritual repetition of the origin.[77] The endlessly debatable nature of that origin ensures that the question, like the future itself, will remain open. As Gordon Wood has written, "Americans' interpretation of their Revolution could never cease; it was integral to the very existence of the nation" (*Radicalism of the American Revolution*, 336).

Throughout the nation's history various groups have sought redress of grievances, equal protection, or basic rights by appealing to some previously unstressed or unacknowledged meaning of the constitutional text that, they claim, was present all along *in potentia* but unrecognized, like shapes in clouds or figures in blotches on the wall. Slaves, women, workers, religious groups, gun rights advocates, abortion opponents, political advocacy groups, and other aggrieved parties have come before the courts seeking to persuade the justices to see what they see, reading the Constitution as if it were the expression of their commitments and desires. Their occasional success in doing so proves that the Constitution is as flexible as it is unchanging. Indeed, the very fixity of the Constitution has enabled it to be reimagined and repossessed by people who read in its lofty and unchanging generalities an abiding assurance of the legitimacy of their own struggles against hierarchy, power, privilege, and the consensus of the moment.[78]

From America to English

Both Douglass and Lincoln represented their conclusions as the result of deeper or more probing insights than others had achieved into the unchanging intentions of the Framers. If either man had based his case on the premise that times had changed and the country now needed new laws that conformed to current convictions, the result might have been an immediate gain in justice or equity in a few areas, but a loss of faith in the law in general. The founding, the Founders, and the fundamental law would become less venerable, and the character of the country would change.

But the law would also be compromised by claims that the Founders were men of such transcendent wisdom that their formulations had to be regarded as iron laws fixed for all time. Such claims would imply that the founding was the enemy of the future, that people must conduct their lives in the shadows of belatedness and inadequacy, aspiring at best to faithful repetition. This, too, would defeat the purpose of founding not just a new order but an order dedicated to newness. Living within the limits of a text, we nevertheless want to feel that the fundamental law of the nation assists us as we grope toward a more perfect union, that the Constitution is on the side of progress, and that the nation is founded on the promise of an open future.

Hence interpretation. The textuality of the Constitution suggests the reassuring fixity of the law, while the Constitution's responsiveness to interpretation allows us to exercise the freedom of self-discovery and self-invention. The interpretable text allows us to think well of the Founders, the law, and ourselves. With a license to interpret the text, we are able to understand the thinking behind the founding of the nation as if it were in a sense our own thinking, appearing before us with, as Emerson said, "a certain alienated majesty" that both dignifies the present and vitalizes the past. And so—one could argue—the nation was founded on the interpretation of foundational documents as the highest calling of opinion, the secular and political fulfillment of the principle of separation.

Foreign visitors to the United States in the nineteenth century often commented on the extraordinary prominence of public opinion in the nation's social and political life, which they saw as the ambivalent consequence of majority rule. Not all were reassured that democracy or its citizens would flourish under the unstable regime of the majority. Tocqueville was appalled by the tropism toward demagogy and tyranny in the American elevation of public opinion, a tendency to enforced conformity that produced a "courtier spirit" and discouraged the emergence of "that manly openness, that male independence of thought" that characterized American society at the time of the Revolution and before.[79] The dominance of the all-mastering majority constrained the exceptional spirit and disciplined the nonconforming citizen not through force but through the influence of "corporate thinking upon the intelligence of each single man" (501). This subtle violence against the free intellect, this suppression of debate among competing views, was particularly striking in a country in which "everyone is more or less called upon to give an opinion of state affairs" (301). The range of opinions on any issue of significance seemed to Tocqueville depressingly and dangerously narrow, to the point that American democracy was threatened.

Over time, the deeper wisdom of the Constitution's separation of powers became apparent, especially to foreign visitors, who recognized that the inefficiency of the American government was designed as a check against the irrationalities and excesses of democracy. In an 1893 tome even more immense than *Democracy in America*, the British liberal politician, jurist, and historian Viscount James Bryce updated Tocqueville's comments on public opinion in light of half a century of experience. Bryce saw the system of checks and balances, which created a "waste of power by friction" between branches of government and produced a "want of unity and vigor in the conduct of affairs by executive and legislature," as an entirely intentional way of countering the tyranny of the majority. The Founders, Bryce wrote, wanted "not so much to develop public opinion as to resist and build up breakwaters against it," forcing "the current of the popular will into many small channels instead of permitting it to rush down one broad bed."[80] Neither Tocqueville nor Bryce would have been surprised by the arguments made in the twentieth century by

Walter Lippmann and Noam Chomsky that public opinion was vulnerable to the deliberate "manufacture of consent" by those who wished to create a majority on their side of an issue.[81]

Lincoln, too, well understood the singular authority of public opinion in America. "Our government," he wrote in 1856, "rests in public opinion. Whoever can change public opinion, can change the government."[82] He did not say that opinion inclines toward justice, or that the popular will must command moral respect, or that all differences of opinion could be worked out through earnest good-faith dialogue. Indeed, he concluded a speech delivered in the same year by warning that if appeals to popular opinion on the questions of slavery and the union did not achieve the desired result, "WE MUST MAKE AN APPEAL TO BATTLE AND TO THE GOD OF HOSTS!!"[83] Five years later, Lincoln himself was leading the battle, which he characterized, in the Gettysburg Address, as a mighty conflict fought over the interpretation of the phrase "all men are created equal."[84] For Lincoln, public opinion was something that morally serious people were obliged to recognize and try to control, by, as a later political leader would say, any means necessary.

If democracy was not to destroy itself, if the tropism toward tyranny embedded in majority rule was to be held in check, if a confident, responsible, and reflective Emersonian individualism was to flourish—if the principle of separation was not to degenerate into anarchy—opinion had to be disciplined, channeled, and regulated so there could be some agreed-upon way of evaluating competing arguments. The potential for a destructive frenzy of opinionating—"aggressive, unreasoning, passionate, futile, and a breeder of mob violence," as Bryce put it—had to be limited by the general if tacit acknowledgement of protocols of responsible persuasion, the "rules of interpretation" Douglass referred to (*American Commonwealth*, 2:926). Such rules would regulate the process by which some opinions were able to clear a space in the general cacophony and bend others in their direction. The right to an opinion may have been inalienable, but the power to influence others had to be earned. The success of the democratic experiment hung on the competence of the people to acquire and interpret facts, to deliberate with one another in a spirit of respect, and to arrive at solutions in which the interests and perspectives of all parties were at least acknowledged. In the course of this process, opinion had to transcend itself, to become something more than "mere," so it could exercise authority by what Douglass called "honorable means." Authoritarian governments could hold their societies together by diverse measures, but republics, as Gordon Wood says, "possessed few of the adhesive attributes of monarchies," and had to rely on "the moral quality of the people themselves" as the only power capable of keeping them from being torn apart by the centrifugal forces of factionalism and division.[85]

Nobody was born with the requisite qualities. People had to be trained. The best place to train them was in the schools. And the people best suited to do the training were, as gradually became clear, English teachers.

III

The Peculiar Opportunities of English

We do suggest that . . . [English] is the central humanistic study—that it offers peculiar opportunities for achieving the goals [of general education].
« *General Education in a Free Society* »

English and Wisdom

The responsibility for creating the habits, assumptions, and skills that would equip people for individual and collective self-governance in a decentralized, diverse, widely scattered, and secular society fell to the nation's schools. Education was to be the solution to the problems created by popular sovereignty. To this end, many institutions of higher education in the second half of the nineteenth century offered courses in classics, rhetoric, and elocution or public speaking, courses that reflected the oratorical culture John Quincy Adams had wanted to reinvigorate.[1] This culture was eventually buried under the avalanche of print and mass communications, which, by hastening the end of courses in rhetoric and elocution, created a vacuum that was eventually filled by "the humanities," and, more particularly, by the discipline of English. By the mid-twentieth century, English had emerged as, in the words of the Redbook, "the central humanistic study," the core discipline of the curriculum, the moral and even political anchor of the entire educational system, the curricular site of democratic aspirations (Redbook, 107).[2]

How did this happen? Why English? And how did English organize itself in such a way that when the nation called, it was ready to serve?

In order to qualify as the central humanistic discipline, English had to be a certain kind of discipline. There were many forms it could not take. An orientation toward linguistics of the kind that had characterized the discipline of literary study throughout the nineteenth century would not serve; nor would literary history. If literature were considered an unchanging repository of timeless truths or a system of genres, English could play no more than a small and largely decorative role in the education of a citizenry. If literature were held to be a lively way of presenting abstract arguments or a miniaturized representation of social or historical circumstances, the ends of society would be more immediately and productively served by the study of philosophy, sociology, or history. If literary study were a second-order social science studying the ways in which literature cast a fictive sidelight on issues of the day or provided colorful instances of social or intellectual trends, it would hardly merit the sustained attention of serious people. If society is burdened by an aging population, why study *King Lear*? Is Franz Kafka really a more reliable guide to justice than John Rawls?

English could only be as important as the Redbook insisted it was if it was a humanistic discipline in the Redbook's terms. The primary term the Redbook uses is "wisdom," which it identifies as the goal of education in a democracy. The aim of all education, the Redbook says, is "mastery of life, and since living is an art, wisdom is the indispensable means to this end" (75). This association of the humanities and wisdom was not original. In a 1939 essay titled "The History of Art as a Humanistic Discipline," the German-Jewish émigré art historian Erwin Panofsky had written, "The ideal aim of science would seem to be something like mastery, that of the humanities something like wisdom."[3] In the German tradition Panofsky inhabited, such wisdom was reserved for the few who could obtain advanced degrees. The premise of the Redbook is entirely different, that wisdom should be diffused, through education, throughout the populace.

What is wisdom? The Redbook does not go into detail, but the term seems in context to designate a higher competency, the ability to live one's life in conformity with the deeper constraints and responsibilities associated with the human condition. Irreducible to learning or intelligence, wisdom takes the form of interpretations, evaluations, and judgments—speculative determinations made prematurely, as it were, in advance of the evidence by an individual willing to take risks. Autocracies demand that subjects know their places, that they be content; communes demand that people act collectively, that they be cooperative. A democratic society requires each person to assume responsibility both for his or her own welfare and for the society as a whole; it requires wise citizens. The National Endowment for the Humanities, formed in 1965, identified the rationale for a national investment in the humanities with a phrase rooted in Redbook rhetoric that continues to be featured in its mission statement a half century later: "Democracy demands wisdom."[4]

All the humanistic disciplines are wisdom disciplines in that they solicit acts of interpretation, evaluation, and judgment, and resist translation into quantitative terms. But literary study during the thirty years after the Second World War enjoyed special distinction as a tutelage in wisdom, in part because the study of literature in America at the time was devoted to the question of meaning, a question that could only be settled by close analysis of the text combined with a speculative account of the author's intentions. Literary study in the second half of the twentieth century in the United States acquired a peculiar significance, matched by no other discipline in the American academy or by any comparable discipline in any other nation's curriculum, in large measure because of the coincidence between the emphasis on wisdom as the key to democratic citizenship and the prevailing mode of understanding literature.

English had not always been a humanistic discipline in this sense. At the beginning of the twentieth century, the discipline of English in the leading colleges and universities remained grounded in the Germanic discipline of philology. But, partly as a consequence of wars with Germany, English began to assume other, more indigenous responsibilities. The first of these was to construct and curate forms of cultural tradition, including both a cosmopolitan culture of "the West" that Americans were invited to claim as their own and, more specifically, an American tradition that could serve to bind together a diverse and multiethnic society that, a century and a half after the founding of the nation, still saw itself as exploratory, experimental, and undefined.[5] Spurred particularly by the First World War, the argument for a national identity expressed through imaginative literature was made implicitly by the curricula, and often explicitly by the professors, of the nation's English departments. This claim was advanced on the basis of the subject matter and sensibility expressed in American literature, but it was, as I argued in the previous section, made plausible by the deep investment of a self-created or invented nation in imaginative and especially literary creation.

The assertion of a cultural identity established through a literary tradition entailed a second responsibility, the development and refinement of competence in the judgment, evaluation, and especially interpretation of the printed word. Since these were the very faculties that most other academic disciplines—especially the ones that saw themselves as "hard" rather than "soft"—sought to minimize or marginalize in favor of more method-driven, rigorous, or empirical forms of knowledge, English had nearly sole possession of this humanistic project. In the postwar American academy, English acquired a place of privilege by claiming to be the discipline in which the objective of much of the scholarly labor and most of the undergraduate pedagogy was the determination of value and, preeminently, meaning. Students of English were required to interpret imaginative literature and to argue for their interpretations in public discourse, the most rudimentary forms of which were assigned essays and the classroom interactions of the sort that humiliated but then inspired Mr. Ramirez, in which the student's opinion of the creative intentions of a long-deceased stranger was solicited. In a made-up country governed by made-up principles and ideas whose application to the world of today was always to be determined, such exercises had national implications.

The connection between the demand placed on Mr. Ramirez and that placed on citizens in a constitutional democracy to interpret the law is not, perhaps, difficult to grasp. But there is, in addition, a deeper, less self-evident affinity between literary interpretation and American national identity. As the Redbook authors put it, "There is a sense in which education in the great books can be looked at as a secular continuation of the spirit of Protestantism. As early Protestantism, rejecting the authority and philosophy of the medieval church, placed reliance on each man's personal reading of the Scriptures, so this present [general education] movement, rejecting the unique authority of the Scriptures, places reliance on the reading of those books which are taken to represent the fullest revelation of the Western mind" (44). As the discipline responsible for imparting both cultural heritage and interpretive skills, English became identified with a project of national importance, one that extended all the way back to the origin of the country. By learning to interpret—and to do so with the goal of recuperating *mind*, whether of God, an author, or "the West"—a student not only could come to an understanding of the text but could keep faith with the nation-building project begun by the Puritans and ratified by the Constitution. And by applying to other areas the interpretive skills learned in English classes, citizens could function as responsible private spirits in a democratic society bound by a written Constitution.

In short, when Mr. Ramirez was asked his opinion about Shakespeare, he was being invited not just to make a blind guess about the meaning of a poem, but to participate in the national conversation.

The Meaning of Literature

The story of the fortuitous conjunction of an academic discipline and the needs of the nation is not simple or straightforward. Many things had to happen, and happen in a certain order, to result in the discipline of English taking a certain form at a certain time. For the sake of efficiency and clarity, we can retrace the first part of this sequence of developments through the story told by M. H. Abrams in *The Mirror and the Lamp* (1953).[6] Abrams's subject is the shift from the neoclassic to the Romantic understanding of literature, but his book can also be read as a chronicle of the changes wrought in the concept of literature that ultimately produced a literary object that could be not merely appreciated by the public or by amateur critics, but studied and taught by professionals working in an academic discipline.

The story of the Romantic revolution as Abrams tells it begins with the effort by a new generation of thinkers to revitalize what had come to be seen as the dead universe of the materialists—Descartes, Hobbes, and the French mechanists of the latter eighteenth century. This younger generation argued that humankind was not adrift in a meaningless world of extension, quantity, and motion, but was deeply anchored in a living cosmos in which subjects and objects, emotions and reason, matter and purpose were intertwined in an organic unity. The subject on which many of these thinkers converged, and the lever of many of their arguments, was poetry.

Prior to the Romantic revolution, a poet was considered an artisan who was expected to attend respectfully to the external world, to established literary models, and to the reasonable expectations of his audience. On the basis of this agreement, literature qualified as a "fine art" that appealed to the taste and judgment of the public.[7] "Gradually, however," Abrams writes, "the stress was shifted more and more to the poet's natural genius, creative imagination, and emotional spontaneity, at the expense of the opposing attributes of judgment, learning, and artful restraints" (*Mirror and the Lamp*, 21). Hence the title of Abrams's book: the metaphor that guided thinking for most of the eighteenth century was the mirror, with the poet holding up a reflecting glass to the external world; the Romantics, by contrast, thought of poetry on the model of a lamp that illuminated the inner world of the poet.

A small thing in itself, this exchange of one metaphor for another in the discussion of poetry signaled an immense alteration in the understanding of the world—a change "as sharp and dramatic as any the history of ideas can show"—and in the practice of literature (Abrams, *Mirror and the Lamp*, 158). In the new order, poetry was not an imitation of reality crafted by an astute observer, but the "expression" of a superior being endowed with extraordinary powers of sympathy, penetration, and articulation—a genius of a special kind, a figure of commanding authority with access to otherworldly sources of energy and value that were available only to those who, in Coleridge's phrase, had "drunk the milk of Paradise." Even when the ostensible subject of the poem was mundane and the language unadorned and simple, the premise was that the poet had an uncanny capacity to give voice to dimensions of experience hidden from or otherwise unavailable to most people. The path to the wellsprings of poetry ran down and back. Trying to retrieve and re-create "natural" speech unencumbered by cultural accretions, Wordsworth, for example, chose subjects that would have seemed preposterous to poets of a previous generation—a mad mother, an idiot boy, a child, and men "who lead the simplest lives, and most according to nature."[8] Such people seemed to him particularly rich with significance because their speech—untutored, rhythmic, and insistently figurative—was closer than learned or polite discourse to the elemental thought-forms of humanity, the archaic sources of poetry. The poet who could articulate the profundity to which these people gave unwitting voice hardly needed external standards of judgment or taste, or even an audience. As John Stuart Mill put it, poetry written in the wake of the Romantic revolution had "the nature of soliloquy," or of a transcript of a poet's conversation with himself.[9]

Abrams's book centrally concerns the way in which metaphors and figures of speech—especially, in the case of the Romantics, metaphors drawn from the natural world—structure the concepts that circulate through society. Some of these figures were geological, as when Byron described the language of poetry as "the lava of the imagination whose eruption prevents an earthquake."[10] But most were organic. Indeed, so powerful was the conviction that poetry was a reanimation of the natural condition of speech or the precivilized constitution of the human mind that the entire discussion among poets and philosophers alike became invaded by a principle of organicism, with poetry being described as a living system that developed in obedience to some inner impulse, like a shell spiraling out from a conch or, more characteristically, like a plant.

Once rooted, this metaphor itself spread like a weed, coming to dominate all concepts associated with the creation of poetry. "Indeed," Abrams writes in a striking passage, "it is astonishing how much of Coleridge's critical writing is couched in terms that are metaphorical for art and literal for a plant; if Plato's dialectic is a wilderness of mirrors, Coleridge's is a very jungle of vegetation. Only let the vehicles of his metaphors come alive, and you see all the objects of criticism writhe surrealistically into plants or parts of plants, growing in tropical profusion. Authors, characters, poetic genres, poetic passages, words, meter, logic become seeds, trees, flowers, blossoms, fruit, bark, and sap" (*Mirror and the Lamp*, 169). The figure of the organism explained a great deal about poetry, and had the further desirable effect of situating human existence, and particularly human creativity, in the rhythms and materials of the natural world. But it had unintended consequences as well, for under the spell of the organism, poetry had to be considered an unconscious invention, emerging spontaneously from a part of the mind that was inaccessible to awareness or control. In an even more audacious version of the organic metaphor, the poet became host to a blind spontaneity, a creative agency that operated beyond his authority, such that the poet himself was but an "unconsciously growing plant . . . unaware of his own powers and potentialities" (205). "I have written this poem," William Blake said of his *Milton*, "from immediate Dictation . . . without Premeditation and even against my Will." "Nor is it I who play the part," Wordsworth wrote in the verse postscript to "The Waggoner," "But a shy spirit in my heart."[11]

The very metaphors that had described the poet's exaltation could also imply his irrelevance. In the new ethos, the poet could be humbled before a conception of genius that reduced his personal agency nearly to zero, making him a kind of high-performing savant, a secretary to the spirit, a "vegetable genius" (Abrams, *Mirror and the Lamp*, 201–13). Several of those responsible for the Romantic revolution attempted to think their way out of this self-insulting conception by constructing more nuanced accounts of poetic creation that reserved a modicum of agency for the poet. F. W. J. von Schelling, for example, argued that while the poet was driven involuntarily to write, his work manifested an oceanic feeling of infinite harmony that could be attributed if not precisely to himself, then to what Abrams calls "a voluntary grace of his nature" (210). Similarly, Coleridge, in his accounts of the poetic process, tacked ambiguously back and forth between an emphasis on a kind of creative homunculus, a "genius in the man of genius," and a more integrated account in which the "whole soul of man" was engaged in the act of creation.[12] Coleridge described Shakespeare, and by diminishing implication all those who write poetry, as the mysteriously privileged but not altogether undeserving possessors of "a genial understanding directing self-consciously a power and an implicit wisdom deeper than consciousness."[13]

Both the natural and supernatural conceptions of poetry placed the reader at a serious disadvantage. When the poet is figured in Romantic terms as a nightingale pouring forth his soul abroad in ecstasy, a genius with superhuman powers of feeling and expression, or a seer of the Divine Idea, the reader cannot claim to be the arbiter, much less the generator, of aesthetic norms. Indeed, the reader is reduced to gazing in admiration at the miracle of the poem, exercising his will only in consenting to be improved—his sympathies awakened, subtilized, strengthened, and refined, his understanding of the human condition enriched—by submitting to the uplifting influence of the poem. While the poet, under the new regime, acquired powers that made him more than human, the reader suffered a devastating loss. As Abrams says, "There is something singularly fatal to the audience in the romantic point of view" (*Mirror and the Lamp*, 25).

Let us pause the story here in order to assess some of the effects wrought by the Romantic revolution. Perhaps the most conspicuous is that the category of literature had acquired a new, more restricted application. Previously, the term "literature" had been used very generally to describe not only dramatic, poetic, or fictional works but also works of history, philosophy, and even science, with Locke, Newton, Aristotle, Aeschylus, and Donne all being regarded as equally literary. But with "literature" now denoting "imaginative" works exclusively, a hierarchy emerged in which the most imaginative works—the works whose content or style owed least to the conventions or features of the common world—were seen to be the most literary. Poetry, with its conspicuous and traditional formal characteristics, came to represent the general category of literature, with the highest place reserved for the hitherto minor genre of lyric. Construed in this way, literature acquired not only a history, with poets thinking of themselves as heirs to the tradition of Dante, Shakespeare, and Milton, but a theory as well, with poets such as Wordsworth and Coleridge discoursing authoritatively about their art.

By creating a limited class of objects with a history and a theory, the Romantic revolution had begun to establish literature as an object of knowledge. But this establishment was far from complete. We might say that for the Romantics the poem was definitely an object, but not an object of knowledge. For by identifying poetry with both nature and transcendence, and attributing its appearance to an impersonal, even inhuman superagency operating beyond the volition of the poet, the Romantics had placed poetry in a realm that was inaccessible and even resistant to the rational intellect.

If theorizing about poetry had remained fixated on the extraordinary and essentially inhuman powers welling up within the poet, there might be no academic discipline devoted to the study of literature. Amateur admiration would suffice. But the revolution made further turns that had the effect of humanizing the author and restoring an active role for the reader. Unfolding the full implications of a commonly voiced analogy between God's creation of the world and the poet's creation (a new term for poetic composition, applied for the first time by the Romantics) of the poem, writers described the poem as a "second nature" whole and complete, a self-contained artifact subject only to its own laws—a "heterocosm," as Abrams describes it (*Mirror and the Lamp*, 272–85). This analogy carried the reassuring suggestion, voiced by Mill, Matthew Arnold, and many others, that poetry could serve as a gentling, spiritualizing, all-but-religious force that might counter the brutalities and vulgarities of modern industrial and commercial life. More important in the present context, the concept of the heterocosm also underscored the special character of poetic language as opposed to the literal or representational language of science or facticity in general. The formal features and occasional obscurity of poetry, combined with suggestions of an otherworldly or nonhuman origin, indicated an encrypted poetic intention to communicate messages of exceptional importance, on the model of God's communication with the world through signs and portents.

The effort to understand these messages took the form of a zealous scrutiny of the poetic text, which led in turn to a new kind of attention to the author. With the small allowance granted by the figure of the genius within the genius, the concept of expression arose. This, too, was a by-product of the analogy between God and the poet, applied in this case not to the creation but to the creator, who was said to be "visibly invisible" in his work (Abrams, *Mirror and the Lamp*, 272). In what Abrams calls a "strange innovation, which swept everything before it in applied criticism for more than a century," poems became interrogated for traces of their authors, whether to find the cause of the poem in the character of the author, to illuminate the character of the author by studying the poem, or to explore in a deeper sense the soul of the author through the lens of the poem (227).[14] Strange though it may have been, the idea that the poem was a self-contained and independent unit of language produced by an author whose intentions and even character could be inferred from his work made possible a concept that has since become thoroughly naturalized: a critical approach to the question of meaning.

At this point, we leave the period canvassed by *The Mirror and the Lamp* and approach the era of Modernism. Vanished completely, in the twentieth century, are the notions that the poet is a vegetable, a volcano, or a demigod. Poetry in the twentieth century is a species of language that, while distinctive in its formal features, is produced, like other kinds of language, by people living in the world, people whose intentions we should be able to understand. For the Romantics, obscurity was hardly a problem: one does not expect transparency from oracles, deities, or shy spirits, much less from plants. But in the drier climate of Modernism, questions of meaning could not be evaded, all the more so since many of the literary works most closely associated with the spirit of Modernism were puzzling or opaque, their motivation uncertain, their significance or value obscure. If the difficult or problematic work of art is present before us and the author is considered to be a person like us, inhabiting the same world we inhabit, we are entitled and even compelled to ask such questions as, why am I being told this? what is the author's intention? and what does this mean? Such questions could never yield certainty, for they could only be answered by the interpretive and necessarily exploratory activity of the reader, who thus gains under Modernism what had been lost under Romanticism.[15] Having been forced by the Romantic revolution to relinquish the role of discriminating judge and generator of artistic norms, the reader in the era of Modernism is granted a belated compensatory responsibility for a new and daunting task: the determination of meaning.

The Romantic revolution and its aftermath yielded a number of specific concepts that continued to influence the ways in which literature was understood, especially in the Anglo-American context, for many decades: that literature was the product of purposeful creative action, that the crucial question was meaning, that the heterocosmic artifact was the primary evidence for creative intention and therefore for meaning, and that intention could only be determined through an act of speculative interpretation that combined close attention and divination. None of these concepts had any force in the eighteenth century; in the twentieth, they were not uncontested, as we will see, but they were commonplaces.

We have reached the point where all this turbulence in the upper stratosphere of history, philosophy, psychology, religion, and literature is beginning to approach the Florida coastline, where Mr. Ramirez will one day be challenged to produce an opinion about the meaning of a literary work written by a man who lived long ago and far away. Still to be explained is how all this high argumentation was translated into classroom procedures—in other words, how literature became teachable, and teachable in a particular way.

The Birth of Criticism from the Spirit of Compromise

In the late nineteenth and early twentieth centuries, the study of literature in the American academy took two forms. With poetry dominating critical and theoretical approaches to literature, the first of these forms focused on the poem as an object of inquiry, a self-contained and freestanding artifact that demanded to be understood not as a representation of the world but on its own poetic terms. The second concentrated on the poem as an object of meaning, significance, and value, an object suffused with subjective energy waiting to be discovered and liberated by responsive minds from the object in which it was immured. The first approach emphasized the correct perception and understanding of the literary work; the second the necessarily speculative interpretation of the author's intentions. This, at least, is the way Gerald Graff describes the opposing sides in his classic *Professing Literature: An Institutional History* (1987), which chronicles the ragged and contentious struggle that would result in the discipline of English becoming the "central humanistic study," the core of the general education project, and the heart and soul of the American educational system.

Graff describes prolonged trench warfare between two groups that, a tendency to self-caricature aside, had little in common. On one side was arrayed a group he describes variously as Scholars, Investigators, or Philologists, who traced their practices to the kind of linguistic scholarship conducted largely in German research universities. For the Scholars, as I will refer to them collectively, language was the object of a scientific academic discipline that required deep erudition, scrupulous attention to detail, and a patience that seemed, to those who were not Scholars, nothing short of perverse, with the Reverend Mr. Casaubon in George Eliot's *Middlemarch* serving as a chilling icon of the scholarly personality at its most extreme.[16] Setting aside an older and broader conception of philology as the multidimensional study of linguistic and cultural origins, the Scholars committed themselves to an extremity of disciplined perseverance in the notation and documentation of textual or linguistic microdetails. A monkish acedia was the price to be paid for ultimate reward: if the Scholars did their work properly, they believed, their results might one day form part of a more complete account that might be merged with others, enabling Scholars yet unborn to venture more synthetic analyses that might eventually form parts of a permanent contribution to human self-understanding because they rested on a firm foundation of accurate and informed observations precisely rendered. At the end of the rainbow: a full and definitive understanding of primordial thought-forms, a scientific description of human origins and precious insight into the human condition and human nature—the key to all mythologies. For now: the scrupulous notation of orthographic irregularities, anomalous verb forms or case terminations, the geographical extent of certain usages, and first uses of words.

Scholarship of this kind was dreary but honorable work, and provided, in its sobriety, method, and rigor, a model for other disciplines, including the sciences, that were seeking to modernize themselves. In the last quarter of the nineteenth century, many academic disciplines were acquiring markers of professionalization by organizing themselves into departments, creating learned societies, offering advanced degrees, and publishing journals. The newly specialized faculty in research universities were insisting on the right to judge their own work without submitting to any external standard, be it social, political, religious, or administrative. In this context, the image of the credentialed philologist— obsessed with research and renown, stonily indifferent to the interests or needs of students, defiantly resistant to calls for change, a law unto himself—was for many ambitious professors in a number of fields the desired face of the future.[17]

In the American context, however, this Germanic guild was not unchallenged. Some faculty members, more sensitive to the interests and abilities of undergraduates, approached the study of language and literature differently. Beginning to appear in numbers in the last third of the nineteenth century, those whom Graff describes as Generalists, Dilettantes, or Critics regarded the Scholars not as boldly secularizing modernizers but as hoary relics, an incorporate death force of zealous pedantry unsuited to the new and robust American context, while they themselves were exciting, fresh, and passionate in their devotion to the "awakening touch" of inspired and inspiring teaching (*Professing Literature*, 86). Charismatic, sometimes uncredentialed, the Generalists would commune before their astonished undergraduate students with the master-spirits of the literary past. Their ranks included, by Graff's reckoning, such formidable figures as Henry Wadsworth Longfellow, James Russell Lowell, Charles Eliot Norton, William Lyon Phelps, Irving Babbitt, and, surprisingly, Woodrow Wilson.

Generalist teaching was of a particular kind. As Graff reports, one of the primary sources of the Generalist's magic was that he seemed able, as one student recalled, to "reincarnate the poetry and personality and thoughts of poets who are dead" (*Professing Literature*, 86). In order to do so, the teacher had to introduce considerations beyond the text. Personalities and thoughts do not develop in isolation, and so if the teacher was going, as the cliché has it, to "talk about Aeschylus as though he lived down the street," he had to summon up a phantasm of the historical author, and re-create all the historical and other contexts in which the author was embedded—the "street" he lived on—that might contribute to an understanding of the work. If philological research focused on the challenging inertness of the text, Generalist teaching was necessarily centered on the fascinatingly vital figure of the author.

From the perspective of the Generalists, the Scholars were simply missing the point, ignoring the unique and indisputable power of literature to engage the emotions and edify the spirit. From the perspective of the Scholars, the Generalists represented a corruption of academic study, a kind of performance more suited to the evangelical church than the lecture hall. The Scholars were not entirely wrong, for the goal of Generalist teaching as Graff describes it was taken directly from evangelical Protestantism. The connection is legible in an 1834 entry Emerson made in his journal: "The whole secret of the teacher's force lies in the conviction that men are convertible. And they are. They want awakening. Get the soul out of bed, out of her deep habitual sleep."[18]

Perhaps the purest instance of the Generalist spirit at the end of the nineteenth century was Hiram Corson of Cornell University. Corson's teaching method was essentially vocal. He read extended passages in class while his students stood before him, and every Saturday morning he declaimed to large campus audiences the works of English and American writers. In one memorable year he worked through all thirty-seven plays of Shakespeare, following this marathon the next year with a reading of the entirety of Browning's *The Ring and the Book*, "with requisite comment."[19] He gave these performances in the conviction that the universal, eternal, and spiritual value of literature—especially as it related to development of "the whole man," a phrase he used deliberately—could best be realized by "interpretative vocal rendering" undertaken by a supremely skilled lector (himself) capable of giving breath and life to the letter of the text. This program, focused, like John Quincy Adams's lectures on eloquence, on undergraduates, was quasi-religious, antischolarly, and even anti-intellectual. Feeling, Corson felt, must precede understanding: "The premature forcing open of the bud of reason, which now prevails to a lamentable degree, must receive its due condemnation. It is a thing to be condemned from Christian pulpits."[20]

For Corson and other Generalists, a small thing—an English teacher trying to keep his students awake—was burdened with immense if diffuse and even contradictory aspirations. Generalists often represented themselves as a force for modernization compared to the Scholars, but Harvard professor Bliss Perry registered a certain reactionary potential implicit in the Generalist approach, writing of his hope that "the amateur spirit" might be able to "penetrate, illuminate, idealize the brute force, the irresistibly on-sweeping mass, of our vast industrial democracy."[21] While perhaps only a few shared Corson's faith in the exceptional benefits to students of extended professorial declamations, his sense of the mission and curricular centrality of literary study was widely shared and remarkably durable. Writing in the same volume as Corson in 1895, Albert S. Cook of Yale described English as the best subject for the full development of the whole man: "To this end, no study can be better suited than English, its comprehensiveness, variety, and richness of content rendering it an unsurpassed aliment of the spiritual life."[22] The greatest triumph of the Generalists, the Great Books course at the University of Chicago, was described in 1936 by President Robert Hutchins as "an evangelistic movement . . . which shall have for its object the conversion of individuals and finally of the teaching profession to a true conception of general education."[23]

The division of labor, and indeed the outright antagonism, between Scholars and Generalists presented problems of coherence within the discipline of English, but was reinforced by the structure of the American academy, in which undergraduate and graduate programs were combined in a single institution. In research universities, this arrangement ensured the dominance of the graduate school over the curriculum and the reward system. The critic-theorists W. K. Wimsatt and Monroe Beardsley argued in their famous essay "The Affective Fallacy" (1954) that a professional practice of criticism was incompatible with the extravagant classroom performances of faculty members who adopted the style of "the soul adventuring among masterpieces, the contagious teacher, the poetic radiator."[24] But the Generalist impulse, oriented not toward expertise, theory, method, publication, or field-mastery but toward a more generalized awakening, has endured, with popular lecturers suffering the contempt of their more rigorous colleagues for the sake of undergraduate applause, which sometimes becomes alumni loyalty and support, which in turn often results in administrative encouragement and protection. A pattern emerged in many institutions that continues to this day, with the undergraduate curriculum in English devoted to the exciting of interest and engagement—getting the undergraduate soul (and body) out of bed—and the graduate program dominated by intellectual or literary history, theory, professionalism, research, and apprenticeship. As radical as the division was, departments typically accommodated both—as did Cornell, where the German-trained philologist James Morgan Hart coexisted with the flamboyant Corson.

John Williams's 1965 novel *Stoner* describes the way in which this division was often experienced.[25] A boy coming from the farm in the early years of the twentieth century to study agronomy at the University of Missouri is at first confused but then enraptured by his English class, which forces him to think thoughts never entertained on the farm. He experiences a transformative but cruelly protracted "Mr. Ramirez" moment when his teacher asks him for his response to a Shakespeare sonnet. "Mr. Shakespeare speaks to you across three hundred years, Mr. Stoner; do you hear him? . . . What does he say to you, Mr. Stoner? What does his sonnet mean?" Completely fuddled, the young man can only stammer, "It means" (13). Later, the teacher suggests to Stoner that his agitated response to literature has taken the form of "love." To the bewildered disappointment of his parents, the young man decides to major in English. He goes on to graduate school, writes a dissertation on classical influences on the prosody of Chaucer, accepts a teaching position at the same university, and eventually turns his dissertation into a book described in reviews as "pedestrian" and "a competent survey" (102). Stoner seems to have gone over to the dark side in his commitment to philological research of a particularly dull kind, but very late in his long career, and somewhat to his own surprise, he discovers in himself the capacity to be an inspiring undergraduate teacher. Versions of this bipolarity, in which the Scholar-Generalist debate was somehow reconciled not just in the same department but the same person, were apparently not uncommon. As René Wellek wrote, many English teachers "taught graduate students bibliography and sources . . . and meanwhile they read poetry to undergraduates in a trembling or unctuous voice."[26]

Such a double commitment to conflicting goals and approaches was a consequence of the commitment to the literary text considered as an expressive artifact. The Scholarly focus on the literary text secured the academic status of literary study in a university environment increasingly dominated by science and social science, while the spellbinding Generalists, treating literature as expression, ensured undergraduate enrollments. And so, although each side had its partisans, the need for compromise became evident to all. That compromise, when it came, was called "criticism."

Appearing with some regularity in professional publications around the turn of the century, the term "criticism" was, according to Graff, agreeable to both sides because it embraced and reconciled the imperatives of each. The process of argumentation by which the compromise was reached is displayed in compressed form in an essay by a twenty-nine-year-old scholar named Martin Wright Sampson that appeared in the same volume as the essays by Corson and Cook cited earlier.[27] Fascinating as a snapshot of a rapidly evolving profession at the end of the nineteenth century, *English in American Universities* (1895) consists of a collection of brief essays that describe the program in twenty colleges and universities. Speaking for the Department of English at the University of Indiana, Sampson began by arguing, as if to a skeptical observer, that the study of literature was to be considered altogether distinct from the simple enjoyment of literature, which he held to be a pleasant and even a vaguely honorable thing but a waste of classroom time. The goal of literary study, he insisted, was to bring students to an intelligent understanding of "the works themselves, viewed as their creators wrote them . . . pure literature only." As Sampson saw it, university literary study was no amateur pursuit of "the beauty of the poet's utterance," but neither was it merely a scholarly inquiry into literary history, grammar, or etymology, important as all these were. The task of the professor of literature was to force students to "systematically approach the work as a work of art, find out the laws of its existence as such, the mode of its manifestation." And how does the study of literature accomplish all its objectives without sliding off into amateurism or hyperprofessionalism? How does mere reading become transformed into criticism? Sampson offers a one-word prescription: "the mode of its manifestation—in brief, to have his students interpret the work of art" (96). In Sampson's brief account, we can see the fading lineaments of both the excitable Generalists, whose claims were recognized but firmly set to the side, and the withdrawn but defiant Scholars, whose myopic obsessions were noted with respect but subordinated to the larger project of an interpretive understanding of the art of literature.

Sampson could not have made such an argument without the support of the concept of the text as heterocosm, the self-sufficient but expressive and therefore interpretable verbal artifact. This concept, now so naturalized that its history has become all but invisible, constitutes the bridge from the Romantics to the academic discipline of English at the end of the nineteenth century and beyond, its influence extending into the twentieth century.

In the first decades of the twentieth century, the concept of criticism, which Arnold had defined loosely in 1864 as "*a disinterested endeavor to learn and propagate the best that is known and thought in the world*," was still relatively undefined, embracing not only judicious appreciation but source studies, close scrutiny of language, personal response, explication, and general commentary.[28] What it emphatically and increasingly did not denote was either the personal inspiration of the Generalists or the stultifying pedantry of the Scholars, both of which it sought to replace. Criticism was advanced as a blended mode, a soberer species of Generalism that Scholars might just tolerate and a livelier form of Scholarship that Generalists could just about accept.

Focus on the text, Mr. Ramirez. What is Shakespeare trying to say to you?

The consensus view that emerged from the time of the Great War was that criticism, if properly disciplined, could both reconcile divisions within the English department and provide invaluable service to individuals and to the nation. In his presidential address to the Modern Language Association in 1915, Jefferson

Fletcher of Columbia University argued that, with nations fighting for their ideals, the overriding need was for a rejection of all forms of sentimentality and pleasure seeking in favor of discipline and commitment, which he described as a "munitioning of the spirit."[29] Professors could help the cause, but only if they abandoned their former factional ways. Neither the grammarians nor the beauty worshippers (lumped together as "Impressionists, Intuitionists, Croceans, Bergsonians") could be of service in this hour; only an approach that permitted the *"natural magic"* and *"moral profundity"* of literature to shine forth would be capable of counteracting the partisanship, ideology, and propaganda now threatening the world (lv). It was evident to Fletcher that the challenge of perilous times could only be met by a critical practice focused on literary interpretation: "as interpreters of the written word of nations to themselves and to their neighbors," he argued, professors "might do something towards the correction of misunderstanding, the purging of hate" (liii). The conclusion Fletcher reached in this most urgently time-sensitive of addresses was pregnant with significance for the future of literary study: "Our present opportunity lies through a renewed emphasis on interpretative criticism" (li).

In the years just after the war, the discipline of English, newly organized around and anchored in the activity of interpretation, emerged as what one of the writers Graff quotes called the "heart of the school."[30] English was able to claim this preeminence because, in the first instance, it could expose students not just to the monuments of culture but, more particularly, to the documents in which "the march of the Anglo-Saxon mind" was recorded, thus contributing to the training for citizenship thought to be so important in the postwar world. Graff goes into punishing detail on the ways in which American literature was interpreted by philologists and literary historians alike "according to the old Aryan racial theories" (*Professing Literature*, 131). But he also notes a surprisingly strong reaction against racialist jingoism in the form of a promotion of an international republic of letters. The means through which this more humane and cosmopolitan end was to be achieved was, Graff reports, criticism, which had become "associated with the skeptical dissection of destructively chauvinistic arguments, and with distinguishing between politically partisan and disinterested interpretations." Going forward, "the vehicle of . . . heightened consciousness was criticism" (132).

I. A. Richards and the Emergence of an American Humanities

When Jefferson Fletcher was making his case for critical interpretation as the American contribution to world peace, the "general tendency of British criticism," as Ezra Pound was later to write, "was toward utter petrifaction or vitrification."[31] An overripe aestheticism, the decadence of the Romantic revolution chronicled by Abrams, had degenerated into loose talk of sublimity, the elevation of the soul, the transcendent superiority of the poet's sensibility, and the celebration of the exquisite sensations afforded by poetry. But the man who would undo all that was matriculating at Cambridge University, studying logic, philosophy, ethics, psychology, history, and linguistics—and undoubtedly reading Ezra Pound, T. S. Eliot, and other Modernist innovators. By the age of thirty-one, Ivor Armstrong Richards, having written *Foundations of Aesthetics* (1922), *The Meaning of Meaning* (with C. K. Ogden, 1923), and, most important, *Principles of Literary Criticism* (1924), had begun to issue forth a flow of books that would continue unabated for decades. This last text inaugurated a movement that would provide criticism with all the tools required to become a university discipline, including an articulated theory, an analytical method designed for classroom use, and a worldly rationale. Drawing especially on linguistics and psychology, Richards proposed radical new ways of modernizing criticism by subjecting it to the rigors of the scientific method so that it might be deployed in the service of human flourishing, as he understood it.

An endlessly energetic polemicist and iconoclast, Richards was in confident possession of the truth of things, and was consequently in a state of perpetual grave concern. The advance of humanity, he was convinced, had been blocked by propaganda, dogmatism, discord. The old beliefs had been shattered, language had been debased, and public discourse was dominated by vulgarity of thought and expression. Poetry, he thought, might help. A traditionalist in some respects, Richards believed, with Shelley, that poets were the vanguard of the species, and poetry the record of the best and happiest minds. "We shall," he wrote, "be thrown back, as Matthew Arnold foresaw, upon poetry. It is capable of saving us; it is a perfectly possible means of overcoming chaos."[32] But he was convinced that the mere reading of poetry, no matter how sensitive or intelligent, was not going to save anyone. Reading had to be done in the right way, a way he undertook to prescribe, beginning with a theory, a specialized vocabulary, and a clear sense of methods and goals. While the method was intended for university professors, Richards's ambitions extended far beyond them and the tiny group to which they had direct access, to the general public, who were, he felt, badly in need of the training in sensibility provided by disciplined exposure to great literature.

In both his specific recommendations for critical method and in his larger ambitions for criticism, Richards exhibited a compelling extremism. More than any other individual, he was responsible for raising criticism to the status of an important academic field in British elite universities. Considerable as his influence was in Britain, however, his impact in the United States was far greater. Not only did Richards have a considerable following among American literary critics just at the crucial moment when criticism was emerging as the discipline-saving compromise between Scholars and Generalists, but his participation on the Redbook committee enabled him to shape the general education curriculum for postwar American secondary and postsecondary schools. At midcentury, it was essentially Richards's version of criticism that was accepted by many of the country's leading critics. And it was Richards's ability to secrete his spiky and idiosyncratic agenda for criticism, infused with his immense social and even spiritual ambitions, into the larger context of the humanities that was largely responsible for the high status of English in the postwar university as the central discipline of the general education program. Without Richards soldering the connections between English, the humanities, and general education, such connections might not have been made, or imagined.

His fellow committee members must have wondered what to make of him. They were largely Harvard veterans, while he had only recently arrived from the other Cambridge. They were trying to craft an educational system that would awaken Americans to the glorious opportunities and solemn responsibilities of all citizens, while he was committed to creating an apolitical and maximally efficient "mind of the future."[33] They proposed a curriculum based on heritage; he was disdainful of such concepts, which seemed to him ideological and intellectually primitive. And yet in many respects, Richards must have appeared to his fellow committee members as general education incorporate: a literary critic with scientific training, social-scientific methods, and philosophical pretentions—a whole man.

Richards's modernized version of the whole man—intense, severe, scientific, moralistic—would have crossed the street to avoid meeting the committee's more gregariously Rotarian version. But on other issues, Richards and his colleagues would have found themselves in smiling agreement. They would have been in complete accord on the proposition that education ought to be oriented toward broadly moral ends, seeking wisdom rather than the mere accumulation of knowledge or simple training for a task. They would have found common ground on the desirability of educating all the people in a given society. They would have shared concerns about the fragmentation of knowledge in the modern university and the dominance of technology in modern society. The committee might have been favorably impressed by, if silently skeptical of, his confident prediction that in the foreseeable future the human brain would become such a supple, responsive, complex, self-mastering instrument that "our current critical activities would compare with those of such a mind much as the physical conceptions and experimental technique of an Aristotle compare with these of an Eddington" (*Practical Criticism*, 325n). And, probably because of Richards's insistence, they were willing to agree on the natural prominence of English in the core curriculum.[34]

As virtually all those who came into his wide orbit attested, Richards was an extraordinary man. Before coming to Harvard he had been a spectacularly successful scholar and teacher at Cambridge; he had taught for some years in China; with his remarkable wife, Dorothy, he had become seriously involved in trekking and high mountaineering in the Himalayas; he had developed and promoted an ambitious program for Basic English, which was to be a new international language; in furtherance of this project, he had studied cartooning at Disney Studios in order to be able to produce a book for the mass market; he had written influential works on a wide range of linguistic and literary subjects; and he had been named by Conant as one of Harvard's five University Professors a few months before the formation of the committee. Brilliant and accomplished men were proud to call themselves disciples.

Imperious, visionary, ambitious, internationally famous, Richards was an exceptional instance of the kind of teacher that Emerson was thinking of when he thought of students being roused from their habitual slumbers. Richards had begun his professional life at Cambridge University as an unsalaried lecturer whose pay was derived entirely from student fees, which he collected at the door; but by the late 1920s, so many were signing up that on occasion the room could not hold them and he had to lecture in the streets. He may have been one of the very few Cambridge dons to care deeply about teaching, but at Harvard, the figure of the life-changing pedagogue was (and is) a local tradition.[35] This was entirely to Richards's liking, and he inserted into the Redbook a vivid account of the moral influence of the charismatic professor: "The best way to infect the student with the zest for intellectual integrity is to put him near a teacher who is himself selflessly devoted to the truth; so that a spark from the teacher will, so to speak, leap across the desk into the classroom, kindling within the student the flame of intellectual integrity" (72).

A last point of consensus on the committee appears to be that everyone was willing to have Richards draft a good deal of the final report.[36] Having helped formulate the university-wide policy for English studies at Cambridge in the 1920s, Richards undoubtedly communicated to his colleagues an air of informed authority, and was given ample opportunity to influence thinking and to draft language on both general principles and private fixations. He was, it strongly appears, given unchallenged dominion over the sections on English, which are utterly distinct in tone and approach from the rest. Much of the Redbook contents itself with generalities presented in a tone of patrician assurance, but the passages describing English leave little to chance, with lists of approaches to be avoided and adopted. There should, Richards insists, be no attention to "factual content," no "literary history" or "generalizations as to periods," no "strained correlation with civics," no "didacticism," and no "irresponsible attitude to the implications of what is being read." There must, on the other hand, be a close attention to "quickened imagination, heightened delight, and clearer perspective"; "close study of well-written paragraphs"; a respect for "the normal ingredients of full meaning"; and a prescribed acknowledgment of "the utility, almost the necessity, of metaphor" (110–12).

This program is presented in the Redbook, as it undoubtedly was to the committee, as "the consensus on the art and science of teaching English, a middle-of-the-road policy" (113). But it was Richards's private road, for it represented a condensed version of the close reading style that, under his influence, had become known back in Britain as "Cambridge English," and which, again under his influence, had taken root in the United States under the rubric of the New Criticism. The section on English put the Redbook seriously out of phase with itself, but it put the discipline of English on a path that was straight and narrow with respect to its methods and extraordinarily ambitious with respect to its aspirations.

The program for English outlined in the Redbook would have been recognizable to any reader of Richards's most influential work, *Practical Criticism* (1929). This book famously documented an experiment in behavioral psychology conducted through a classroom exercise in which students were asked to write their responses to "protocols," sheets of unsigned and therefore effectively authorless poems—perfect instances of the heterocosm without the expressive dimension in that they were, in this form, self-sufficient texts shorn of external associations. In class, and then in print, Richards anatomized and categorized the many deficiencies he found in his students' responses, including "mnemonic irrelevancies," "sentimentality and nauseation," "inability to construe," "immaturity," "bewilderment," "doctrinal adhesions," "stock responses," "exhilaration," and so forth. He then sought through "a direct study of interpretation" to develop critical approaches and terms that would eliminate such confusions and maximize cognitive performance (317).

Poetry was selected for this experiment not for its aesthetic values—Richards ridiculed the "phantom aesthetic state"[37]— but for its complexity and organization. Poetry is "the unique, linguistic instrument by which our minds have ordered their thoughts, emotions, desires . . . in the interest of our standard of civilization" (*Practical Criticism*, 301). The language of poetry is not to be measured against the world or nature, for it is "emotive" rather than "referential," capable only of "pseudo-statements" rather than positive knowledge. The poem thus detached from author and world would challenge the reader's capacity to focus on an object and to perceive it without the filters of fantasy, the irrelevance of random responses, or the distractions presented by the general dreck flowing ceaselessly through the channels of the brain. In the Richards classroom, the poem served as a kind of whetstone on which to sharpen the mind: "The critical reading of poetry is an arduous discipline; few exercises reveal to us more clearly the limitations under which . . . we suffer. But, equally, the immense extension of our capacities that follows a summoning of our resources is made plain. The lesson of all criticism is that we have nothing to rely upon in making our choices but ourselves" (328–29). Note that the object is not a true understanding of the poem but the training of the mind to the task of clearheaded independent judgment, a skill with universal applicability. If we can respond to poetry properly, without bewilderment, irrelevance, exhilaration, or nauseation, then, Richards believed, we can begin to accommodate ourselves to the hard realities of the human condition.

Intellectually, Richards managed to combine social science and philosophy, but temperamentally, he was evangelical if altogether secular. "Our purpose," he wrote, "is saving society and our souls."[38] A saved soul would be an independent soul, one capable of taking in a mass of conflicting and ambiguous information, sorting through it, and coming to a decision. The future of democracy and all its individual citizens thus depended, in Richards's view, on the cultivation of the cognitively and politically crucial skills involved in the interpretation of poetry.

Practical Criticism is the better-known work, but it is *Principles of Literary Criticism*, written five years earlier in 1924, that more plainly reveals Richards's intellectual commitments. It is unashamedly behaviorist, antimetaphysical, and even antihumanist. Beginning with the startling pronouncement that "a book is a machine to think with," *Principles* takes the form of an extended polemic against the picaresque peregrinations of ungoverned subjectivity (vii). Virtually all previous or popular thinking about the mind is wrong, Richards argues, beginning with the notion that mind is a "spiritual thing" (74). In fact, the mind is directly reducible to, and best understood as, "the nervous system," the behavior of which Richards describes in terms of "autogenous emotions," "inhibitions," "fixations," and so forth. When the nervous system encounters a complex stimulus such as a poem, it jangles into disorderly action with a host of inefficient, inappropriate, and counterproductive responses that typically involve some considerable measure of "curtailment, conflict, starvation and restriction" (53). It is only on rare occasions that synthesis and coordination are achieved. Artists have such experiences more frequently and intensely than most people, but they are not for this reason to be considered exceptional. In fact, Richards argues, the sustained state of harmony and equilibrium they experience in the act of creation qualifies them as more "normal" than ordinary people, a curious proposition to which he devotes an entire chapter. Reading great literature in the right way presents opportunities for nonartists to attain such frictionless optimality, re-experiencing the author's experience, with immense benefit to reader and indeed to the species. "We should not forget," he writes, "that finer organization is the most successful way of relieving strain, a fact of relevance in the theory of evolution" (182).

I have cited Richards's words so extensively in order to suggest the thoroughness, tenacity, and distinctive tone with which he pursued the project of making literary criticism into a discipline that could command respect in an academic environment increasingly dominated by scientific research. For him, the professional critic of poetry had little in common with the common reader. The latter was buffeted about by inner surges and drives, veering this way and that, while the former was professionally obligated to be cold, precise, exact, methodical, prescriptive. Richards was remarkably successful in his efforts to professionalize criticism, but in making literary study into a near science he sacrificed many of the hard-won principles of the Romantic revolution, chief among them the concept of expression. What Richards gave to the poem, he took from the poet, whom he drained of any psychological richness or even interest for the critic. The Romantics and their successors treated the poem as a self-sufficient verbal structure that registered and made manifest the poet's conscious and unconscious intentions, so that the reader puzzling out the meaning of "Ode to the West Wind" could with justification think that he or she was trying to "understand Shelley." For Richards, the "Ode" was the object, while Shelley—was not.

Richards's severity on this point often suggests a curiously motivated refusal even to think about the mind of the poet except as the generator of the poetic "experience." There is, he comments in *Principles of Literary Criticism*, "nothing particularly mysterious about the imagination," and nothing to be gained by speculating about it (177). Although he sometimes represented himself as a psychologist, he regarded the "unconscious" as singularly barren territory for scholarly exploration, offering "far too happy a hunting-ground for uncontrollable conjecture" (24). "Had I wished to plumb the depths of these writers' Unconscious," he says in *Practical Criticism*, he could have done so, but he decided that "little progress would be made if we attempted to drag too deep a plough. . . . even as it is, enough strange material is turned up" (9).

The disordered oddity of individual minds was greatly compounded when they attempted to communicate with one another, a project so fraught with possibilities for confusion that success in the entire laborious and unnatural undertaking seemed almost inconceivable. "We start then," Richards writes, "from the natural isolation and severance of minds" (*Principles of Literary Criticism*, 162). Readers sunk in their condition of natural isolation would, he believed, be poorly advised to attempt so unpromising a task as the understanding of the poet's mind, and should restrict their efforts to the already formidable project of understanding the poem. In this respect, the authorless or orphaned poems distributed in the protocols of *Practical Criticism* clarified the essential condition of poetry as Richards understood it, and removed what he regarded as a primary source of misunderstanding, the persistent tendency to fantasize about historical contexts and the personal peculiarities of the poet.[39]

Richards's thinking was idiosyncratic to the point of eccentricity, but he was an exceptionally effective polemicist for his own views, which were taken up by others who dropped his jargon and translated his general precepts into a sustainable and teachable critical practice. In this translated form, Richards was immensely effective in orienting the field of English, especially in the United States, around a few fundamental premises:

that exposure to great literary works had potential cognitive and moral
benefits, exerting a "formative and ordering power on minds still
plastic, growing, and active" (Redbook, 110);

that these benefits could only be realized by a reading practice that
focused intensively on the work itself, independent of any context
of emergence or general ideas the work might suggest;

that this kind of reading was not natural or intuitive but the result of
deliberate method and discipline; and

that a proper reading method could be taught by trained professionals
in a university environment.

Together, these premises constituted a compelling argument for
centering a project of general education on English.

Richards was no patriot of any country, certainly not the
United States; he was, if anything, more heavily invested in
China, and his deepest commitments were internationalist. And
yet, the other members of the Redbook committee may have
sensed, in addition to Richards's general air of command, a deep
alignment between their understanding of America as a land of
limitless opportunity and ideal freedom—a nation that, having been victorious in a war that had devastated much of the
rest of the world, was self-sufficient in a singular way—and his
understanding of the object of literary study. There is a fresh-
green-breast-of-the-new-world quality to Richards's approach
to literature, with its insistence on immediate, direct, and kinetic
experience, its intolerance of general ideas or isms, and its confidence that the detritus of the past and the fog of generalities
and ideologies could be swept away, resulting in a clear and un-
obstructed view of the poem itself. Like the poem, America at
midcentury was, or felt itself to be, unencumbered by the past,
free from any ideology, and as untethered as the poems in the
protocols Richards passed out to his students.

And so, Richards, in almost every respect an outlier on the
Redbook committee, was in some ways its central and essential
member, the one who could define the core discipline of the core
curriculum in "American" terms, and provide disciplinary integrity to the committee's attempts to devise a program centered on
ideas of heritage and citizenship. As such, he was perhaps the

single individual most responsible for the shape of not just the discipline of English in the American academy, but the larger category of the humanities in which English played such a dominant role.

Turning Science into the Humanities: The New Criticism

Although Richards had little interest in accumulating disciples or even colleagues, and professed to have little knowledge of the New Critics who traced their origins to him, his influence on literary criticism at midcentury was immediate, direct, and transformative. As R. P. Blackmur reflected in 1952, "no literary critic can escape" the influence of Richards, who "stimulates the mind as much as anything by showing the sheer excitement as well as the profundity of the problems of language." Christopher Isherwood wrote that "[Richards] was infinitely more than a brilliant new literary critic; he was our guide, our evangelist, who revealed to us, in a succession of astounding lightning flashes, the entire expanse of the Modern World." Walter Jackson Bate compared Richards's influence on criticism to that of T. S. Eliot; and Allen Tate ventured that Richards "will probably turn out to be the most instructive, among critics, of our age."[40] When the Redbook committee was meeting, Richards had reached the zenith of his influence. What neither the committee nor Richards himself could have fully grasped at the time was that he was not only a transformative but also a transitional figure who was necessary for the discipline of English to mature but who, once this goal was in sight, had to be superseded and even rejected.

If no contemporary literary scholar could escape Richards's influence, none actually followed either his example or his precepts. One of the distinctive features of Richards's aura was that those most influenced by him disagreed with him on key, even central points. His most devoted and gifted student from the early days in Cambridge, William Empson, wrote his first book under Richards's direct influence, defended him in public, joined him in China and in the Himalayas, and said in the dedication to one of his last books that Richards was "the source of all ideas in this book."[41] And yet he found Richards's diktats impossible to follow in practice and impossible to believe in principle. In dissent, Empson liberated Richards from his own doctrine. Vast as Richards's influence was, it was Empson who demonstrated that Richards could inspire without constraining and did not need to be believed in order to be useful.

That first book, the astonishing *Seven Types of Ambiguity* (1930), published when the author was twenty-four, originated as a kind of gust in a tutorial with Richards, and began with a reference to his teacher as the driver behind the current "scientific" mode of literary criticism, with "'psychological' explanations of everything, and columns of a reader's sensitivity-coefficients."[42] Empson, as would become almost immediately clear, was dubious about this kind of science. Take for example the concept of ambiguity. In *Principles of Literary Criticism*, Richards had discussed poetic ambiguity as "the fault of the poet or the reader," which his methods were designed to clarify (192); for Empson, ambiguity was a function of complexity that could be understood but never eliminated because it was tied directly to meaning as a function of the author's or speaker's intentions. "An ambiguity," as Empson says in his first sentence, "in ordinary speech, means something very pronounced, and as a rule witty or deceitful" (*Seven Types*, 1). A witty or deceitful speech presumes a witty or deceitful speaker, who is welcomed to the scene of analysis even as Richards is respectfully ushered out.

One wonders what Richards made of his precocious student's work, which insistently introduces the authorial intentions and historical contexts that Richards had tried to banish. The first example taken up by Empson is the line from Shakespeare's seventy-third sonnet "Bare ruined choirs, where late the sweet birds sang," the ambiguity of which is said to result from the interplay of "Shakespeare's feeling for the object of the Sonnets, and for various sociological and historical reasons (the protestant destruction of monasteries, fear of puritanism), which it would be hard now to trace out in their proportions" (*Seven Types*, 3).

The scores of readings that constitute the analytical work of the rest of the book are almost invariably grounded in some understanding of the mind of the historical author—Crashaw, Byron, Synge, Chaucer, Sidney, Keats, Wordsworth, Donne, and especially Shakespeare, who earns Empson's respect for packing more cognition into his lines than any other poet. Throughout, the historical author is treated not as a distraction but as the only factor that saves analysis from pointless niggling and arbitrary speculation. Empson's fourth "type," for example, "occurs when two or more meanings of a statement do not agree among themselves, but combine to make clear a more complicated state of mind in the author" (138); the fifth, "when the author is discovering his idea in the act of writing, or not holding it all in his mind at once" (155); in the seventh, "the total effect is to show a fundamental division in the writer's mind" (192). More heretical still, from a Richardsonian standpoint, Empson recognizes that one persistent source of uncertainty about meaning is the diversity of readers, whom no amount of training can force into perfect conformity no matter how lucid the instruction they receive. There is, for Empson, no question of a definitive reading, in part because the critic is no scientist but a social being like the author, and "in so far as people are always reading an author, he is always being read differently" (245). Indeed, for Empson, the greatest poets are those whose conceptual fecundity and expressive originality create the richest possibilities for significant ambiguity.

Attending to the multitudinous possibilities that once thronged in the busy minds of the now-deceased authors he discusses, Empson's critical practice suggests a principle of interpretive infinity that runs in precisely the opposite direction from Richards. Fixing his gaze on a few words of Macbeth— "If th' Assassination / Could trammel up the Consequence, and catch / With his surcease, Success . . ."—Empson gets snagged on the least of the words, and finds himself unspooling a passage that might itself serve as an example of inspired ambiguity: "And *catch*, the single little flat word among these monsters, names an action; it is a mark of human inadequacy to deal with these matters of statecraft, a child snatching at the moon as she rides thunder-clouds. The meanings cannot all be remembered at once, however often you read it; it remains the incantation of a murderer, disheveled and fumbling among the powers of darkness" (*Seven Types*, 50). Critically speaking, Richards never fumbled in the dark, attempted to inhabit the consciousness of a literary character, pondered the disorder of a murderer's mind, or described poetic language in such agitated terms. Empson's empathic rendering both confirms his teacher's insistence on the value of very close reading and detaches that reading from the goal of therapeutic enlightenment by introducing banned notions of intention (in this case Macbeth's), multiplying rather than reducing interpretive possibilities, proceeding in a spirit of precocious exuberance rather than moralized scientific restraint, and dropping without comment Richards's messianic ambitions. The issue, for Empson, is analytical and explicative rather than salvific: not training people to accommodate themselves to reality and thereby save their souls, but helping them understand how poems achieve their meaning.

They achieve them, he argues, in the course of being read by people who must try to sort out complicated matters by making educated guesses about the countless possible meanings of words grouped together, and about the often half-, semi-, or unconscious conflicts and tensions in the poet's mind that were responsible for the grouping. The interpretive problem is compounded by the fact that the poet is working with a language that has over the centuries laid down, like geological deposits, layers of meaning, all retained and present to some degree, that no artist or critic could reduce to one-dimensional clarity. The simplest words— "catch," for example—often compress the greatest number of possible meanings.[43] The diamond-like concentration of the coal of ordinary language achieved in poetry may produce ambiguities, but these invite critical discussion in which the reader, mixing his labor with the text, becomes personally invested. The reader comes alive in the presence of ambiguity, and would falter or wilt if he could not try to sort things out by making guesses about intentions using the evidence of history and biography.[44] In a letter written late in his life, a candid Empson said that the "effect of renouncing [intention] produces dirty nonsense all the time, with a sort of tireless unconscious inventiveness for new kinds of nonsense."[45]

American critics were especially receptive to such arguments. Even more idiosyncratic and sui generis than Richards, and if possible even less disposed to cultivate disciples,[46] Empson was far more attuned than his teacher to a culture in which the struggle to divine the intentions behind a text was an essential part of civil as well as religious life. Empson was, moreover, far more willing than Richards to accept an abundant democracy of interpretations. So while Richards was the key figure in crystallizing the discipline of English around criticism, in encouraging the microscopic analysis of language, in securing the place of English in "the humanities," and in arguing that a soul-saving, humanities-centered liberal education should be offered to the entire nation, it was Empson who demonstrated that such a program could be accommodated to key American traditions and commitments. Empson exerted far less direct or personal influence over American criticism than Richards—he had no systematic theory, and who could follow his practice?—but it is in Empson's extreme, obsessive, almost at times hallucinatory work that we can see something like the modern American humanities emerge from the Richards chrysalis as a group of disciplines in which the search for meaning leads through history and intention, requires imagination and sympathy, and allows for individual interpretation and judgment.[47]

Richards's influence over the American discipline of English was exercised largely through the New Critics, whose dominance extended from the late 1930s to the late 1960s. This period lingers in memory as a time of rare consensus, when the methods and aims of criticism were relatively uncontested, when the discipline had a clear self-understanding, and, perhaps not coincidentally, when American confidence in education and educational institutions was particularly strong.[48] With the general education model being advanced as national policy, and the close reading of literary texts held to be central to the entire project and therefore deeply important to the nation, it should have been Richards's finest hour—except that, like Empson, those leading the crucial discipline of English all found ways of disentangling their work from the uncompromising, antihumanistic, and, they may have sensed, fundamentally anti-American ethos in the work of the great man.

Close interpretive reading found an early American champion in the commanding figure of John Crowe Ransom, the leader of the group known as the Agrarians at Vanderbilt University between 1914 and 1937, the central figure at the improbable epicenter of critical activity at Kenyon College from 1937 to 1958, the founding editor of the important *Kenyon Review*, and author of *The New Criticism*,[49] whose title christened the movement. That movement's agenda was announced in a 1937 essay by Ransom with the provocative title "Criticism, Inc.," the first sentence of which suggests the unsettled state of literary studies at that moment: "It is strange, but nobody seems to have told us what exactly is the proper business of criticism."[50] The "Inc." indicates the direction of Ransom's argument, which is that literary study would benefit greatly from being understood as a business to be conducted not by reviewers and not by the "amateurs" lauded by an earlier generation of Generalists, but by professional critics working in universities. The incorporated critic would take a "scientific, or precise and systematic"—in short, an "ontological"—approach to "the nature of the object rather than its effects on the subject"; he would "attend to the poetic object and let the feelings take care of themselves."[51]

This was to be a rigorous exercise, a discipline for the heroic few: "It is not anybody who can do criticism" ("Criticism, Inc.," 336). Not even the philologist-scholars were professional enough for Ransom, for they were doing a kind of noncritical or pre-critical work that belonged more naturally to history.[52] Only a discipline organized around the practice of criticism—"the attempt to define and enjoy the aesthetic or characteristic values of literature"—could fly the noble banner of English (332). All this might have struck many of Ransom's readers as a homegrown set of variations on Richards's themes. And indeed, Ransom wrote in *The New Criticism* that the "new criticism"—a descriptive phrase, not yet the name of a group—"very nearly began with" Richards and "his pupil" Empson (3).

Surface affinities between Ransom's arguments and Richards's masked, however, deeper differences about the assumptions and ends of criticism. Richards was heavily invested in a series of distinctions (as between "emotive" and "referential" language, or between scientific and poetic ways of knowing) that would restrict the possibilities of legitimate interpretation. Even while calling for a scientific or corporate spirit in criticism, Ransom is far more responsive to open forms and interpretive undecidability, which he treats as central to the essence and mission of poetry. Prose was the normal state of language, he wrote, but poetry contained in addition to a prose "core" other elements that he grouped under the general name of "texture," including "differentia, residue, or tissue, which keeps the object poetical or entire" ("Criticism, Inc.," 349). Texture signaled the poet's resistance to prose and to the values of communicative efficiency, utility, and generality that Ransom found regrettably rampant in modern culture. The critic's task was to come to an understanding of the differentiae through "studies in the technique of the art," by which Ransom meant all the ways in which the poet converts the world into poetry, including "inversions, solecisms, lapses from the prose norm of language, and from close prose logic; its tropes; its fictions, or inventions, by which it secures 'aesthetic distance' and removes itself from history" (346, 347). The larger issue for Ransom is cultural and moral, but the lever of his argument is critical: not the reformation of the reader but the understanding of the poem, not how the reader ought to read but what makes a poem poetic.

Like Empson, Ransom found it impossible and undesirable to restrict the critic's attention to the words on the page. Something more than close inspection was needed to understand a poem. One wants to know why the words are there, in just that way; one wants, in a word, to understand the intention behind them. "The critic," he writes at the end of "Criticism, Inc.," "speculates on why poetry, through its devices, is at such pains to dissociate itself from prose at all, and what it is trying to represent that cannot be represented by prose" (347). Such a question is not, of course, properly addressed to poetry, but to the painstaking poet. And so the professional critic finds himself contemplating a richly psychologized scene of creation. Richards might have averted his eyes from such a turgid and ultimately irrelevant scene, but Ransom finds it darkly fascinating: "The critic should regard the poem as nothing short of a desperate ontological or metaphysical manoeuvre. The poet himself, in the agony of composition, has something like this sense of his labors. The poet perpetuates in his poem an order of existence which in actual life is constantly crumbling beneath his touch. His poem celebrates the object which is real, individual, and qualitatively infinite. . . . The poet wishes to defend his object's existence against its enemies, and the critic wishes to know what he is doing, and how" (347–48). A simple, crucial question—why poetry and not prose?—provokes a meditation on the high drama of creation, with the poet, writhing in a state of agonized inspiration as he attempts the nearly impossible feat of transforming the world into something commensurate to his dreams and desires.

The poem may be a complex integrated verbal object, and criticism may be a business for certified professionals, but the meat of the matter for Ransom is a sympathetic understanding of the desperate stratagems of beleaguered humanity. Ontology leads directly to psychology, sociology, and history, forces that are not just churning beneath the surface of the object but are responsible for creating the object entire, including the surface. The office of criticism requires not just a scholar's training and judgment but a deeper insight into human ambition, human achievement, and human frailty. If one makes allowances for Ransom's idiosyncratic vocabulary about residues and tissues, the rarely cited conclusion to the oft-cited "Criticism, Inc." could have been written by any late Romantic critic under the spell of the concept of expression: "The character of the poem resides for the good critic in its way of exhibiting the residuary quality. The character of the poet is defined by the kind of prose object to which his interest evidently attaches, plus his way of involving it firmly in the residuary tissue. And doubtless, incidentally, the wise critic can often read behind his poet's public character his private history as a man" (349). The interest and significance of this passage are difficult to overstate. While making the case for the study of poetic ontology, Ransom freely acknowledges the need for "pure speculation," to cite the title of one of his essays. In that essay, Ransom makes the same point Empson had made, pointing out that the poet's words "are the words the race has already formed, and naturally they call attention to things and events that have been thought to be worth attending to" over the entire course of their history ("Criticism as Pure Speculation," 97). Like icebergs, words, and the intentions that select and organize them, exist mostly below the surface. As a result, criticism could never be more than "a rude and patchy business" ("Criticism, Inc.," 349).

For all his indebtedness to Richards, Ransom felt that the great man was so infatuated by modernity that he was unable to perceive the real nature and value of poetry. In a wickedly witty essay in *The World's Body* called "A Psychologist Looks at Poetry," Ransom acknowledges Richards's considerable influence, but attributes that influence primarily to the intimidating assurance with which Richards brandished "an unusual set of terms" that, in Ransom's unintimidated account, sound determinedly obtuse, even ridiculous, the jargon of "a scientist who has got into the wrong science" (149, 148). Richards's deep if not altogether disabling limitation, in Ransom's view, is his eagerness to embrace what Ransom and his fellow Agrarians deplored as the alienated, scientistic, urbanized, efficiency-driven culture of modern market capitalism, with its entailments of disillusion, abstraction, skepticism, introspection, and anxiety. Neither poetry nor the study of poetry, Ransom believed, should participate in such a culture; indeed, his emphasis on poetic inversions, solecisms, and lapses was meant to draw attention to the ways in which poetry deliberately opted out of the culture of prose in order to speak more evocatively for particularity, locale, and tradition.

On occasion, Ransom suggested that any locale and any tradition would be an improvement on rootless capitalist modernity, but as he and his closest friends and colleagues were loyal Southerners, they generally took their bearings from, and their stand on, what they saw as the patriarchal, mannerly, well-ordered culture of the plantation, a kind of organic community that, they sometimes implied, remained a viable ideal. The implication flickering around the edges of the Agrarians' theorizing was that organic poems would and should issue from organic communities. Poets writing such poems were in effect speaking to contemporary culture from the perspective of the past, and using the language that the race—or at least the white race—had bequeathed them in order to do so. It was the job of the critic to complete the message by saying precisely what the poet had done and why he had done it. Informed by a rich and radical agenda, poetry could never, Ransom thought, be as self-contained as Richards seemed to think it could, and could never be satisfactorily explicated in the technical and hyper-rational terms Richards favored.

The Agrarian argument has not worn well, and the battle with modernity itself now seems an ancient artifact.[53] But Ransom's insistence on the social and historical dimension of language represents a deeper insight than Richards, for all his sophistication, was able to achieve. Moreover, among American critics, Ransom's sympathetic attention to the poet's struggle proved a more appealing and productive guide than Richards's object-centered and directive pedagogy. Because he insisted on the specificity of poetic art, Ransom could represent criticism as a professional affair to be undertaken by properly trained and credentialed people. But because he understood interpretation as a form of speculation on many fronts, he opened the door to a more democratic practice of criticism as a rude and patchy business that could be done, if not always done well, by anyone. As we saw, Richards believed that criticism supported democratic values in that it forced readers to experience moments of sheer decision in which their interpretations were unsupported by any external authority. But Ransom saw other and deeper democratic potentialities in poetry. He compared prose to a "totalitarian state" that subordinated all its elements to a single design, while poetry was "like a democratic state" in which the elements had far greater independence ("Criticism as Pure Speculation," 88). With so much about the poem unsettled or uncertain, readers also have great independence. They are all in the same position, doing their best to understand, with no predetermined authority, no privileged access, and no hope of certainty. No method, no amount of erudition, can fully illuminate the darkness of the poem or rationalize critical practice. In the Ransom classroom, Mr. Ramirez's opinion about Shakespeare, if he had been able to come up with one, would have stood, for a moment at least, on an equal footing with anyone else's.

In the work of Ransom, we can see the American discipline of literary studies coming rapidly into focus as an academic practice of research and analysis that used the close reading of texts as a way of understanding the specificity of the literary work. In order to support such a discipline, literature had to be conceived as a distinct form of language, one that, unlike nonliterary and especially scientific discourse, was exceptionally rich and meaningful but also to some degree difficult and mysterious. For Ransom and other New Critics, poetry was the purest form of literature because it was in poetry that the differences between literary and nonliterary language were most clearly marked. These differences began with the nature of the poem as a self-contained linguistic entity, an organic whole subject only to its own laws—a heterocosm with a specific ontology. Second, the poem, unlike prose, did not speak its meaning plainly, and yielded its riches only to the reader willing to labor through a disciplined practice of critical reading. These two assumptions were uncontested.

A third was contested in an unusual way, being denied in New Critical theory but conceded in practice. It was that the poem must be understood as an expression, as an artifact shaped by the author's intentions. Both the denial and the concession were essential to the formation of an American discipline of English capable of bearing the weight of a nation's intellectual and political aspirations.

The doctrinal core of the New Criticism was the concept of the "intentional fallacy," the title given it in a famous article by W. K. Wimsatt and Monroe Beardsley that states the position with uncompromising clarity: "The design or intention of the author is neither available nor desirable as a standard for judging the success of a work of literary art."[54] Adapted directly from Richards's insistence in *Practical Criticism* that the author's intention must be derived solely from the evidence in the poem itself, the intentional fallacy holds that the author's state of mind during the act of creation—like the emotional responses of the reader that were duly banned in a second coauthored essay on "the affective fallacy"—belongs to the vast mass of "external" factors that can only distract from the "object of public knowledge," the "object of specifically critical judgment," the poem on the page.[55] Drawing a series of bright lines between approved practices and various fallacious, heretical, or otherwise rogue deviations, Wimsatt and Beardsley defined the "true and objective way of criticism" as a professional academic undertaking: restrict yourself to the poem itself; deny yourself the easy pleasures of psychobiography and general ideas; do not confuse your responses to the poem with the poem; be hard, cold, severe in the pursuit of understanding; avoid imprecision ("Intentional Fallacy," 18). The assumption was that not even the author, if he or she could be found and questioned, could tell us more about the poem than the poem itself reveals to the discerning critic; or as Wimsatt and Beardsley put it, "Critical inquiries are not settled by consulting the oracle" (18).

Given the reputation of the New Critics for doctrinal severity, many of their essays and books make for surprising reading today.

While arguing for restriction, focus, exclusion, and constraint, they are not know-nothing screeds against erudition or learning, nor do they offer narrow prescriptions for orthodoxy. What often strikes the eye are qualities of sophistication, erudition, assurance, ambition, and a manifest desire to situate criticism in larger philosophical and scholarly contexts. Ransom made his case in "Criticism, Inc." through a reading of Kant against Hegel; he presumed that critics, like the poets he most admired, would have knowledge of several languages and a broad understanding of history. Wimsatt and Cleanth Brooks included in their 750-page *Literary Criticism: A Short History* (1964) their own translations from Greek and Latin. René Wellek and Austin Warren, whose *Theory of Literature* (1942) was widely considered the most commanding exposition of New Critical theory, expressed hope for a renewal of the kind of "general literary historiography" exemplified by Ernst Robert Curtius's *European Literature and the Latin Middle Ages* and Erich Auerbach's *Mimesis*.[56]

Such expansiveness and range were not rare or exceptional. If the New Criticism had simply insisted on the repeated discovery of tensions, ambiguities, ironies, and paradoxes undertaken in the service of cultural and political views that once may have qualified as conservative but had by midcentury come to seem reactionary to the point of delusional, it would have languished as a perhaps arresting but finally unimportant branch on the tree of liberal education, a historical event with a short tail, even a misguided attempt, as Empson charged in *Using Biography* (1985), at "destroying all literary appreciation" (225). But the influence of the New Criticism continued long after its founding moment in the late 1930s, long after its main polemicists had aged out, long after its early doctrines had been softened or recanted, long after its crippling limitations of perspective and practice had been exposed, long past the point where the discovery of tensions and ambiguities seemed an adequate response to the issues of the day. One of the primary reasons for this survival was that the severities and conformities insisted on by the New Critics with respect to method were relaxed, sometimes tacitly and sometimes through asides or codicils, with respect to meaning.

The critic, according to Wimsatt and Beardsley, is "a teacher or explicator of meanings" ("Affective Fallacy," 34). And as they and other New Critics understood, a meaningful poem implies and even requires a poet who meant something. The lives of the poets are not "extrinsic" to the poem, but essential, even part of the poetic organism. "There is," Wimsatt and Beardsley concede in a striking passage, "a gross body of life, of sensory and mental experience, which lies behind and in some sense causes every poem, but can never be and need not be known in the verbal and hence intellectual composition which is the poem." Trying to screen off the undefended poem from this gross body, they posit "an action of the mind which cuts off roots, melts away context," without which "we should never have objects or ideas or anything to talk about" ("Intentional Fallacy," 12). The argument appears to be that in order to study or even perceive any manmade thing, we need to forget, if only temporarily, about the processes that brought it into being. This is not a bold or controversial position. But the deeper and more suggestive argument, the one Wimsatt and Beardsley scarcely seem to be aware they are making and would reject if it were presented to them, is that any assessment of meaning must include an account of intention, even if intention can never be determined with perfect accuracy or precision.

The New Critics did their best to cordon this intuition off from the critical method they were promoting, but the line was always being breached. Take, for example, the work-around concept developed by Wimsatt and Beardsley of "the speaker," a disembodied pseudoperson who could stand in for the interdicted author. If we consider the poem as a dramatic utterance performed by a speaker, they suggest, we can retain the concept of expression while avoiding the confusion that would beset us if we tried to think about the actual author. But even as they lay out the argument for the speaker, they build a bridge to the author. We ought, they say, "to impute the thoughts and attitudes of the poem immediately to the dramatic *speaker*, and if to the author at all, only by an act of biographical inference" ("Intentional Fallacy," 5).[57]

In practice, New Critics imputed with impunity, creating hermeneutical circles or feedback loops in which the received wisdom about a given poet is marginally enriched by new information provided by a given poem, which is in turn decoded as an expression of that person. Ransom accounts for the defective construction of Shakespeare's sonnets by pointing not to poorly formed emotions or simple ineptitude but to the poet's fortunate lack of "literary training" (*World's Body*, 272). "I have tried to read the poem, 'The Horatian Ode,'" Brooks once said, "not Andrew Marvell's mind."[58] But it is Marvell's mind in particular that he is "not reading," and if the poem had been written by Vladimir Lenin, John Wilkes Booth, Queen Elizabeth, or P. T. Barnum, the reading would undoubtedly have taken a different direction. In any event, Marvell's poem is in Brooks's reading firmly stapled to its author, as are other poems he considers in *The Well Wrought Urn* by Wordsworth, Donne, Shakespeare, Pope, Keats, Tennyson, Yeats, Gray, and Milton.[59]

Given that *The Well Wrought Urn* is often thought to represent the purest distillation of New Critical practice (which had, Brooks noted with chagrin, become known in some quarters as "well-wrought-urn-ism"), such moments cannot be counted as mere lapses in attention, especially since Brooks specifically allows for them. He will, he says, read Wordsworth's "Intimations" ode "as a poem, an independent poetic structure, even to the point of forfeiting the light which his letters, his notes, and his other poems throw on difficult points"—but immediately adds that the forfeiture "need not be permanent" and that at a suitable moment, when dues had been paid, the poet may be readmitted to the discussion (124). That moment comes immediately and repeatedly. His essay on Wordsworth concludes with the suggestion that the virtues and weaknesses of the "Ode" are best understood "if we see that what Wordsworth wanted to say demanded his use of paradox" (150). In other essays, we read that Keats "meant what he said and . . . chose his words with care"; that a difficulty in Shakespeare may be accounted for by the possibility that "Shakespeare could not make up his own mind" (155); that certain passages in Milton suggest either that "Milton meant to be noble" or, if "he knew what he was doing, he can only have meant to be funny" (29, 52); and that Gray "was plainly conscious" of some echoes in his verse (106).

And Pope. Brooks's chapter on *The Rape of the Lock* reads as an extended speculation about how conscious Pope was of the salacious wickedness of his double meanings, beginning with the word "rape," and coming to rest on the conclusion that "Pope himself, we may be sure, was perfectly aware" (*Well Wrought Urn*, 94). There is almost no limit to what Brooks is willing to say Pope knew: "Pope knows too how artificial the social conventions really are and he is thoroughly cognizant of the economic and biological necessities which underlie them—which the conventions sometimes seem to mask and sometimes to adorn" (103). In a small-print footnote near the end of his book, Brooks concedes what has by then become obvious, that "we are, of course, always forced to go outside the poem for the unit meanings on which the poem is founded. . . . Every poem is rooted in language and in the language of a particular time. We *start* outside the poem" (255). It is very late in the day, and in the book, to make such a statement, and yet a close reader of *The Well Wrought Urn* will long since have grasped the point and conceded it, grateful for the critic's willingness to commit heresies and fallacies in order to comment on matters of larger human concern—while remaining focused on the poem itself.

It is useful to recall that while the New Criticism took the form of an elaborated theory of literature and criticism, it began—as far back as Richards—as an undergraduate pedagogy, with its leading figures devoting themselves to producing, in addition to critical books and essays, teaching anthologies and textbooks. These were manifestly intended to embed the New Critical doctrine in pedagogical practices in colleges and universities across the land, but the sheer ambition of the endeavor created the need for an open, flexible, and nondogmatic approach. While some undergraduates might find it bracing to learn the counterintuitive skill of reading poems without poets—

and teachers might be grateful for a method that only held them accountable for knowing the words on the page and not the vast amount of contextual information that another approach would require them to master—in the long run, literature without authors is a dry experience unlikely to please many or long. Sensitive to this threat, the New Critics repeatedly found ways to distance themselves from their own formulations, even criticizing others for formalist zealotry compared to their own more holistic and flexible approach.[60]

Theoretical debates in which the New Criticism belabored such issues often turned on the crucial question of intention, which had been exiled from the realm of criticism by Wimsatt and Beardsley but kept reappearing under special dispensations or allowances. In *Theory of Literature*, for example, Wellek and Warren, trying to draw a circle around the "intrinsic" or "real" poem, suggest that intention could be considered if by intention one was referring not to the mind of the author at the instant of creation but to "the total conscious and unconscious experience during the prolonged time of creation" (148). Richards would never have entertained such a suggestion, but Wellek and Warren insisted that this second sense of intention must be allowed into the circle of intrinsicality.[61] "There can be," they say, "no objections against the study of 'intention,' if we mean by it merely a study of the integral work of art directed towards the total meaning" (149). *No objection* to opening up the "real poem" to the author's conscious *and unconscious* experience? How, given this exposure to the unknowable, can the meaning of the poem be determined with any assurance at all? In fact, Wellek and Warren concede, it cannot. The proper and indeed the only way to know the real poem is through "perspectivism," "a process of getting to know the object from different points of view" (156).[62]

This more pluralistic and less technical or doctrinal approach to meaning is consistent with the version of New Criticism that students encountered in *Understanding Poetry*, a teaching anthology, the first of its kind, edited by Brooks and his colleague at Louisiana State University, Robert Penn Warren.[63] First appearing in 1938, *Understanding Poetry* was revised and expanded every few years, earning the reputation of being "one of the truly revolutionary books of our times . . . the single most important influence upon a whole generation of teachers."[64] One would expect the doctrine promulgated by this text to be exceptionally pure and assertive, but in fact it is strikingly tolerant of heterodoxy. The 1938 edition begins not with a crisp definition of the real poem but with the humane acknowledgment that poetry "springs from a basic human impulse and fulfills a basic human interest" (25). Students are assured that this "basic" understanding of poetry will be respected by the authors, who merely wish to propose ways of studying metrics, tone, attitude, imagery, and theme as preparation for "a critical and perhaps more advanced treatment" to be undertaken in "careful private study" (xii, xiii). With each successive edition, *Understanding Poetry* became less committed to the New Critical orthodoxy it was thought to represent, with the fourth edition in 1976 describing poetry as a vivid instance of "the lived fullness of the world," to be approached in a spirit of "immediacy, naturalness, effortlessness."[65] Recognizing that it is natural and easy to impute thoughts and feelings expressed in the poem to the poet, Brooks and Warren, like Brooks in *The Well Wrought Urn*, did not ban, but simply deferred such imputations: "Ultimately, the sayer is, of course, the poet, but *for present purposes* let us look at the matter more narrowly" (13; italics mine).

The more they thought about it, the shorter this "present" lasted. In an appendix to the 1976 edition, Brooks and Warren note that the private lives of writers, the inherited language, literary conventions, and general context can all contribute to an understanding of what the poet was trying to say. Like René Wellek and Austin Warren, Brooks and Warren come around to the necessity of the concept of expression as the basis for a study of meaning.[66] In fact, expression, intention, and even the gross body of life behind the poem are not late arrivals or resented guests at the New Critical banquet. They are all there from the beginning. The concept of irony, which joins with paradox and ambiguity to form the New Critical trinity of poetic devices, requires a speaker or author. As one authoritative reference work says, "Verbal irony ... is a statement in which the meaning that a speaker implies differs sharply from the meaning that is ostensibly expressed."[67] By insisting that any rich, mature, or complex work of art must display some measure or form of irony, the New Critics were, their own pronouncements notwithstanding, committing themselves to the study of intention as a necessary component of literary understanding.

The reputation of the New Criticism has suffered grievously despite its remarkable effectiveness on so many fronts because it has become seen as a practice of narrow conformity marked by critical predictability, political withdrawal to the point of reaction, antipathy to fresh currents of thought from other quarters, and hostility to history and historicism. The New Criticism, its more recent detractors have charged, exhibited many unworthy Cold War tendencies, including an "end of ideology" naïveté, a neutralization of dissent, excessive credulity toward science, and, organicist preferences notwithstanding, tacit complicity with "the technological system."[68] Other forms of criticism that labored in relative obscurity in the shadow of the New Criticism now seem more fertile, less compromised. Neo-Aristotelian formalism, Freudian and Jungian forms of psychoanalytic criticism, Marxist criticism, archetypal criticism, American studies, literary history, and traditional philology were all being practiced alongside the New Criticism, with attacks on the dominant practice being launched from several of these strongholds. Such formidable critic-theorists as Kenneth Burke, Edmund Wilson, Northrop Frye, Leslie Fiedler, Erich Auerbach, R. P. Blackmur, Lionel Trilling, and, in England, G. Wilson Knight, C. S. Lewis, F. R. Leavis, Frank Kermode, and others were largely indifferent if not hostile to the New Criticism. From the perspective of the present, these exciting figures seem larger and more appealing, more pregnant with the future, than the New Critics. In a sense, literary studies in the era of New Critical ascendancy might be considered a stagnating enterprise. And yet, while other golden age disciplines, particularly in the social sciences, seemed robust, confident, and unconflicted, none was as institutionally successful as literary studies under the aegis of the New Criticism.

How to explain this?

The New Critics dominated not through the brute force of brilliance but because they were effective and dedicated advocates, industrious organizers, gifted pedagogues committed to a well-defined and eminently reducible set of arguments, and—a factor not to be underestimated—convinced of their own collective importance and disciplinary centrality. No other school of thought made the claim that the entire discipline of literary studies should be organized around a single approach, much less that the discipline so organized should be the heart of the entire curriculum, entrusted with ownership not just of heritage and citizenship but of the practice of interpretation and therefore of the general question of meaning. While they claimed that their methods would toughen up and routinize the study of literature, making interpretation something more than the ungoverned whims of the private spirit, they also managed to open up literary study to considerations of history, biography, emotional impact, the drama of creation, and the infinite variety of individual perspectives. In short, despite their reputation for being exactingly doctrinaire, the New Critics managed to create a discipline that could be deployed on behalf of many of the broader objectives of the general education program that was at that time being designed to meet the needs of the American democracy.

To be sure, the match between the disciplined critical practice and the larger cultural agenda of general education was far from perfect. While the cultural politics of some New Critics coordinated fairly well with the Redbook's emphasis on heritage and American identity—one sticking point being that many leading New Critics seemed to consider themselves more Southern than American—the New Critics were wary of general education. They were specialists, not generalists. Translated texts of great books could not be read closely, civic responsibility was not scholarship, and heritage was not research. Some New Critics, following Ransom, may have associated poetry with democracy, but the New Critics did not, in general, see themselves engaging in a pedagogy of patriotism, instructing Americans in the responsibilities that fell to them, as the Redbook had put it, "because they are Americans and are free" (xv). Their contribution to general education, and to the nation, was of another kind.

Perhaps without intending to—intention being hard to determine—the New Critics were relaying, renewing, and translating into modern academic terms some of the most deep-laid assumptions in American culture, beginning with the singular importance of the individual interpretation of a certain kind of text. The concept of a "special ontological status" claimed by the New Critics for the poem had already been naturalized and domesticated by the reading practices applied to the Bible and then to the Declaration and the Constitution, texts treated with reverence as objects of supreme if sometimes mysterious import that imposed on all people a duty of proper construal. Given the venerable status and potentially immense significance of these texts, the task of interpretation becomes a matter of great significance. A fierce, disciplined, and respectful attention to textual detail—a strict construction of textual ontology—undertaken in a spirit of chastened humility is required in order to see the text as in itself it really is. But correct perception is not enough. To determine the meaning of the text, one has to grasp the intention of the author, whether divine as in the Bible, collective as in the Constitution, or authorial as in the poem. Since the text speaks equally to all, and since any determination of intention is to some extent speculative, interpretation is both individual and infinite, with all interpretations having some basis for a claim to validity and no single interpretation representing a final settlement of the question of meaning. In all three cases, the entire process is understood to be a practice of freedom predicated on a respect to the separate and diverse opinions of mankind.

Anyone can read closely, and nobody could claim that Americans read more closely than others. But the form taken by American close reading under the influence of the New Critics was of a very particular kind. One of the most decisive contributions of the New Critics to the professional study of literature is registered in the statement with which Cleanth Brooks begins *The Well Wrought Urn*: "The language of poetry is the language of paradox" (3). This is an American innovation, a distant echo of other national paradoxes, beginning with the act of self-founding and including the concept of representation according to which the people hold the power but must obey their rulers, the tropism toward tyranny in a system of popular democracy, the tolerance of slavery and other inequalities in a country dedicated to universal equality and freedom, and the fact that the nation is composed almost entirely of immigrants. In discussing the New Critics, I have focused on repeated concessions to the very arguments they insist they are rejecting, but the point has not been that the New Critics are simply confused or inconsistent; rather, it has been that such concessions strengthen arguments that would otherwise be manifestly weak and improbable. Indeed, one could argue that these complicating concessions are signs of sympathetic affinity between criticism and its paradoxical object. But they could with equal warrant be considered as tokens within critical method of the paradoxical character of the nation.

Mr. Ramirez's teacher may not have considered himself a New Critic— (professionally marginal as he was, he may not have held any position at all on the questions being hotly debated at Yale and Vanderbilt) but, on the evidence provided by Mr. Ramirez, his teaching method—regarding the poem as an expressive object, and focusing on the meaning the author intended to convey by the words he chose—was informed and authorized by New Critical theory, and underwritten by a long tradition of American hermeneutics.

While the New Critics' attachment to the idea of America was formed before the Second World War—and in some cases looked back to the time before the Civil War—the discipline of interpretation that they proposed proved to be adaptable as a national practice in a postwar environment in which America saw itself as the standard of democracy, a moral and intellectual beacon to the world. Perhaps the New Critics and their disciples, situated at major research universities and elite colleges all over the country, did not have Mr. Ramirez in mind when they thought about icons, urns, or the organic work of art. But as specialists in irony, they might have appreciated the fact that their intentions counted for little as the nation looked to the future.[69]

The Persistence of Intention

Like all such movements, the New Criticism passed from the scene, eclipsed by more dramatic struggles within literary studies not over questions of critical method or specific readings, but over theoretical issues. Informed and inflamed by European, primarily French, theorizers, scholars began to discourse on larger subjects. With debates often centering on language, which many have considered the defining human trait, positions taken in these debates could claim or appear to have consequences for an understanding of the human condition in general. Because the issues raised by Continental philosophy, linguistics, psychoanalytic theory, feminism, and Marxism could often be reframed as issues of interpretation, these influences found their most receptive audience in, and had the greatest impact on, English departments. Inspired by the possibilities for pronouncement made available by theoretical accounts of language, American English teachers began to discourse not just about poems but about literariness, textuality, or meaning in general, as well as about science, reason, the Enlightenment, law, power, identity, justice, the West, and other large subjects.

Professors of English were widely criticized during the period of the "theory wars" (ca. 1968–90) for many things: abandoning truth and beauty, professionalizing the innocent love of literature, subordinating teaching to research and publication, rejecting the cultural traditions they supposed to curate and transmit, and displaying a host of unseemly attitudes and behaviors associated with careerism. But perhaps the gravest fault, in the eyes of critics, was that English teachers, who had in the general education program been entrusted with teaching heritage and the interpretive skills necessary in a constitutional democracy, had suddenly sworn allegiance to foreign masters who did not share American values, beginning with the values of humanism, the humanities, and even the human. Behind the debates dominating the theory wars was a thinly veiled struggle between American and foreign modes of thinking.

The foreign powers never concealed their hostile intentions. As the French anthropologist Claude Lévi-Strauss said, the goal of the human sciences was "not to constitute, but to dissolve man."[70] The rhetorical style of theory could be highly aggressive, with abstract propositions phrased in a vocabulary that inclined toward the lethal, even the genocidal. Jacques Derrida spoke of the "dead letter" of the text; Roland Barthes, of the "death of the author"; and Michel Foucault, of the "end of Man."[71] In the general onslaught, the New Criticism, with its roots in a fantasized Agrarian order and its prim insistence on the pitfalls of heresies and fallacies, was mere unmourned collateral damage, generally ignored by those who assumed they were operating on an entirely different plane. But in a curious way the onslaught had been anticipated and even precipitated by the New Criticism itself, which had raised in such an equivocal way the issue that now dominated the scene: intention. In a sense, the theory wars simply replayed in different terms the irresolution within the New Criticism on the subject of intention.

This was not how the combatants saw themselves at the time. Advanced French thinking in the 1960s regarded American New Critics as cautious to the point of cowardice and contemptibility. A bolder analysis, Barthes insisted, would do away with all concepts related to the author: instead of literature, he proposed writing; instead of expression, translation; instead of interpretation, decipherment; instead of the author, the scriptor, "born simultaneously with his text" ("Death of the Author," 4). With these substitutions the old order would be overthrown, the Author and all his conceptual relations or entailments guillotined, and a new day dawn (5). *Aux armes, citoyens*; we now know

that a text does not consist of a line of words, releasing a single
"theological" meaning (the "message" of the Author-God), but is
a space of many dimensions, in which are wedded and contested
various kinds of writing, no one of which is original. . . . Thus literature (it would be better, henceforth, to say writing), by refusing
to assign to the text (and to the world as text) a "secret," that is, an
ultimate meaning, liberates an activity which we might call counter-
theological, properly revolutionary, for to refuse to arrest meaning is
finally to refuse God and his hypostases, reason, science, the law. (5)

A vague but hectic politics ensued from this new understanding of language. The death of the author was traced to a revolution, specifically the atheistic French Revolution. Indeed, the
word "revolution" slithered through the writings of a number
of French intellectuals, increasing in frequency in the wake of
1968.[72] From the Parisian perspective, nothing exciting much less
subversive was to be expected from the New Criticism, or, indeed from a country whose mediocre revolution was, by comparison with 1789, a "bourgeois" and even "theological" upris-
ing, not "properly revolutionary" at all. One did not hear, in the
chorus of properly revolutionary voices, any regard for a Creator
whose intent must be divined, much less a decent respect to the
opinions of mankind.

The new concept of language to which Barthes referred was
distinguished from the old primarily in that it was detached from
any human agency. "For us," Barthes wrote in "Death of the Author," "it is language which speaks, not the author" (3). The "us"
included a number of European thinkers: Walter Benjamin, who
wrote in 1916 that "language is the mental being of things"; Martin Heidegger, whose 1950 essay "Language" included the memorable pronouncement "*die Sprache spricht*" (language speaks); and
Teodor Adorno, who wrote in 1957 that in the highest forms of
lyric poetry, "language itself acquires a voice."[73] Advanced thinking at the time that Barthes was proclaiming the death of the
author had crystallized around the idea that language was not
the expression of subjectivity but its origin, and that in order for
human beings to communicate or even to think at all, they had,
as Adorno put it in a phrase that captured the tendency of intel-

lectuals to think of human beings as the servants of language, to submit themselves "to language as to something objective" ("On Lyric Poetry and Society," 43).[74]

This "foreign" argument determined the trajectory of advanced American literary theory in the 1970s and 1980s, reaching a kind of maximum in the late work of the Belgian-born theorist Paul de Man. De Man deployed a host of vivid metaphors that had the effect of displacing accountability and agency from human beings to language. Some of these—"defacement," "decomposition," "radical annihilation," "sheer blind violence," all describing the actions of language—involved extreme aggression. Others involved concepts of seduction or temptation, with language bewitching people into confusion through sensual or aesthetic mirages. At the end of his career, de Man had settled on the notion that language was an inhuman mechanism composed of structures, figures, and events that not only rebuked humanistic fantasies but had actually created the idea of humanity in the first place.[75] People might naïvely believe that they could understand someone else by interpreting their language, but in the cold reality for which de Man argued, complex texts interpreted themselves, and the honest reader was compelled to recognize this fact. In de Man's late work, language was both inhuman and more human than humans. A more deeply foreign argument is hard to imagine.

What I have been calling the foreign position had, of course, many advocates among American academics, a fact that would seem to count against the argument that there are American or foreign positions at all. But the issue is not the nationality of individuals; it is the set of largely tacit assumptions that provide a silent context for both theory and practice. It is not irrelevant in this context that many of the Americans who found foreign theory most compelling had strong commitments to European intellectual traditions that had developed in institutional settings geared more toward the creation of empirical and theoretical knowledge than toward the production of an interpretively competent and self-governing citizenry.

Take for example the distinguished literary theorist Jonathan

Culler, who has for forty years argued for the superiority of Continental theory to an American approach to literary study that had, under the influence of the New Criticism, become myopically obsessed with the question of interpretation and with the snarl of secondary debates about the status of intention.[76] A more productive point of orientation, Culler has argued, would be the study of poetics, the generic conventions and techniques that make meaning possible. His most recent work, *Theory of the Lyric* (2015), is framed as an extended refutation of the assumed primacy of interpretation as the goal of both ordinary reading and scholarly inquiry. Lyric poetry, on Culler's account, is valuable not only in itself but because it resists any reading that goes in search of meaning or authorial intent. As his many readings of individual poems demonstrate in abundance, lyric is best approached not as a fictional representation or an expression, but rather as a singular genre that invites and rewards a noninterpretive responsiveness to its ritualistic, musical, rhythmical, incantatory, and even magical aspects.

Generously conceived and theoretically compelling, Culler's book has a breathtakingly emancipatory effect on lyric poetry, which he would liberate from the prison of meaning. But a poetics of enchantment and sensation does not aspire to contribute to democratic practice, nor is the ability to respond to lyric poetry, however admirable and rare, among the capacities required of people who wish to take full advantage of their rights and privileges in the democratic polis. Culler's work is certainly not antidemocratic in its intention or effect, but it does register a pronounced resistance to the general education project of conscripting the educational system, and especially the humanistic disciplines, to the task of creating a certain kind of citizenry.

Like Culler, the Marxist theorist Fredric Jameson attacks the primacy of interpretation, extending his critique to the entire concept of a self-determining private spirit. Heavily invested in French and German theoretical traditions of hermeneutics and political theory, Jameson is even more pointedly hostile than Culler to the American emphasis on the decipherment of authorial intention. He begins "Metacommentary" (1971), one of his most programmatic and widely cited articles, with the blunt statement that "in our time, exegesis, interpretation, commentary have fallen into disrepute."[77] The very notion of "my *private* interpretation of an *individual* text" seems to Jameson politically suspect, a late derivative of the age of imperial exploitation in which the "sovereign individual" would plumb the depths of texts and emerge with triumphs of divination, the spoils of interpretive conquest (7). The time for interpretation, Jameson asserts, has passed; we have moved beyond such retrograde practices and the ideologies that sustained them, and the task now is to produce a reading—a metacommentary—that seeks not to render the deep and hidden meaning of the text, but to explain the historical processes that resulted in the encryption of meaning in the first place. Stimulating and provocative as it has proven to be, Jameson's argument owes nothing to the American project I have been describing, which it treats only as a politically and intellectually compromised foil to the manifestly "foreign" program he favors.

Other theorists and critics who saw themselves as insurgents, if not precisely as foreign agents, also grounded their arguments in a critique of the ideology of individualism they associated with traditional American culture. What united the various critical schools that arose in the 1980s—feminism, African American criticism, New Historicism, postcolonial studies, queer theory, cultural studies—was the conviction that the emphasis on the individual author was misplaced because it ignored the determining role of larger impersonal forces such as history, culture, or ideology. If they did not, like Jameson, reject the very idea of interpretation, they dismissed either explicitly or implicitly the notion that the goal of interpretation was a reconstruction of the author's intention. The suggestion that the truth of a text reposed in the creative mind of the individual author—or even that truth could be determined at all—seemed to the advanced critic of the 1980s critically naïve, historically untenable, and politically reactionary.[78]

Threatened by numerous and powerful antagonists, America fought back. The most serious and combative response to foreign theorists and their domestic sympathizers came in the course of an exchange that ran in the pages of the leading American theoretical journal, *Critical Inquiry*, from 1982 to 1987. Two young American academics, Steven Knapp (later president of George Washington University) and Walter Benn Michaels (subsequently the leading Americanist of his generation and author of *Our America*[79]), both of the English Department at the University of California, Berkeley, inaugurated the controversy by publishing an article called "Against Theory"[80] that sought to demonstrate that the issues with which literary theory had concerned itself were phantom problems easily solved by a simple recognition of the truth.

Knapp and Michaels began this frontal assault on the then-entrenched theoretical movement by reducing the immense field of theory to a single issue, the American obsession: "By 'theory' we mean a special project in literary criticism: the attempt to govern interpretations of particular texts by appealing to an account of interpretation in general" ("Against Theory," 11). All differences between theoretical schools or approaches were immediately dissolved by this definition because, in Knapp and Michaels's view, all of them came down to different ways of committing the same blunder of imagining that meaning could be divorced from intention. Those convinced that the only valid meaning is the author's intended meaning and those who insisted that there are no valid meanings because the author's intent can never be determined both implicitly hold to the belief that meaning and intention can be separated. The truth, Knapp and Michaels argued, is that meaning just is intended meaning, and that, absent the concept of intention, language has no meaning at all; indeed, they argued, without the positing of a governing intention, written words merely resemble language. Their briskly stated but, at the time, outrageous conclusion was that "the whole enterprise of critical theory is misguided and should be abandoned" (12).

By reducing all of theory to the very issue that the New Critics had focused on, Knapp and Michaels seemed to suggest that the debate should return to the terms announced by Wimsatt and Beardsley in "The Intentional Fallacy," the only difference being that the truth was precisely the opposite of what they said it was. In fact, however, Knapp and Michaels differed only with the more reductively programmatic New Critical pronouncements about the irrelevance of intention. They were in perfect accord with those moments when the New Critics anticipated a more comprehensive approach in which the ironies and ambiguities duly noted were folded into a more comprehensive understanding of the poem as a human expression.

In retrospect, the Americanness of "Against Theory" stands forth with greater clarity. With the details of the theoretical arguments no longer commanding fascinated attention, we can see that the real issue is political and national. An imperial power of theory is attempting to "govern" the interpretation of texts from afar. A tiny group of brave, clear-eyed citizens rises up against this intolerable imposition of force, listing injuries and usurpations, and declaring the causes which impel them to their separation from the project of theory. The reasoning behind this separation, while rebellious in intent and effect, reflects, they say, nothing more than common sense. They hold these truths to be self-evident: that meaning and intended meaning are one and the same, that the attempt by theory to distinguish between them is therefore misguided, and that the theoretical enterprise should come to an end so that texts can be governed, as they should be, by their authors.[81]

By the mid-1990s, when the final grenade in the "Against Theory" debate had finally been lobbed, Continental theory was no longer the dominant force in American English departments. The discovery of the "wartime journalism" of Paul de Man—over two hundred articles in Belgian publications now condemned as collaborationist—proved to be a decisive blow against a movement that had prided itself on its apolitical but vaguely liberal cosmopolitanism.[82] In the "canon wars" and "culture wars" of the

1990s, Continental theory was no longer considered the most interesting, much less the most dangerous thing about English. But in a sense, theory had won the day. With the discipline of English becoming more professionalized, and professors speaking more to other professors than to their undergraduate students and ignoring altogether the public at large, the entire question of interpretation no longer seemed of compelling importance. Indeed, during this time printed literature itself seemed to lose ground, yielding its position as the cultural mode in which society most immediately or directly expressed its desires, fears, obsessions, or aspirations.

By the 1990s, those who wanted to make personal or political statements were not doing so by proposing new readings of literary works. The implicit compact between university education and the public interest had been questioned or even dismissed as a reactionary humanist fantasy. Soliciting the opinions of people like Mr. Ramirez no longer seemed central, or even marginal, to the discipline, certainly not at the leading research universities. The assumption that English was the central discipline in the humanities and indeed in the entire educational system had come to seem an anachronism, a dream from long ago, like Paris as recalled by Bogart and Bergman in *Casablanca*. Science and technology, fueled by extraordinary funding opportunities supported by the federal government, grew rapidly, filling the void. As it generally does, the world came to seem increasingly dangerous and uncertain, and a liberal education anchored by the humanities came to seem an extravagance, a luxury, a distraction from the urgent tasks at hand, whatever those might be.

And so the last echoes of the golden age died away.

But within the shrinking and beleaguered American discipline of literary studies, these issues have refused to vanish altogether because American critics have continued to insist on the primacy of interpretation and of intended meaning as indispensable points of orientation for the discipline, and have done so with a determined conviction that suggests that there are still large stakes involved. In 2012, the eminent theorist and critic Stanley

Fish—who left a prestigious private university (Duke) to become dean at an urban public university (The University of Illinois at Chicago, to which he subsequently recruited Michaels)—began his new book *Versions of Antihumanism: Milton and Others* with the statement that the entire book was animated by "a position on the relationship between intention and interpretation. Indeed," he continued, "my argument is that it is not a relationship, but an identity. Interpretation just is the act of determining what someone meant by these words. . . . So the answer to the very old question, 'What is the meaning of a text?' is: 'A text means what its author or authors intend,' period."[83] Several pages later, Fish announced an even more audacious and provocative position: "One consequence of the fact that a work means what its author or authors intend is that the meaning of a work cannot change, although our understanding of what that meaning is can and does change" (4). Then, in 2015, another leading critic, Gordon Teskey, began his six-hundred-page tome, *The Poetry of John Milton*, with a declaration of principle—the same principle, that "the task of the criticism of a poem is to explain what the intended sense of a poem is, what the poem *says*."[84] Perhaps it is significant that the intentions in both cases are those of the Puritan Milton, whose conviction that the individual had greater moral authority than the state had been so important to the American Revolution.[85] Both critical statements represent forms of originalism, the doctrine that not only aligns literary study with a legal system based on a written Constitution, but also throws a line from the present to the theologico-political origins of the nation.

Like the nation itself, the American system of education is decentered, plural, resistant to top-down direction—hardly systematic at all—and, of course, derivative from ideas and traditions developed elsewhere. Still, the American system is different in ways that reflect a national self-understanding that has been articulated and affirmed throughout the course of its history.

The most foundational of the ideas I have been discussing is the right of each person to his or her opinion even on matters of great consequence. This right entails not only a commitment to a civil society predicated on difference, dissent, and persuasion, but also a determination to refine and discipline the process of opinion formation and argumentation in order to limit the potential for anarchy and tyranny that threatens a society in which public opinion plays such an important role. Responsibility for creating a citizenry capable of recognizing and playing by the rules of argumentation fell to the educational system, which assumed forms not seen elsewhere. The set of disciplines that became known as the humanities emerged as ways of studying cultural history and, just as important, as ways of determining meaning through interpretation, skills required of citizens if not of "laborers," "subjects," "employees," or "inhabitants." The discipline of English acquired particular prominence not just because language is the instrument of personal and political reflection, but also because its own disciplinary development had brought about a consensus in which the primary critical activity was the close reading of an "iconic" text with the objective of determining its meaning. This reading would focus on the text in itself, but would necessarily if paradoxically include a reconstruction of intention—precisely the activity required of the citizen in coming to an understanding of the law of the land.

Textual interpretation is particularly appropriate as a focus for an educational system that aspires to be universal, liberal, and general. The interpretation of signs, marks, or symbols is "universal" in that it is a human constant, a behavior as automatic as respiration: we do it not because we can but because we must. Interpretation is a species as well as an individual imperative for everyone from professional literary critics to the young Mr. Ramirez, and an educational system that strengthens the interpretive faculty provides its students with a fundamental skill.

Second, interpretation, broadly considered as the act of determining meaning, is required across an immense range of activities, including many if not all academic disciplines. Interpretation is therefore intrinsically "liberal," and the behaviors learned and practiced in the classroom are properly considered as essential components in what the Redbook calls "the art of living."

And last, interpretation is "general" in that it is a comprehensively good thing when done right, especially when done right by all. Unlike, for example, aesthetic appreciation, which can be enjoyed, in an often-used example, by the concentration camp commandant relaxing to the strains of a symphony after a trying day in the slaughterhouse, disciplined textual interpretation has an all but moral value as a focused and intensified form of the ordinary activities of observation and reflection, and then of conversation and persuasion, in which we "read" and are read by our fellow citizens. These activities constitute the molecular structure of a democratic civil society. When conducted responsibly, they require attention, judgment, consideration, and self-awareness; they manifest a willingness and even a desire to know and be known, to understand and be understood. This openness to others can be manipulated or feigned for reasons honorable or dishonorable, conscious or unconscious. We do not always know what we want, or want the right things. But the process of discovering, making, and arguing for meaning can be improved by discipline and experience, and corrupted by sloth, incompetence, ignorance, or bad faith. Proper methods must be learned, and school is a good place to learn them.

This, at least, is the theory behind a system of education oriented around the pragmatic needs of a democratic society. The system whose underlying philosophy I have tried to describe in these pages is not the only one that can serve the ends of democracy, and improvements can always be made. But advocates for any system that claims to serve the ends of the nation that supports it should be obliged to spell out the connection between those ends and the educational means they propose. For it may be that the means are unsuited to the ends, or the ends unworthy of the beginning, of the nation. If so, that would be good to know.

Postscript:
In Praise of Depth

No return to the general education program of the golden age can now be contemplated. Nor is the curriculum of the 1950s appropriate to the world of the present day. Our thinking about education must continually adapt to present realities. At the same time, the educational system must resist premature overhauling that would sever the connection with the past and provoke an uncontrolled cascade of readjustments. The educational system should be an engine for necessary and desirable change, and a brake on unnecessary and undesirable change. We do not need to reinvent the wheel, but the argument of this book is that we do need continually to rediscover America by identifying the principles and practices that will best realize, in the contemporary world, certain fundamental principles that have served the nation well.

The first of these principles is that education should play an important role in the formation of a citizenry, conceived as a body of people diverse in its composition but united in its commitment to a civil society in which claims of justice are constantly being weighed against those of personal freedom. The curriculum best designed to achieve that end would include a range of disciplines and approaches, with the totality designed to encourage mental habits and dispositions characterized by sensitivity, precision, and flexibility. An American system serving a nation of immigrants and the descendants of immigrants must include cultural knowledge, and, more generally, the humanities, which give people access to the past. The study of literature should be encouraged on the grounds that literature stimulates the imagination, exercises the capacity for empathy and understanding, and informs us about other times and places, but also on the specific grounds that literary study helps us understand the imaginative and "literary" character of a nation that made itself up, a nation more created than inherited. The concept of authorship has particular significance in the American context, and a study of literature can provide efficient and intuitive access to that concept.

Interpretive competence is required for the full exercise of citizenship rights in a constitutional democracy. Individual interpretation was at the core of the Protestant Reformation, and particularly of the Puritan version of Protestantism, and was soldered into the concept of American citizenship with the Constitution. In both cases, people are enjoined to read with close and exacting attention in an effort to extract from the text its meaning, which is to say, the intention behind it. The requisite skill can be developed by a course in literary study that includes training in the determination of meaning. This is not the only direction that literary study can or should take, but it is the one most directly pertinent to the demands of citizenship in a democracy like that of the United States.

The concept of a determining intention behind the text provides something that a mere pluralist hospitality to any and all interpretations does not—the prospect, at least, of discovering the true meaning beyond all interpretive guesswork. At the same time, the impossibility of determining with perfect certainty the subjective state of an author—or of anyone, even oneself—ensures that the quest for intention will never reach a final resting point, that our time will be taken up with assertions and counter-assertions, refutations, attempts at persuasion, and a general collective groping after the truth. All these constitute core activities of a society that Michael Walzer describes, in *What It Means to Be an American*, as permanently and appropriately "unfinished."[1] The other word Walzer uses in this context is "incoherence." "Indeed," he says, "American politics, itself plural in character, *needs* a certain sort of incoherence" (48–49). General education programs go wrong when they attempt to provide an unwarranted coherence by prescribing essential knowledge, as in a list of Great Books. On the question of what everyone should know, one should, I believe, remain humbly agnostic. But general education programs address directly the needs of the nation when they model a dynamic, exploratory, multidimensional approach to the world that can be applied to problems of all kinds and dimensions. Science and mathematics have an obvious, even unquestionable importance in this respect, as do the social sciences. But the interpretive disciplines of the humanities have a strong claim in the American context, since it is in them that the qualities of incompletion and incoherence—that is, openness and pluralism—are not obstacles to be overcome in the quest for truth but constitutive features of the inquiry, with their own kind of value, their own kind of truth.

It might seem quixotic to lay the responsibility for preserving the character of the nation on the educational system, much less on the liberal arts, much less on the always-in-crisis humanities, much less on a medium—literature—whose market share has been declining, much less on English teachers, much less on an interpretive quest for intended meaning that is actively discouraged by all the movements currently contending to be the salvation of the discipline.[2] But consider Walzer's argument that the distinctive characteristics of American society are registered in and secured by the two-part Constitution. The original Constitution, Walzer says, outlines the structure of the state, while the strongly individualist Bill of Rights reflects a society composed of individuals who remain to some extent "inaccessible to the state" (*What It Means to Be an American*, 123). The practical negotiation and reconciliation of these two kinds of claims is the ongoing project of the legal system, and of social life in general. But the deeper question is, what *is* an individual? How can someone be a member of an interdependent society, with bonds and linkages and obligations to his or her fellows, and at the same time partly hidden away in a zone of license shielded by "rights"?

This question might be considered one of the mysteries of life on which thought is wasted. In peaceful and predictable times, we might be content to live our lives without an answer to it, confident that our indifference would have no consequences. But there may arise occasions when the traditional concept of a citizen is challenged, when such terms as privacy, community, democracy, freedom, and rights are stressed, their adequacy or legitimacy questioned. What seems self-evident now might seem less so then, with noise and disorder on all sides, and our hesitation might expose us to the arguments of those more certain of themselves.

Consider in this context the interpretable text, which is at once open and accessible to the public, and yet filled with an elusive significance that can only be guessed at. "Intention" is a word for that part of the text—the key, the crucial, the vital part—that never achieves full public visibility, that remains inviolate, unfixed and unmastered, held in reserve, deep. The interpretable text gives us an immediate and intimately familiar model for a concept that should be precious, the rights-bearing individual living in a lawful civil society, the kind of society—or so I would argue—in which citizens in a democracy should expect to live.

Notes

PREFACE

1. *The Heart of the Matter: The Humanities and Social Sciences* (Cambridge, MA: American Academy of Arts and Sciences, 2013), accessed 25 May 2016, http://www.humanitiescommission.org/_pdf/hss_report .pdf, 17. For the argument that the humanities are an "American invention," see Geoffrey Galt Harpham, "Melancholy in the Midst of Abundance: How America Invented the Humanities," chap. 6 in *The Humanities and the Dream of America* (Chicago: University of Chicago Press, 2011), 145–90. On the current state of the humanities worldwide, see the cluster of essays in "The Humanities in Historical and Global Perspectives," *American Historical Review* 120, no. 4 (2015): 1247–1367.

2. "Vilnius Declaration: Horizons for Social Sciences and Humanities," http://www.eera-ecer.de/fileadmin/user_upload/Documents /Vilnius-declaration.pdf. See also "Horizon 2020," http://ec.europa.eu /programmes/horizon2020/what-horizon-2020. Both accessed 25 May 2016.

3. "Social Sciences and Humanities," accessed 25 May 2016, http://ec .europa.eu/programmes/horizon2020/en/area/social-sciences-humani ties.

4. Horizon 2020 has stimulated considerable creativity among scholars, who have had to find ways of situating their work in one of the stipulated categories. Thus, a longstanding literature-oriented project in "utopian studies" has obtained funding under the food security pro-

gram by, as the project participants put it, "expanding the horizons of utopian studies" to include a new multidisciplinary and international field of food studies that explores the "innovative solutions" to food security found in utopian literature and promises "community engaged scholarship in critical pedagogy." See "Expanding the Horizons of Utopian Studies," in "Utopian Studies Society, 16th International Conference, 1–4 July 2015, Newcastle University, Book of Abstracts, by Day, Time, Panel," accessed 25 May 2016, https://conferences.ncl.ac.uk /utopianstudies/programme/USS%202015%20Abstracts%2029%2006 %2015.pdf.

5. The goal of projects funded under Vilnius is to "generate new knowledge, support evidence-based policymaking, develop key competences, and produce interdisciplinary solutions to both societal and technological issues." See Laura Hetel, Tom-Espen Moller, and Julia Stamm, eds., *Integration of Social Sciences and Humanities in Horizon 2020: Participants, Budget and Disciplines* (Luxembourg: Publications Office of the European Union, 2015), 4, accessed 25 May 2016, http:// ec.europa.eu/programmes/horizon2020/en/news/integration-social -sciences-and-humanities-horizon-2020-participants-budget-and -disciplines. One of the central goals of the entire vast European Union program is to increase the "employability" of EU citizens, in part by "adjusting educational systems to labour market needs." See "Role of the Bologna Process," #5, in "Motion for a European Parliament Resolution," 31 March 2015, accessed 25 May 2016, http://www.europarl .europa.eu/sides/getDoc.do?type=REPORT&reference=A8-2015-0121 &language=EN#title1.

6. Caltech, "Mission Statement," http://www.caltech.edu/content /mission-statement; MIT, "MIT Story," http://mitstory.mit.edu/. Both accessed 25 May 2016.

1. THE AMERICAN REVOLUTION IN EDUCATION

1. Failing to realize what use I would make of his story, I threw away the card. I have not tried to identify or locate the man, so while I can vouch for the accuracy of my story, I cannot do so for his.

2. The phrase "golden age" is used without irony by David A. Hollinger, introduction to *The Humanities and the Dynamics of Inclusion since World War II*, ed. Hollinger (Baltimore, MD: Johns Hopkins University Press, 2006), 5; Thomas Bender, "Politics, Intellect, and the American University, 1945–1995," in *American Academic Culture in Transformation*,

ed. Bender and Carl E. Schorske (Princeton, NJ: Princeton University Press, 1997), 17; and Louis Menand, *American Studies* (New York: Farrar, Straus and Giroux, 2003), 108.

3. As Arendt puts it, the recurring American "crisis in education" had, in the decade following the Second World War, become "a political problem of the first magnitude," albeit one that arose only due to "certain peculiarities of life in the United States which are not likely to find a counterpart in other parts of the world." Hannah Arendt, "The Crisis in Education" (1958), in *Between Past and Future: Eight Exercises in Political Thought* (New York: Penguin Books, 2006), 170.

4. According to Roger Geiger, between 1965 and 1972, new community colleges were appearing at the rate of one every week. Roger Geiger, "The Ten Generations of American Higher Education," in *American Higher Education in the Twenty-First Century: Social, Political, and Economic Challenges*, ed. Philip G. Altbach, Robert O. Berdahl, and Patricia J. Gumport (Baltimore, MD: Johns Hopkins University Press, 1999), 61.

5. "Freedom" has long been a central and contested term in American political theory, and of course in American society. See Eric Foner, *The Story of American Freedom* (New York: W. W. Norton, 1999); and Orlando Patterson, *Freedom in the Making of Western Culture* (New York: Basic Books, 1991).

6. John Adams to Abigail Adams, 12 May 1780, accessed 25 May 2016, http://www.masshist.org/digitaladams/aea/cfm/doc.cfm?id= L17800512jasecond. In this direct transcription from Adams's manuscript, it is clear from words written but stricken out that Adams at first thought his progeny could leap in a single generation from "Politicks and War" to "Painting and Poetry." Upon consideration, he interposed a buffer generation, his sons, who would study mathematics, philosophy, geography, and other practical subjects, deferring the appreciation of the arts to the third generation. Less often cited than this humanistic passage is Adams's letter to Abigail in which he firmly crushes the hopes of a young man of, as Abigail had put it, "sprightly fancy" and "warm imagination" for his daughter's hand. Writing from Paris, Adams says bluntly, "I am not looking out for a Poet, nor a Professor of belle Letters." Abigail to John, 23 December 1872, and John to Abigail, 22 January 1783, in *My Dearest Friend: Letters of Abigail and John Adams*, ed. Margaret A. Hogan and C. James Taylor (Cambridge, MA: Belknap Press of Harvard University Press, 2007), 272, 276.

7. Thomas Jefferson, *Notes on the State of Virginia*, in *Thomas Jefferson: Writings*, ed. Merrill D. Peterson (New York: Library of America, 1984), query 14, "Laws," p. 274, http://web.archive.org/web/20080914030942 /http://etext.lib.virginia.edu/toc/modeng/public/JefVirg.html.

8. Thomas Jefferson to George Wythe, 13 August 1786, in *Crusade against Ignorance*, ed. G. C. Lee (New York: Teachers College Press, 1961), 99.

9. Adams's conviction, reinforced by his constant study of classical and Enlightenment political thought, that society would inevitably, and properly, contain inequalities and divisions prevented him, in the view of Gordon S. Wood, from approving or even understanding the real force and direction of the American experiment in self-governance that he was leading. Adams's belief in the necessity of a strong executive, like his distaste for the very word "federal," registered his sense that American society, like other societies, contained "orders created by nature." See Wood, *The Creation of the American Republic, 1776–1787* (Chapel Hill: University of North Carolina Press, 1998; orig. pub., 1969), 589. See esp. chap. 14, "The Relevance and Irrelevance of John Adams," 567–92.

10. Thomas Jefferson to John Adams, 28 October 1813, in *The Adams-Jefferson Letters: The Complete Correspondence between Thomas Jefferson and Abigail and John Adams*, ed. Lester J. Capon (Chapel Hill: University of North Carolina Press, 1987), 389. This was not the only friction point between these two Founding Fathers. In fact, they often despised and distrusted each other, as Joseph Ellis demonstrates in *Founding Brothers: The Revolutionary Generation* (New York: Vintage Books, 2002), 168–72.

11. Thomas Jefferson et. al., "Report of the Board of Commissioners for the University of Virginia to the Virginia General Assembly" ([4 August] 1818), Founders Online, National Archives, last modified October 5, 2016, accessed 26 October 2016, http://founders.archives.gov /documents/Madison/04-01-02-0289. Jefferson compared the condition of the educated society he wished to found with that of two other groups: first, the "indigenous neighbors" condemned to "barbarism and wretchedness" by their "bigoted veneration for the supposed superlative wisdom of their fathers, and the preposterous idea that they are to look backward for better things, and not forward, longing, as it should seem, to return to the days of eating acorns and roots"; and second, to those citizens of European nations laboring under the mighty alliance

of "Church and State," which opposed any alteration in the status quo (ibid.).

12. Jefferson took the pigmentation of the African as a difference "fixed in nature" that, regardless of whether it resided in "the reticular membrane between the skin and scarf-skin, or in the scarf-skin itself," marked differences of other kinds that were just as ineradicable (*Notes on the State of Virginia*, 264).

13. John Guillory, "Who's Afraid of Marcel Proust? The Failure of General Education," in Hollinger, *Humanities and the Dynamics of Inclusion*, 30. For a historical account of general education, see Gary E. Miller, *The Meaning of General Education: The Emergence of a Curriculum Paradigm* (New York: Teachers College Press, 1988). See also Sheldon Rothblatt, "General Education on the American Campus: A Historical Introduction in Brief," in *Cultural Literacy and the Idea of General Education*, ed. Ian Westbury and Alan C. Purves (Chicago: National Society for the Study of Education, 1988), 9–28; Alan C. Purves, "General Education and the Search for a Common Culture," in Westbury and Purves, *Cultural Literacy*, 1–8; and Louis Menand, "The Problem of General Education," in *The Marketplace of Ideas* (New York: W. W. Norton, 2010), 21–57. Even today, "general education" is an accepted term to describe that part of any curriculum that involves required courses, or kinds of courses, of all students. See *General Education in the 21st Century: A Report of the University of California Commission on General Education* (Berkeley: Center for Studies in Higher Education, 2007), accessed 25 May 2016, http://www.cshe.berkeley .edu/publications/general-education-21st-century-report-university -california-commission-general.

14. Irving Babbitt, *Literature and the American College: Essays in Defense of the Humanities* (Boston: Houghton Mifflin, 1908); Robert Maynard Hutchins, *Higher Learning in America* (New Haven, CT: Yale University Press, 1936).

15. On the effort to promote "democratic values within exclusionary institutions," see Anne H. Stevens, "The Philosophy of General Education and Its Contradictions: The Influence of Hutchins," *Journal of General Education* 50 (2001): 175.

16. *General Education in a Free Society: Report of the Harvard Committee, with an Introduction by James Bryant Conant* (Cambridge, MA: Harvard University Press, 1945) (hereafter cited in text and below as

Redbook). The committee of twelve included Arthur M. Schlesinger, Paul H. Buck (chairman), John H. Finley Jr., Raphael Demos, and, crucially, the literary scholar I. A. Richards.

17. Daniel Bell, *The Reforming of General Education: The Columbia College Experience in Its National Setting* (New York: Columbia University Press, 1966), 38 ("bible of general education"); Ernest L. Boyer, *College: The Undergraduate Experience in America* (New York: Harper & Row, 1987), 65 ("national symbol of renewal").

18. The elective system was introduced during the presidency of Charles William Eliot (1869–1909). See George M. Marsden, *The Soul of the American University: From Protestant Establishment to Established Nonbelief* (New York: Oxford University Press, 1994), esp. 181–96.

19. Guillory, "Who's Afraid of Marcel Proust?," 28; Menand, *Marketplace of Ideas*, 29–30.

20. See Christopher P. Loss, *Between Citizens and the State: The Politics of Higher Education in the 20th Century* (Princeton, NJ: Princeton University Press, 2012), 113–19.

21. John Kenneth Galbraith, *The Affluent Society* (Boston: Houghton Mifflin Harcourt, 1998; orig. pub., 1958). Galbraith's argument, which became central to the "neoliberal" movement of the time, was that in the postwar period, America was confronting a number of problems associated with growing inequality and should devote its energies to three large projects: the elimination of poverty, government investment in public schools, and the growth of the "new class" of professionals.

22. John Dewey, *The School and Society* (1900), in *"The School and Society" and "The Child and the Curriculum"* (Chicago: University of Chicago Press, 1990), 29. For the reference to Dewey in the Redbook, see 47. As Dewey put it, "The aim of education is to enable individuals to continue their education. . . . The object and reward of learning is continued capacity for growth." John Dewey, *Democracy and Education: An Introduction to the Philosophy of Education* (New York: Macmillan, 1922; orig. pub., 1916), 117.

23. Andrew Jewett, *Science, Democracy, and the American University: From the Civil War to the Cold War* (Cambridge: Cambridge University Press, 2012), 2. See also Julie A. Reuben, *The Making of the Modern University* (Chicago: University of Chicago Press, 1996), esp. chap. 2 (pp. 36–60) and chap. 6 (pp. 176–210). Although both emphasize values, Jewett stresses democracy while Reuben focuses on morality.

24. Vannevar Bush, *Science, the Endless Frontier: A Report to the President on a Program for Postwar Scientific Research* (Washington, DC: National Science Foundation, 1960; orig. pub., 1945), accessed 25 May 2016, https://www.nsf.gov/about/history/nsf50/vbush1945_content.jsp #sect6_5g.

25. On the place of the Bush report in the subsequent discourse of science and society, see Jessica Wang, "Merton's Shadow: Perspectives on Science and Democracy since 1940," *Historical Studies in the Physical and Biological Sciences* 30, no. 1 (1999): 279–306.

26. James B. Conant, "Education and the Prospects of World Peace," speech given 8 September 1947, cited in James G. Hershberg, *James B. Conant: Harvard to Hiroshima and the Making of the Nuclear Age* (New York: Alfred A. Knopf, 1993), 398.

27. See Babbitt, *Literature and the American College*; Norman Foerster, ed., *Humanism in America: Essays on the Outlook of Modern Civilisation* (Port Washington, NY: Kennikat Press, 1967; orig. pub., 1930); and J. David Hoeveler Jr., *The New Humanism: A Critique of Modern America, 1900–1940* (Charlottesville: University of Virginia Press, 1977). See also Reuben, chap. 7 in *Making of the Modern University*, 211–29. For his part, Dewey was not passive in his own defense. "It would be hard," he wrote, "to find anything in history more ironical than the educational practices which have identified 'the humanities' exclusively with a knowledge of Greek and Latin . . . [and] to regard them as par excellence the humane studies involves a deliberate neglect of the possibilities of the subject matter which is accessible in education to the masses, and tends to cultivate a narrow snobbery: that of a learned class whose insignia are the accidents of exclusive opportunity." Dewey, *Democracy and Education*, 268–69. For an account of humanism that begins with "the invention of humanity" in the Renaissance, see Tony Davies, *Humanism* (New York: Routledge, 1997).

28. Hollinger, introduction to *Humanities and the Dynamics of Inclusion*, 1.

29. *Higher Education for American Democracy: A Report of the President's Commission on Higher Education*, vol. 1, *Establishing the Goals* (Washington, DC: US Government Printing Office, 1947). For an argument that the Truman Report still provides a useful stimulus in today's education environment, see Philo A. Hutcheson, "The Truman Commission's Vision of the Future," *Thought and Action*, Fall 2007, 107–15.

For a more equivocal view of the report's effects, see Diane Ravitch, *The Troubled Crusade: American Education, 1945–1980* (New York: Basic Books, 1983), 16–19.

30. *Higher Education for American Democracy*, vol. 2, *Equalizing and Expanding Individual Opportunity* (New York, Harper & Brothers, 1948), 39–40.

31. Andrew Carnegie, who had himself risen from almost desperately humble origins, was especially sensitive to the disappearance of opportunity in the era of "immense concerns," which had made it "harder and harder . . . for a young man without capital to get a start for himself." Andrew Carnegie, "The Road to Business Success: A Talk to Young Men," delivered at Curry Commercial College, 23 June 1885, in *The Empire of Business* (Garden City, NJ: Doubleday, Page, 1917), 15.

32. In *The Diverted Dream: Community Colleges and the Promise of Educational Opportunities in America, 1900–1985* (New York: Oxford University Press, 1989), Steven Brint and Jerome Karabel argue that the vocational emphasis that prevails in community colleges today—an emphasis that represents, for them, the diversion of the dream—is a recent innovation, appearing only after 1970, in response to external pressures, primarily "the decisive influence of business elites," who pressured the colleges to provide them with trained workers (13; see also 201–2).

33. "The Teaching of the Arts and Humanities at Harvard College: Mapping the Future," pp. 23–24, accessed 25 May 2016, http://artsandhumanities.fas.harvard.edu/files/humanities/files/mapping_the_future_31_may_2013.pdf. See Redbook, 24, 42–51.

34. Phyllis Keller, *Getting at the Core: Curricular Reform at Harvard College* (Cambridge, MA: Harvard University Press, 1982), 17.

35. Guillory, "Who's Afraid of Marcel Proust?," 44.

36. Miller, *Meaning of General Education*, 134. For an account of this mood, see chap. 7, "General Education for Democracy," 111–42.

37. James B. Conant, *My Several Lives: Memoirs of a Social Inventor* (New York: Harper & Row, 1970), 366.

38. An increased sophistication in the theoretical understanding of ideology has exposed the ideological roots of general education. To many recent theorists (and to practitioners such as Joseph Goebbels), the most fundamental feature of ideology is its self-concealing ubiquity, its efficacy never greater than when people are convinced that they

have escaped its grasp. By describing general education as an altogether benign ideology, or even as an effective antidote to ideology, advocates for general education commit what is to postmodern eyes a theoretical foot fault. The sociologist Daniel Bell, one of the main postwar architects of Columbia University's general education program, the famous humanities-based Core Curriculum, used the term in just this way when he argued in an influential book that Marxism trapped people in an ideological simulacrum, a "frozen mimicry of reality," while Western liberalism gave them access to reality itself. See Bell, *The End of Ideology: On the Exhaustion of Political Ideas in the Fifties* (Cambridge, MA: Harvard University Press, 2001; orig. pub., 1960), 444. For Bell's account of general education, see *The Reforming of General Education*.

39. Such criticisms may be obvious to later generations but they were not common at the time. As Joseph Ben-David has written, "The utopian idea that it was possible to create a synthesis of Western culture and impart it through a course in general education to all college students was widely acclaimed and accepted" in the postwar era. Ben-David, *American Higher Education: Directions Old and New* (New York: McGraw-Hill, 1972), 71–72.

40. Erich Auerbach, *Mimesis: The Representation of Reality in Western Literature*, trans. Willard R. Trask (Princeton, NJ: Princeton University Press, 1953; 2nd ed., 2003), 307, 308. Page references are to the 2003 edition. Montaigne served as a courtier in the court of Charles IX.

41. Samuel Eliot Morison, *The Founding of Harvard College* (Cambridge, MA: Harvard University Press, 1995; orig. pub., 1935), 51.

42. John Henry Newman, *Apologia pro vita sua* (London: Longman, Green, Longman, Roberts, and Green, 1864), 285. The biblical reference is 1 Thessalonians 5:23. The concept remains central to the mission of some religious institutions today. Oral Roberts, for example, described the mission of his eponymous university as a "quest for the whole man." Cited in David Edwin Harrell Jr., *Oral Roberts: An American Life* (Bloomington: Indiana University Press, 1985), 219.

43. Richards had written on Coleridge's use of the term "the whole man" in *Coleridge on Imagination* (Bloomington: Indiana University Press, 1960; orig. pub., 1934), 171. Richards's biographer, John Paul Russo, attributes the appearance of the figure of the whole man in the Redbook largely to Richards's influence. See Russo, *I. A. Richards: His Life and Work* (Baltimore, MD: Johns Hopkins University Press, 1989), 487.

44. S. T. Coleridge, *The Friend*, pt. 1, in vol. 4 of *The Collected Works of Samuel Taylor Coleridge*, ed. B. E. Rooke (Princeton, NJ: Princeton University Press, 1969), 457.

45. The cultural portability of Shakespeare is the guiding premise behind a project launched in 2008 by Stephen Greenblatt. In this project, a lost Shakespeare play served as the basis of a text composed by Greenblatt and playwright Charles Mee. This play, now called *Cardenio*, was offered to theater companies around the world, with the instructions that they were to adapt the play freely to their own cultural circumstances. For an account of a performance of *Love's Labour's Lost* in Afghanistan, see Stephen Landrigan and Qais Akbar Omar, *Shakespeare in Kabul* (London: Haus, 2012).

46. Jonathan Culler, *The Literary in Theory* (Stanford, CA: Stanford University Press, 2007), 33.

47. In a recent article, Paul A. Kottman argues that Shakespearean tragedy represents a new literary genre devoted to the exploration of human and individual capacities. The essence of this new genre is the attempt to grasp human existence in the absence of such givens as nature, God, or Fate on the one hand and social bonds or institutions on the other. Shakespearean tragedy accordingly focuses on character, and on an extraordinary multiplicity of characters, defeating any attempt to assume a single Archimedean point from which human existence can or ought to be viewed. These premises, Kottman argues, support the eminently modern and democratic concept of the freely self-determining individual. Paul A. Kottman, "What Is Shakespearean Tragedy?," in *The Oxford Handbook of Shakespearean Tragedy*, ed. Michael Neill and David Schalwyk (New York: Oxford University Press, 2016), 1–18.

48. Ernst Cassirer, *An Essay on Man* (New Haven, CT: Yale University Press, 1944), 62. This book was originally undertaken as a condensed redaction and translation of Cassirer's *Philosophy of Symbolic Forms* (1923–29), but became, as Cassirer insisted, an original and freestanding project, "an outcome of my work at the Graduate School of Yale University" (ix).

49. Ernst Cassirer, *The Myth of the State* (New Haven, CT: Yale University Press, 1946).

50. Ernst Cassirer, *Mythical Thought* (1925), vol. 2 of *The Philosophy of Symbolic Forms* (1923–29), trans. Ralph Mannheim (New Haven, CT: Yale University Press, 1955).

51. Cassirer had, of course, a deep familiarity with pictorial art prior

to his arrival in the United States, having worked closely with both fellow German-Jewish scholars Aby Warburg and Erwin Panofsky in Hamburg. See Emily J. Levine, *Dreamland of Humanists: Warburg, Cassirer, Panofsky, and the Hamburg School* (Chicago: University of Chicago Press, 2013).

52. Arendt seems here almost to be responding directly to the Redbook, which includes the assertion that "living is an art" (Redbook, 75).

53. Arendt was deeply impressed by John Adams's vision of an education that would be at once practical, various, and moral. She cites the section "The Encouragement of Literature, etc." in the Constitution of the Commonwealth of Massachusetts (1780), of which Adams was the sole author, which begins: "Wisdom, and knowledge, as well as virtue, diffused generally among the body of the people, being necessary for the preservation of their rights and liberties." "The Constitution of Massachusetts," in *The Political Writings of John Adams*, ed. George A. Peek Jr. (Indianapolis, IN: Hackett, 2003), 103. As Adams's biographer, David McCullough says this passage "is like no other to be found in any constitution ever written until then, or since." McCullough, *John Adams* (New York: Simon & Schuster, 2001), 221. For other references by Arendt to Adams, see Hannah Arendt, *On Revolution* (New York: Penguin, 2006; orig. pub., 1963), passim.

54. Hannah Arendt, *The Human Condition* (Chicago: University of Chicago Press, 1958).

55. To this list of distinguished intellectuals whose emigration to the United States effected a significant alteration in their scholarship as they "emigrated" from European "humanism" to the American "humanities" might be added the names of Erwin Panofsky, Leo Spitzer, and Edward Said. The first two were fully developed intellectually before their arrivals in the United States, Panofsky in 1931 and Spitzer in 1936. But it was in the United States that Panofsky, who had worked alongside Cassirer in Hamburg, became less concentrated on debates within the tradition of German scholarship, less invested in theoretical speculation, and more open, capacious, and responsive to the American context in which "the humanities" were coming into focus as an academic category composed of disciplines with a subjective and interpretive character. His *Studies in Iconology: Humanistic Themes in the Art of the Renaissance*, with its then-controversial emphasis on meaning and interpretation, was published in English in 1939, followed the next year by his remarkable essay "The History of Art History as a Humanistic

Discipline." See Erwin Panofsky, "The History of Art as a Humanistic Discipline," in *Meaning in the Visual Arts* (Garden City, NY: Doubleday Anchor Books, 1955), 1–25. For a subtle and informed account of the relation of early to late Panofsky, see Michael Ann Holly, *Panofsky and the Foundations of Art History* (Ithaca, NY: Cornell University Press, 1984), esp. chap. 6, "Later Work: An Iconological Perspective," 158–94. Spitzer's first book published in America, *Linguistics and Literary History: Essays in Stylistics* (Princeton, NJ: Princeton University Press, 1948), begins with an assertion that would not have been framed in the same way in postwar Germany: "Today the humanities are under attack" (1). While Said (1935–2003) received his secondary and postsecondary education in the United States, he never forgot or abandoned his Palestinian roots, and became a vehement critic of Western, and specifically American, imperial policies and practices. Nevertheless, he was in some respects an ardent traditionalist. His last book, *Humanism and Democratic Criticism* (New York: Columbia University Press, 2004), celebrates the democratic credentials of the humanistic tradition and explicitly states that the United States was the natural contemporary sponsor of that tradition. For many years, and nearly to the end of his life, Said taught in the Core Curriculum of Columbia University, one of the original and most durable institutional sites of the general education movement. On the internationalist character of literary scholarship in the twentieth century, see William Calin, *Twentieth-Century Humanists: From Spitzer to Frye* (Toronto: University of Toronto Press, 2007).

56. The concept of "American exceptionalism," often attributed to Tocqueville and proclaimed by contemporary conservatives, was announced, and denounced, in 1929 by an outraged Joseph Stalin, who was rebuking (in Russian) the explanations offered by an American communist, Jay Lovestone, for America's failure to evolve beyond capitalism, its "right deviation" from the laws of historical evolution established in Marxist theory. See Ted Morgan, *A Covert Life: Jay Lovestone, Communist, Anti-Communist, and Spymaster* (New York: Random House, 1999), 91.

57. See Ben-David, *American Higher Education*, 71.

58. The transitions from "elite" to "mass" and then to "universal" are the recurring subjects of the educational historian Martin Trow. See Trow, "From Mass Higher Education to Universal Access: The American Advantage," *CSHE* 1.00 (Spring 2000): 1–16; and Trow, "Reflections on the Transition from Elite to Mass to Universal Ac-

cess: Forms and Phases of Higher Education in Modern Societies since World War II," in *Twentieth-Century Higher Education: Elite to Mass to Universal*, by Martin Trow, ed. Michael Burrage, (Baltimore, MD: Johns Hopkins University Press, 2010), 554–610.

59. Conant discusses community colleges in *Education in a Divided World: The Function of the Public Schools in Our Unique Society* (Cambridge, MA: Harvard University Press, 1948).

60. Conant was instrumental in forming the first version of the Committee on the Present Danger, a Cold War advocacy group that has since had several neoconservative iterations. See Hershberg, *James B. Conant*, 491–537. And while Conant continually promoted tolerance, he also insisted that members of the Communist Party should be excluded from teaching positions (607–8). For a highly critical account of Conant and anti-Semitism, see Stephen H. Norwood, "Legitimating Nazism: Harvard University and the Hitler Regime, 1933–1937," in *The Third Reich and the Ivory Tower: Complicity and Conflict on American Campuses* (Cambridge: Cambridge University Press, 2009), 36–74. For a brief but measured appraisal of Conant's character, political and governmental activity, and impact on educational theory and practice, see Louis Menand, "The Long Shadow of James B. Conant," *American Studies*, 91–111.

61. James Bryant Conant, "Education for a Classless Society," *Atlantic Monthly* 165 (May 1940): 593–602; and James Bryant Conant, "Wanted: American Radicals," *Atlantic Monthly* 171 (May 1943): 41–45. Harvard Corporation members were among the most surprised of Conant's readers. Soon after the article appeared, an attempt was made within the corporation to relieve Conant of his duties. See Menand, *American Studies*, 103.

62. Robert Maynard Hutchins, "The Threat to American Education," *Collier's* 30 (December 1944), 21, accessed 25 May 2016, http://www.unz.org/Pub/Colliers-1944dec30-00020?View=PDF. Hutchins was also critical of the Truman Report.

63. Alexis de Tocqueville, *Democracy in America*, ed. H. S. Commager (Oxford: Oxford University Press, 1952), 48. This is the edition quoted in James Bryant Conant, *Education and Liberty: The Role of the Schools in a Modern Democracy* (Cambridge, MA: Harvard University Press, 1953), 45.

64. Conant, *Education and Liberty*, 46 ("combine a belief"), xi ("engine of democracy"), 81 ("to use taxpayers' money"); Conant, *Education*

in a Divided World, 4 ("ladders of opportunity"). The greatest triumph of the progressive education movement, comprehensive high schools had grown at about thirty times the rate of population growth between 1870 and 1940 (Redbook, 7), and were widely considered to have played a crucial modernizing and democratizing role in the growth of the nation during this time. For authoritative treatments of the comprehensive school, see William G. Wraga, *Democracy's High School: The Comprehensive High School and Educational Reform in the United States* (Lanham, MD: University Press of America, 1994); and Lawrence A. Cremin, *The Transformation of the School: Progressivism in American Education, 1876–1957* (New York: Vintage, 1964).

65. Cremin, *Transformation of the School*, 347.

66. See Wraga, "'Educational Wastelands': Crisis and Cold War," chap. 4 in *Democracy's High School*, 87–117; and Andrew Hartman, "Progressive Education is *Red*-ucation: Conservative Thought and Cold War Educational Vigilantism," in *Education and the Cold War: The Battle for the American School* (New York: Palgrave Macmillan 2008), 91–116.

67. Charles E. Silberman, *Crisis in Black and White* (New York: Random House, 1964), 252.

68. Diane Ravitch, *Left Back: A Century of Failed School Reforms* (New York: Simon & Schuster, 2000), 363; James B. Conant, *The American High School Today* (New York: McGraw Hill, 1959). Despite his belief that academically gifted students were not being challenged, and his dissatisfaction with the fact that males tended to gravitate to math and science while females went into English and social studies, Conant felt that no major curricular reformations were required. His major recommendation was that the many smaller schools in a given community should be consolidated into larger comprehensive schools, a recommendation he linked directly to the values of American democracy.

69. Ravitch, "The Great Meltdown," in *Left Back*, 322–65. See also Andrew Hartman, "From Hot War to Cold War for Schools and Teenagers: The Life Adjustment Movement as Therapy for the Immature," in *Education and the Cold War*, 55–72. This battle continues today in some community colleges, with "life skills" classes in time management or "leadership" competing for curricular space with courses in logic and Western civilization.

70. Ernest Gellner, "The Crisis in the Humanities and the Mainstream of Philosophy," in *Crisis in the Humanities*, ed. J. H. Plumb (Baltimore, MD: Penguin Books, 1964), 75.

71. Often criticized for its inattention to diversity, the Redbook is in fact obsessed with it, although, in focusing on socioeconomic diversity, it had no adequate response to, or even conception of, the scale and kinds of differences that would eventually be covered under that term. See sec. 3, "Problems of Diversity," 79–102. Still, Louis Menand describes the Redbook's emphasis on "socioeconomic diversity (a subject rarely addressed in discussions of higher education today)" as "the frankest and the most admirable thing about it" (*American Studies*, 107).

II. RIGHTS OF THE PRYVAT SPYRIT

1. Transcript in "The Joint Writings of Henry Barrow and John Greenwood," in *Elizabethan Non-Conformist Texts*, vol. 4, *The Writings of John Greenwood, 1587–1590, Together with the Joint Writings of Henry Barrow and John Greenwood, 1587–1590*, ed. Leland H. Carlson (London: George Allen & Unwin, 1962), 114. For a vivid account of this conversation in the context of the attempt by the English Crown to control the Church of England, see Adam Nicolson, *God's Secretaries: The Making of the King James Bible* (New York: HarperCollins, 2003), 89–90.

2. Nicholson, *God's Secretaries*, 93. Nicolson suggests that Andrewes was personally responsible for the opening books of the Bible, including such innovative translations as "darknesse was vpon the face of the deepe: and the Spirit of God mooued vpon the face of the waters" (193).

3. Barrow is quoting Matthew 11:19 and Luke 7:35. "Joint Writings," 114, 115n3.

4. See Edmund S. Morgan, *Visible Saints: The History of a Puritan Idea* (Ithaca, NY: Cornell University Press, 1963): "By the mid-seventeenth century, candidates for church membership were subjected to the test of 'signs of grace,' as determined by the community: no matter how pious the individual may appear to be, the community had to be satisfied that he or she was truly sanctified before they were admitted to the congregation" (93). For Morgan's account of the separatist movement generally, see chap. 2, "The Separatist Contribution," 33–63.

5. Quoted in Samuel Eliot Morison, *The Founding of Harvard College* (Cambridge, MA: Harvard University Press, 1995; orig. pub., 1936), 8.

6. Morison, *Founding of Harvard College*, 51.

7. Michael Warner, *The Letters of the Republic: Publication and the Public Sphere in Eighteenth-Century America* (Cambridge, MA: Harvard University Press, 1990), 3. Warner discusses "what printedness means"

as a way for individuals to both assert their autonomy and to imagine themselves as part of a reading public separate from the state (xiii).

8. Christopher Grasso, *A Speaking Aristocracy: Transforming Public Discourse in Eighteenth-Century Connecticut* (Chapel Hill: University of North Carolina Press, 1999), 286. As Grasso says, "Writing in the civic forum was, at least ideally, a disinterested and virtuous participation in the commonweal. In the literary marketplace of print, writing became an expression of individual interests within a highly competitive marketplace of ideas and opinions" (286). On the explosive growth of political discourse in newspapers, pamphlets, and books in the second half of the eighteenth century in America, see Bernard Bailyn, *The Ideological Origins of the American Revolution* (Cambridge, MA: Harvard University Press, 1992; orig. pub., 1967), 1–2. See also Gordon S. Wood, *The Creation of the American Republic, 1776–1787* (Chapel Hill: University of North Carolina Press, 1998; orig. pub., 1969), 3–10.

9. Max M. Edling, *A Revolution in Favor of Government: Origins of the U.S. Constitution and the Making of the American State* (Oxford: Oxford University Press, 2003).

10. John Adams, "A Dissertation on the Canon and the Feudal Law," in *Papers of John Adams*, ed. Robert J. Taylor (Cambridge, MA: Belknap Press of Harvard University Press, 1977), 1:114. On the influence of Puritanism on the republican ideology of the Revolutionary era, see Edmund S. Morgan, "The Puritan Ethic and the American Revolution," *William and Mary Quarterly*, 3rd ser., 24 (1967): 3–43.

11. The vocationalist argument had been voiced in England by no less a figure than John Locke, who complained that students have "their Heads stuff'd with a deal of trash" such as Latin, "which [the student] is never to use in the course of Life, that he is designed to," all the while neglecting the tasks of "writing a good Hand, and casting Accounts." John Locke, *Some Thoughts concerning Education*, ed. John W. Yolton and Jean S. Yolton (New York: Oxford University Press, 1989), 157, 217. Locke is fortunate that he lost this debate; if he had won, the cause of individual liberty would have suffered a setback, and the chief English proponent of such liberty—Locke himself—would have been lost to history.

12. Edmund Burke, "Speech on Conciliation with America," in *The Writings and Speeches of Edmund Burke*, vol. 3, *Party, Parliament, and the American War, 1774–1780*, ed. Warren M. Elofson, John A. Woods, and William B. Todd (Oxford: Clarendon Press, 1996), 121–22.

13. Edmund Burke, *Reflections on the Revolution in France* (1790), ed. Conor Cruise O'Brien (London: Penguin, 2004), 211, 212, 213.

14. Hazlitt's writing is as pungent and direct as Burke's. Comparing the two Burkes revealed by his reflections on the American and French Revolutions, Hazlitt notes, "In the latter period, he abandoned not only all his practical conclusions, but all the principles on which they were founded. He proscribed all his former sentiments, denounced all his former friends, rejected and reviled all the maxims to which he had formerly appealed as incontestable. In the American war, he constantly spoke of the right of the people as inherent, and inalienable: after the French Revolution, he began by treating them with the chicanery of a sophist, and ended by raving at them with the fury of a maniac." William Hazlitt, "Character of Mr. Burke," in *The Collected Works of William Hazlitt*, 12 vols., ed. A. R. Waller and Arnold Glover (London: J. M. Dent, 1902), 3:250. One recent proposal on how to square the Burkean circle has been made by David Bromwich, who argues that Burke found ways of "shifting his emphasis without fundamentally changing his ground." Bromwich, *The Intellectual Life of Edmund Burke: From the Sublime and Beautiful to American Independence* (Cambridge, MA: Belknap Press, 2014), 8.

15. While committed to a radical interpretation of the English Constitution that lay far outside the mainstream of English thought, the Americans had no hesitation declaring that it was that constitution itself, unwritten though it was, that justified their resistance. According to the historian Samuel Eliot Morison, "It was an unconscious mission of the United States to make explicit what had long been implicit in the British Constitution." Morison, *The Oxford History of the United States, 1783–1917*, 2 vols. (Oxford: Clarendon Press, 1927), 1:39. For fuller and more recent expositions of this argument, see Bailyn, *Ideological Origins*, 66–77; and Wood, *Creation of the American Republic*, 10–17. The dependence of revolutionary statements on the English Constitution gave the American Revolution, as Wood says, "a curious conservative color" (13).

16. Enoch Huntington, *A Sermon Delivered at Middleton, July 20th, A.D. 1775* . . . (Hartford, [1775]), quoted in Wood, *Creation of the American Republic*, 12.

17. The cord became even stronger during the Second Great Awakening, 1790 to 1840. In *The Democratization of American Christianity* (New Haven, CT: Yale University Press, 1989), Nathan O. Hatch makes

a compelling argument that a central force behind the various sectarian movements that flourished during this time (he explores the Christian movement, Methodists, Baptists, black churches, and Mormons) was a connection between religion and democracy. The separatist fervor of the Reformation took on a political meaning in the new republic, where, however, a spirit of unlettered egalitarian populism constantly threatened the authority not just of the secular government but of the religious movements themselves. See esp. chap. 6, "The Right to Think for Oneself," 162–89. Gordon S. Wood called the early republic "the time of greatest religious chaos and originality in American history." Wood, "Evangelical America and Early Mormonism," *New York History* 61, no. 4 (1980): 362. And Grant Wacker goes even further, describing the "almost unimaginable diversity of religion that emerged in colonial America, a spiritual pluralism unlike that found in any society on either side of the Atlantic." Wacker, "Religion and the American Revolution," in *Religion in American Life*, by Jon Butler, Grant Wacker, and Randall Balmer (New York: Oxford University Press, 2011), 150.

18. For a "global history" of the Declaration, including texts of documents inspired by it, see David Armitage, *The Declaration of Independence: A Global History* (Cambridge, MA: Harvard University Press, 2007). Among the texts inspired by the Declaration were the constitutions that appeared in the various colonies in advance of the federal constitution.

19. Carl L. Becker, *The Declaration of Independence: A Study in the History of Political Ideas* (New York: Vintage, 1958), 5. Garry Wills is more specific, arguing that "there was only one motive" for issuing the Declaration: "It was a necessary step for the securing of foreign [i.e., French] aid in the ongoing war effort." Wills, *Inventing America: Jefferson's Declaration of Independence* (Boston: Houghton Mifflin, 2002; orig. pub., 1978), 325.

20. Hannah Arendt, *The Origins of Totalitarianism* (Orlando, FL: Harcourt, 1976; orig. pub., 1951), 296.

21. Hannah Arendt, *On Revolution* (New York: Penguin, 2006; orig. pub., 1963), 219.

22. Gordon S. Wood begins his *Creation of the American Republic* by saying, "The Americans were not an oppressed people. . . . In fact, the Americans knew they were probably freer and less burdened with cumbersome feudal and hierarchical restraints than any part of mankind in the eighteenth century" (3).

23. Jefferson's indebtedness to the account of innate ideas and "self-evidence" argued in John Locke's *Essay concerning Human Understanding* has been well documented. But as Morton White has demonstrated, self-evidence is not an inherently or unambiguously democratic idea. Locke was acutely aware that what seemed self-evident to some was not so to all, and worried that certain people might become "dictators of principle" to others, influencing what they saw as self-evident. The concept of self-evidence, in short, contains an unresolved element of potential elitism in Locke, which may remain unresolved in Jefferson—hence, we may infer, the necessity of the "we hold," which ensures a place for volition. See Morton White, *The Philosophy of the American Revolution* (New York: Oxford University Press, 1978), esp. "How Democratic Was Locke's Appeal to Self-Evidence?," 23–36. For a subtle discussion of Arendt and Jacques Derrida on the "ambiguity" of the Declaration, see Bonnie Honig, "Declarations of Independence: Arendt and Derrida on the Problem of Founding a Republic," in *Rhetorical Republics: Governing Representations in American Politics*, ed. Frederick M. Dolan and Thomas L. Dumm (Amherst: University of Massachusetts Press, 1993), 200–225.

24. Thomas Jefferson, "A Bill for Establishing Religious Freedom," in *The Papers of Thomas Jefferson*, vol. 2, *2 January 1777 to 18 June 1779, including the Revisal of the Laws, 1776–1786*, ed. Julian P. Boyd (Princeton, NJ: Princeton University Press, 1950), 545–53. The text of the bill has such a complicated history that the modern editor spends nearly five closely printed pages detailing accidental omissions, deliberate alterations, emendations by several hands, and so forth.

25. See Arendt, *On Revolution*, chap. 3, "The Pursuit of Happiness," 106–31.

26. Edmund S. Morgan, *Inventing the People: The Rise of Popular Sovereignty in England and America* (New York: W. W. Norton, 1988), 13.

27. As the author of the phrase "we hold these truths to be self-evident," Jefferson understood that in order to command respect, opinions, though free, could not be altogether or merely subjective. In a sentence subsequently deleted by the Virginia Senate, he began the Statute for Religious Freedom by saying that "the opinions and belief of men depend not on their own will, but follow involuntarily the evidence proposed to their minds." Jefferson, "Bill for Establishing Religious Freedom," 545.

28. Among the books sharing Morgan's title are Garry Wills, *In-*

venting America: Jefferson's Declaration of Independence; Pauline Maier, Merritt Roe Smith, Alexander Keyssar, and Daniel J. Kevles, *Inventing America* (New York: W. W. Norton, 2002); and José Rabasa, *Inventing America: Spanish Historiography and the Formation of Eurocentrism* (Norman: University of Oklahoma Press, 1993).

29. Jefferson would have been dismayed by this suggestion. In an 1818 letter on the education of women, he denounced the "inordinate passion prevalent for novels," which he regarded as a "great obstacle to good education." "When this poison infects the mind," he wrote, "it destroys its tone and revolts it against wholesome reading.... The result is a bloated imagination, sickly judgment, and disgust towards all the real businesses of life." Letter to N. Burwell, 14 March 1818, in *The Writings of Thomas Jefferson*, vol. 7, ed. H. A. Washington (Washington, DC: Taylor and Maury, 1854), 102. Jefferson was not alone in condemning the novel form. Cathy Davidson details a near-hysterical republican opposition to fiction as the genre in which the chaos of democracy and the claims of raw ambition were most sympathetically represented. As Jefferson's letter suggests, women were singled out for censure, as they were not only the main characters but the implied readers of most contemporary fiction. Davidson argues that the opposition to novels was "an attempt by an elite minority to retain a self-proclaimed role as the primary interpreters of American culture." Davidson, *Revolution and the Word: The Rise of the Novel in America* (New York: Oxford University Press, 1986), 42. The rise of the novel in America can be seen as one marker of the shift from a republican to a democratic society after the Revolution.

30. See on this subject Michael Lienesch, "In Defense of the Anti-Federalists," *History of Political Thought* 4 (1983) 1: 65–68.

31. In America, Gordon S. Wood comments, the phrase "the people" had come to refer not to the entire human mass, but to the aggregation of individuals, to "every human creature in the society" (*Creation of the American Republic*, 607). Wood is commenting on Joel Barlow's distinction between the use of the term in America as opposed to the less well-defined meaning of the term in Europe. See Barlow, *Advice to the Privileged Orders in the Several States of Europe* (Ithaca, NY: Cornell University Press, 1966; orig. pub., 1792).

32. Michael Walzer, *What It Means to Be an American: Essays on the American Experience* (New York: Marsilio, 1992), 108.

33. John Quincy Adams, "The Social Compact, Exemplified in the

Constitution of the Commonwealth of Massachusetts," address delivered 25 November 1842 (Providence, RI: Knowles and Vose, 1842), 30, collected in *Massachusetts Pamphlets*, vol. 4, nos. 26–32.

34. This presumption was described with great clarity and conviction by Burke in "Speech to the Electors of Bristol" (1774), in which he declared that that he owed his constituents only the courtesy of listening to their opinions before acting as he thought best: "Parliament is not a *congress* of ambassadors from different and hostile interests; which interests each must maintain, as an agent and advocate, against other agents and advocates; but Parliament is a *deliberative* assembly of *one* nation, with *one* interest, that of the whole—where not local purposes, not local prejudices, ought to guide, but the general good, resulting from the general reason of the whole. You choose a member indeed; but when you have chosen him, he is not member of Bristol, but he is a member of *Parliament*." Edmund Burke, *The Works of the Right Honourable Edmund Burke*, 12 vols. (London: John Nimmo, 1887), 2:96.

35. While representation was, in the rhetoric surrounding the crafting of the Constitution, meant to be a second-best substitute for direct democracy, the Founders well understood that representatives had no completely reliable or accurate way of assessing the shifting views of their constituents, who, in any event, generally lacked the perspective and information of the representatives. One ingeniously Burkean way out of this theoretical-practical difficulty was argued by Benjamin Rush, who proposed that although all power is derived from the people, "they possess it only on the days of their elections. After this it is the property of their rulers." Rush, "On the Defects of the Confederation" (January 1787), in *Selected Writings of Benjamin Rush*, ed. Dagobert D. Runes (New York: Ramage Press, 2007), 29.

36. James Madison, "Federalist Paper #49," in *The Federalist*, by Alexander Hamilton, John Jay, and James Madison, ed. Jacob Cooke (Cleveland: Meridian Books, 1961), 340.

37. *Trenton New Jersey Gazette*, 12 May 1779, quoted in Wood, *Creation of the American Republic*, 276. See also Gordon S. Wood, "The Constitution as Fundamental Law," in *Creation of the American Republic*, 273–82.

38. Hugo Black, *A Constitutional Faith* (New York: Alfred Knopf, 1968).

39. See Sanford Levinson, "The Law School, the Faith Community, and the Professing of Law," in *Constitutional Faith* (Princeton, NJ:

Princeton University Press, 1988), 155–79; see also chap. 1, "The 'Constitution' in American Civil Religion," 9–53.

40. Max Lerner, "Constitution and Court as Symbols," *Yale Law Journal* 42 (1937): 1294–95, quoted in Levinson, *Constitutional Faith*, 12. It is important to note that in both cases the submission is voluntary. As Clinton Rossiter remarks, "The Puritan theory of the origin of the church in the consent of the believers led directly to the popular theory of the origin of government in the consent of the governed." Rossiter, *The First American Revolution* (New York: Harcourt, Brace, 1956), 91. And as Michael Walzer notes, "the aura" of the Bill of Rights in particular "comes from religion. . . . The 'unencumbered self' of liberal doctrine . . . bears in its original form the encumbrances of divinity." Walzer, *What It Means to Be an American*, 109.

41. Thomas Jefferson, *Summary View*, in *The Papers of Thomas Jefferson*, vol. 1, *14 January 1760 to 25 December 1776*, ed. Julian P. Boyd (Princeton, NJ: Princeton University Press, 1950), 134, quoted in Wood, *Creation of the American Republic*, 301.

42. Moses Mather, *Sermon, Preached in the Audience of the General assembly . . . on the Day of Their Anniversary Election, May 10, 1781*, cited in Wood, *Creation of the American Republic*, 303.

43. For a transcript of Roberts's remarks at his confirmation hearing on September 12, 2005, see http://www.cnn.com/2005/POLITICS/09/12/roberts.statement/ (accessed 25 May 2016).

44. In recent years, this argument has been more closely associated with political conservatism. In *The Tea Party and the Remaking of Republican Conservatism* (New York: Oxford University Press, 2012), Theda Skocpol and Vanessa Williamson note that "a persistent refrain in Tea Party circles is the scorn for politicians who fail to show suitable reverence for, and detailed mastery of, America's founding documents"— documents that Tea Party activists believe to be "immediately accessible and obviously clear [and] can be understood by each person without the aid of expertise of intermediaries" (51). But the legibility of the Constitution and the right of citizens to form opinions about it are also unquestioned by those liberals or progressives who see the Constitution as open to continual reinterpretation. On originalism, see Paul Brest, "The Misconceived Quest for the Original Understanding," *Boston University Law Review* 60 (1980): 204–38. For Justice Scalia's views, see Antonin Scalia, *A Matter of Interpretation: Federal Courts and the Law, an Essay*, ed. Amy Gutmann (Princeton, NJ: Princeton University Press,

1997); also Antonin Scalia and Bryan Garner, *Reading Law: The Interpretation of Legal Texts* (St. Paul, MN: West, 2012). Intention, a difficult matter to decide in the best of cases, becomes even more mysterious in the case of transcriptions or copies of handwritten documents, where intention takes material form inscribed by a human hand. In the case of the Declaration, the hand was that of a scribe, whose perhaps accidental and perhaps meaningless mark might have serious consequences for the nation. This at least is the position of Danielle Allen, who notes in *Our Declaration* that a small mark on the signed parchment became a period in the printed transcript. The difference between an accidental or errant spot and a deliberately placed dot may be visually negligible, but, Allen contends, the spot implies a role for the federal government in securing the rights of life, liberty, and the pursuit of happiness, and the dot does not. Allen, *Our Declaration: A Reading of the Declaration of Independence in Defense of Equality* (New York: Liveright, 2015).

45. For a learned and subtle account of Madison's evolving thoughts on constitutional interpretation, see Richard S. Arnold, "How James Madison Interpreted the Constitution," *New York University Law Review* 72, no. 2 (May 1997): 267–93.

46. Madison to Thomas Ritchie, 15 September 1821, in *Letters and Other Writings of James Madison*, 4 vols. (Philadelphia: Lippincott, 1865), 3:228. Madison had made the same point in a speech to the House of Representatives on April 6, 1796, saying that the document that came from the Framers was "nothing more than the draft of a plan, nothing but a dead letter, until life and validity were breathed into it by the voice of the people." In *The Writings of James Madison*, ed. Gaillard Hunt, 9 vols. (New York: G. B. Putnam's Sons, 1900–1910), 6:272. On the process of ratification, see Pauline Maier, *Ratification: The People Debate the Constitution, 1787–1788* (New York: Simon & Schuster, 2011); and Michael Allen Gillespie and Michael Lienesch, eds., *Ratifying the Constitution* (Lawrence: University Press of Kansas, 1989). For a more recent perspective close to Madison's, see M. E. Bradford, *Original Intentions: On the Making and Ratification of the United States Constitution* (Athens: University of Georgia Press, 1993). On Madison's role in the Constitutional Convention, see Jack N. Rakove, *Original Meanings: Politics and Ideas in the Making of the Constitution* (New York: Vintage, 1997). For a brief overview of Madison's role in the Constitutional Convention, see Jack N. Rakove, "Mr. Meese, Meet Mr. Madison," *Atlantic Monthly*, December 1986, 77–86, which argues that jurisprudence of "original in-

tent" is not supported by Madison's own thought and actions. For a synthetic account of the originalist movement, see Johnathan O'Neill, *Originalism in American Law and Politics: A Constitutional History* (Baltimore, MD: Johns Hopkins University Press, 2005).

47. See Christopher Tiedman, *The Unwritten Constitution of the United States: A Philosophical Inquiry into the Fundamentals of American Constitutional Law* (New York: G. P. Putnam's Sons, 1890); William B. Munro, *The Makers of the Unwritten Constitution* (New York: Macmillan, 1930); Thomas Grey, "Do We Have an Unwritten Constitution?" *Stanford Law Review* 27 (1975): 703–18; and Akhil Reed Amar, *America's Unwritten Constitution: The Precedents and Principles We Live By* (New York: Basic Books, 2012). Amar makes the point that we need to go "beyond" the Constitution just in order to establish the Constitution itself, since several versions were circulating at the time of ratification, and the parchment copy in the National Archives has never been the official version.

48. Interpretive infinity is one of the forms of "tragedy" entailed by the Constitution, according to a probing essay by Peter Lancelot Mallios, who draws on Hegel for a definition of tragedy as "a crucially dynamic literary form, best conceived not in terms of abstraction from a single character, but rather in terms of 'opposition' and 'antagonism' between (or within) characters." See Mallios, "Tragic Constitution: United States Democracy and Its Discontents," *PMLA* 129, no. 4 (2014): 708–26. One of the last sections in Gordon S. Wood's *Creation of the American Republic* is titled "The Repudiation of 1776," and it describes the Constitution's creation of a well-nigh "aristocratic" power in the four-year term of the executive and the six-year term of the Senate (519–24). On the "agonistic" theory of democracy, see Bonnie Honig, *Political Theory and the Displacement of Politics* (Ithaca, NY: Cornell University Press, 1993); Chantal Mouffe, *The Democratic Paradox* (London, New York: Verso, 2000); and Chantal Mouffe, *Agonistics: Thinking the World Politically* (London, New York: Verso, 2013).

49. See Arendt, *On Revolution*, 175, 218.

50. John Quincy Adams, *Lectures on Rhetoric and Oratory*, 2 vols (Cambridge, MA: Hilliard and Metcalf, 1810).

51. For an account of Adams's debt to David Hume's essay "Of Eloquence," as well as to biblical and classical sources, see Adam Potkay, "Theorizing Civil Eloquence in the Early Republic: The Road from

David Hume to John Quincy Adams," *Early American Literature* 34, no. 2 (1999): 147–70; see esp. 158–59.

52. The transition from a republican to a democratic society has been described in impressive detail by several leading historians. See Gordon S. Wood, *The Radicalism of the American Revolution* (New York: Vintage Books, 1991); Sean Wilentz, *The Rise of American Democracy: Jefferson to Lincoln* (New York: W. W. Norton, 2005); and James T. Kloppenberg, *Toward Democracy: The Struggle for Self-Rule in European and American Thought* (New York: Oxford University Press, 2016).

53. In *John Quincy Adams: Militant Spirit* (New York, Basic Books, 2016), James Traub argues that Adams, a passionate opponent of slavery, anticipated Lincoln in this insistence on the centrality of the Declaration to the American polis.

54. George Santayana, "Emerson" (1900), in *Emerson's Prose and Poetry*, ed. Joel Porte and Saundra Morris (New York: W. W. Norton, 2001), 634.

55. John Dewey, "Ralph Waldo Emerson" (1929), in Porte and Morris, *Emerson's Prose and Poetry*, 643–48.

56. Ralph Waldo Emerson, "The American Scholar" (1837), in Porte and Morris, *Emerson's Prose and Poetry*, 64, 68, 68, 68, 69.

57. Ralph Waldo Emerson, "The Poet" (1844), in Porte and Morris, *Emerson's Prose and Poetry*, 194.

58. Ralph Waldo Emerson, "Self-Reliance" (1841), in Porte and Morris, *Emerson's Prose and Poetry*, 120. The argument for "Self-Reliance" as the central essay in the Emerson oeuvre is made by George Kateb, *Emerson and Self-Reliance* (Lanham, MD: Rowman and Littlefield, 2002; orig. pub., 1995).

59. In *Emerson and Self-Reliance*, Kateb argues that Emerson's thought does not develop as a series of assertions, but—in keeping with his impeachment of "consistency" as "the hobgoblin of little minds"— rather as a series of "multi-perspectival" collisions that defeat the doctrinal aspirations of any system. The only unifying principle in Emerson's thought, according to Kateb, is the insistence on self-reliance. See esp. chap. 1, "Self-Reliance and the Life of the Mind," 1–36. On Emerson as a thinker of democracy, see also George Kateb, *The Inner Ocean: Individualism and Democratic Culture* (Ithaca, NY: Cornell University Press, 1992).

60. Frederick Douglass, *Narrative of the Life of Frederick Douglass, an*

American Slave (1845), ed. William L. Andrews and William S. McFeely (New York: W. W. Norton, 1996), 33.

61. Ralph Waldo Emerson, "An Address . . . on . . . the Emancipation of the Negroes in the British West Indies," in *Emerson's Antislavery Writings*, ed. Len Gougeon and Joel Myerson (New Haven, CT: Yale University Press, 1995), 31. In the draft of this speech, Douglass was mentioned as one of those who might emerge; with Douglass in the audience, Emerson omitted this mention in his reading. The address strikes a very different note from "Self-Reliance," where Emerson had proudly rejected the "angry bigot" preaching an "incredible tenderness for black folk a thousand miles off " in West Indian slavery (123). For an account of the impact of Emerson's lecture on Douglass, see Len Gougeon, "Militant Abolitionism: Douglass, Emerson, and the Anti-Slave," *New England Quarterly* 85, no. 4 (December 2012): 622–23.

62. Frederick Douglass, "The Constitution and Slavery" (letter to C. H. Chase, 23 January 1849), in *Life and Writings of Frederick Douglass*, ed. Philip S. Foner, 5 vols. (New York: International Publishers, 1950–75), 1:353.

63. Frederick Douglass, "Letter to Gerrit Smith" (1851), in *Life and Writings*, 2:150.

64. Frederick Douglass, "The Meaning of July Fourth for the Negro" (1852), in *Life and Writings*, 2:192, 201.

65. Cass R. Sunstein, "Constitutional Myth-Making: Lessons from the *Dred Scott* Case," *Occasional Papers from the Law School of the University of Chicago*, no. 37 (1996), 8; Dred Scott v. Sandford, 60 U.S. (19 How) 393 (1857) at 407. Others have argued that Taney was a very imperfect originalist and ignored precedents that might have supported a different decision. Taney was seemingly unaware of the fact that black men had fought in the Revolution and that former slaves had been granted citizenship. Sunstein himself denounces the decision as "an abomination" on several grounds ("Constitutional Myth-Making," 23).

66. On Taney's admiration for the "literary" achievements of the Framers, see Barbara Johnson, "Anthropomorphism in Lyric and Law," *Yale Journal of Law & the Humanities* 10, no. 2 (1998): 549–74, esp. 565–66.

67. Frederick Douglass, "The Dred Scott Decision" (1857), in *Life and Writings*, 2:414.

68. H. Jefferson Powell, "The Original Understanding of Original Intent," *Harvard Law Review* 98 (March 1985) 5:945. This long essay is

the definitive treatment of the concept of original intent as applied to constitutional interpretation, and of the continuity between the Protestant approach to biblical interpretation and constitutional interpretation in the American context.

69. Jefferson Davis, "Address of Jefferson Davis at Montgomery, Alabama" (18 February 1861), in *Annals of America*, 238, 240–41, cited by Powell, "Original Understanding of Original Intent," 947.

70. Frederick Douglass, "The Constitution of the United States: Is it Pro-Slavery or Anti-Slavery?" (1860), in *Life and Writings*, 2:468 ("written instrument . . . single word therefrom"), 469 ("mere text . . . plain reading"), 475–76 ("strict construction"). Douglass was not consistent in his enthusiasm for "strict construction." Writing in 1883 on a recent ruling of the Supreme Court that had restricted the application of the Fourteenth Amendment to actions committed by the state, Douglass remarked on a "strange and glaring inconsistency" with the court's prior decisions. As long as slavery was the "base line" of society, Douglass noted, the court had used "intention as a rule of interpretation," with a "generous recognition of [the] broad and liberal spirit" of the law, ungenerous and illiberal though the law itself was; but after Reconstruction, when liberty was the baseline, the court suddenly applied only "the narrowest and most restricted rules of legal interpretation," effectively supporting the same oppressive practices that they had previously justified by appealing to intention. Douglass, "Speech at the Civil Rights Mass-Meeting Held at Lincoln Hall" (22 October 1883), in *Life and Writings*, 4:398, 398–99. In rejecting the argument that the private views of the Framers constituted the relevant intentionality behind the Constitution, Douglass was following the example of the abolitionist Lysander Spooner. In *The Unconstitutionality of Slavery* (Boston: Bela Marsh, 1845), Spooner argued that the Framers were not lawgivers but committee members charged with devising and recommending an instrument that the people could then vote to approve. At the moment of ratification, the Framers were, like everyone else, suddenly bound by the document they had devised, to which they had no privileged relation (135).

71. Waldo Martin, *The Mind of Frederick Douglass* (Chapel Hill: University of North Carolina Press, 1984), x. For a detailed account of Douglass's thoughts about the Constitution during this crucial time, see pp. 36–38.

72. Samuel Johnson, *Taxation No Tyranny. An Answer to the Reso-lutions and Address of the American Congress*, 4th ed. (London: T. Cadell, 1775), 89.

73. Charles W. Mills, "Whose Fourth of July? Frederick Douglass and 'Original Intent,'" in *Frederick Douglass: A Critical Reader*, ed. Bill I. Lawson and Frank M. Kirkland (Malden, MA: Blackwell, 1999), 115.

74. Ralph Waldo Emerson, *Representative Men* (London: John Chapman, 1850), 7.

75. Abraham Lincoln, "Address at Cooper Institute, New York City" (27 February 1860), in *The Portable Abraham Lincoln*, ed. Andrew Delbanco (New York: Penguin Books, 2009), 197–216. On the various real, probable, and possible linkages between Douglass and Lincoln, see John Stauffer, *Giants: The Parallel Lives of Frederick Douglass and Abraham Lincoln* (New York: Twelve, 2008). Three years earlier, Lincoln had argued, in a speech on the Dred Scott decision, for the necessity of public officials to interpret the meaning of the Constitution for themselves, citing Andrew Jackson's statement that "each public officer, who takes an oath to support the Constitution, swears that he will support it as he understands it, and not as it is understood by others." Abraham Lincoln, "Speech on the Dred Scott Decision at Springfield, Illinois," in Delbanco, *Portable Abraham Lincoln*, 92.

76. In many cases, the contemporary debate about interpretation takes place not between originalist and "living document" approaches, but within the originalist approach. This is true even in Supreme Court decisions on statutory law, in which the court must decide the intent not of the Founders but of the less venerable, more fractious, more numerous, but still authoritative Congress. The decision on July 25, 2015, against the plaintiffs in *King v. Burwell*, a case that sought to delegitimate the Affordable Care Act, is a case in point, in which opposing sides each appealed to the intention behind the act. Chief Justice Roberts, writing the majority opinion, refers repeatedly to the "intent" of Congress in drafting this nine-hundred-page bill, but concedes that congressional intent must be divined by the court in the face of "inartful drafting" of the legislation by Congress (3). Some interpretive latitude is in effect compelled, Roberts argues, because the key phrase ("established by the State") at issue in the case is "properly viewed as ambiguous," and thus requires the court to construe it (3). Roberts's interpretation, based on the context of that phrase and the structure of the entirety, represents his best guess as to the most plausible and least "odd" interpretation of

Congress's overall purpose in enacting the bill (11). In a bitter and even contemptuous "textualist" dissent, Justice Antonin Scalia charges the majority with "rewriting the law under the pretense of interpreting it," and argues that if "all the usual rules of interpretation" were followed—virtually the same phrase Douglass had used in "What to the Slave Is the Fourth of July?"—the plaintiffs would prevail (Scalia dissent, 19, 2). On his reading, the four words at issue are not ambiguous but clear, even if they have the effect of rendering the entire massive Affordable Care Act effectively null. Scalia's commitment to a decision based on the dictionary meaning of individual words compels him, he claims, to conclude that Congress meant—or at any rate, did not *not* mean—to eviscerate the act in the process of enacting it. In defense of his method, he cites the principle articulated by John Adams in his 1780 constitution for the state of Massachusetts that "ours is a government of laws and not of men" (18). See King et al. v. Burwell, Certiorari to the United States Court of Appeals for the Fourth Circuit Court, No. 14–114, accessed 25 May 2016, http://www.supremecourt.gov/opinions/14pdf/14 -114_qol1.pdf.

77. On the connection between the veneration of the Constitution and a continual public recommitment to the spirit of progress and self-invention, see Hannah Arendt, "Foundation II: *Novus Ordo Saeclorum*," in *On Revolution*, 171–206.

78. For a discussion of the issues surrounding what he calls "constitutional rights consciousness," see Hendrik Hartog, "The Constitution of Aspiration and 'The Rights That Belong to Us All,'" *Journal of American History* 74, no. 3 (December 1987): 1013–34 (phrase at 1032).

79. Alexis de Tocqueville, *Democracy in America*, in *Democracy in America and Two Essays on America*, trans. Gerald E. Bevan (New York: Penguin Books, 2003), 301.

80. Viscount James Bryce, *The American Commonwealth*, 2 vols. (Indianapolis, IN: Liberty Fund, 1995), 1:274 ("waste of power"), 2:926 ("current of the popular will"). Bryce devotes an entire section to public opinion: "Public Opinion," 2:909–1020.

81. The phrase "manufacture of consent" is from Walter Lippmann, *Public Opinion* (New York: Harcourt, Brace, 1922), where it described the instruction of public opinion by informed experts. Lippmann was in favor of such engineering, arguing that most people entertained false and destructive illusions provided willy-nilly by imperfect sources of pseudo-information. The phrase was appropriated and its valence re-

versed by Edward S. Herman and Noam Chomsky in *Manufacturing Consent* (New York: Pantheon Books, 1988). See also Jonathan Auerbach, *Weapons of Democracy: Propaganda, Progressivism, and American Public Opinion* (Baltimore, MD: Johns Hopkins University Press, 2015).

82. Abraham Lincoln, speech at a Republican banquet, 10 December 1856, in *The Collected Works of Abraham Lincoln*, ed. Roy P. Basler, 9 vols. (New Brunswick, NJ: Rutgers University Press, 1953–55), 2:385.

83. *Lincoln's Lost Speech* (New York: Printed for the Committee of the Republican Club of the City of New York, 1897), 55. The text of this often-reprinted 1856 speech is a reconstruction made years later from notes made by an observer, H. C. Whitney. Scholars have rejected the reconstruction, but the substance and general direction of the speech as printed convinced some who were in attendance that it was a faithful rendering.

84. This, at least, is the interpretation given by Garry Wills, who argues, in *Lincoln at Gettysburg: The Words That Remade America* (New York: Simon & Schuster, 2006), that the famous address sought to influence public opinion about the purpose of the war. Because of his success in doing so, Wills says, the Civil War came to mean "what Lincoln wanted it to mean" (38).

85. Gordon S. Wood, *The Idea of America: Reflections on the Birth of the United States* (New York: Penguin Books, 2011), 324; see also 251–72.

III. THE PECULIAR OPPORTUNITIES OF ENGLISH

1. See *General Education in a Free Society: Report of the Harvard Committee, with an introduction by James Bryant Conant* (Cambridge, MA: Harvard University Press, 1945), 67–69 (hereafter cited in text and below as Redbook); see also Gerald Graff, *Professing Literature: An Institutional History* (Chicago: University of Chicago Press, 1987), 36–51.

2. The centrality of English was a golden age commonplace. Consider: "Literature is the central division of the humanities, flanked on one side by history and on the other by philosophy." Northrop Frye, *Anatomy of Criticism* (New York: Athanaeum, 1969; orig. pub., 1957), 12. "[Of the humanistic disciplines] it is clearly literature that displays the strongest and most consistent commitment" to the basic premises of the humanities, beginning with a conception of Man as the "language animal." Frederick A. Olafson, "Humanism and the Humanities," in *The Philosophy of the Curriculum*, ed. Sidney Hook, Paul Kurtz, and Miro Todorovich (Buffalo, NY: Promethus Books, 1975), 61, 57.

3. Erwin Panofsky, "The History of Art as a Humanistic Discipline," in *Meaning in the Visual Arts* (Garden City, NY: Doubleday Anchor Books, 1955), 25.

4. "About NEH," accessed 25 May 2016, http://www.neh.gov/about.

5. American literature began to emerge as a distinct literary tradition, an expression of a singular national character and sensibility, with the publication of such groundbreaking books as Perry Miller's *The New England Mind: From Colony to Province* (New York: Macmillan, 1939), F. O. Matthiessen's *American Renaissance: Art and Expression in the Age of Emerson and Whitman* (New York: Oxford University Press, 1941), and Alfred Kazin's *On Native Grounds: An Interpretation of Modern American Prose Literature* (New York: Harcourt, Brace & World, 1942).

6. M. H. Abrams, *The Mirror and the Lamp: Romantic Theory and the Critical Tradition* (New York: Oxford University Press, 1971; orig. pub., 1953).

7. For Abrams's account of literature as a fine art, see M. H. Abrams, "Art-as-Such: The Sociology of Modern Aesthetics," in *Doing Things with Texts* (New York: W. W. Norton, 1989), 135–58. For an account focusing more on sociology than aesthetics, see Pierre Bourdieu, *The Rules of Art: Genesis and Structure of the Literary Field*, trans. Susan Emanuel (Stanford, CA: Stanford University Press, 1996).

8. William Wordsworth, "Letter to John Wilson," in *Wordsworth's Literary Criticism*, ed. Nowell C. Smith (London: Humphrey Milford, 1905), 6.

9. John Stuart Mill, "Thoughts on Poetry and Its Varieties," in *Autobiography and Literary Essays by John Stuart Mill*, ed. John N. Robson and Jack Stillinger (Toronto: University of Toronto Press, 1981), 349.

10. Byron cited by Abrams, *Mirror and the Lamp*, 49.

11. Blake and Wordsworth quoted in Abrams, *Mirror and the Lamp*, 215, 214, respectively.

12. Samuel Taylor Coleridge, *Biographia Literaria*, quoted in Abrams, *Mirror and the Lamp*, 222, 224.

13. Samuel Taylor Coleridge, *Lectures 1808–1819: On Literature*, vol. 5 in *The Collected Works of Samuel Taylor Coleridge*, ed. R. A. Foakes (New York: Routledge & Kegan Paul, 1987), 495.

14. See Abrams, "Literature as a Revelation of Personality," chap. 9 in *Mirror and the Lamp*, 226–62.

15. The permanent openness of these questions is one of the fundamental premises of the modern humanistic disciplines. As Abrams says

elsewhere, the humanities "are those disciplines whose concern is with the areas of human action and production where valid knowledge is the aim, where a rational procedure is essential, but where certainty is impossible." M. H. Abrams, "The Language and Methods of Humanism," in Hook, Kurtz, and Todorovich, *Philosophy of the Curriculum*, 90. The question of meaning, and the openness of this question due to the inaccessibility of "intention" to empirical methods, becomes pertinent in all disciplines that see themselves as part of the modern humanities. As Panofsky wrote in "The History of Art as a Humanistic Discipline," the artist's intention "cannot be absolutely determined. In the first place, 'intentions' are *per se*, incapable of being defined with scientific precision. In the second place, the 'intentions' of those who produce objects are conditioned by the standard of their period and environment. . . . Finally our estimate of those 'intentions' is inevitably influenced by our own attitude" (18).

16. On the history of philology, see James Turner, *Philology: The Forgotten Origins of the Modern Humanities* (Princeton, NJ: Princeton University Press, 2014); Seth Lerer, ed., *Literary History and the Challenge of Philology: The Legacy of Eric Auerbach* (Stanford, CA: Stanford University Press, 1996); and Hans Ulrich Gumbrecht, *The Powers of Philology: Dynamics of Textual Scholarship* (Champaign: University of Illinois Press, 2003). In "Roots, Races, and the Return to Philology," I trace the connections between racial theorizing and philological investigation from the late eighteenth to the mid-twentieth centuries and document the various "returns to philology" that in recent years have been advocated as cleansing or chastening therapy for a degenerate discipline of literary study. Geoffrey Galt Harpham, "Roots, Races, and the Return to Philology," in *The Humanities and the Dream of America* (Chicago: University of Chicago Press, 2011), 43–79. It must be noted that while the philology-based pedagogy in the early twentieth-century college classroom was, in Graff's account, often conducted in a manner almost designed to numb the undergraduate mind, the discipline has also produced a number of truly remarkable cosmopolitan intellects, a distinguished genealogy extending from F. A. Wolf and the great scholars of the Germanic tradition, to E. R. Curtius, Leo Spitzer, and Erich Auerbach of the mid-twentieth century, and, more recently, Sheldon Pollock and Anthony Grafton.

17. On this point, see William Clark, *Academic Charisma and the Ori-*

gins of the Research University (Chicago: University of Chicago Press, 2006).

18. Ralph Waldo Emerson, entry for 20 April 1834, in *The Journals and Miscellaneous Notebooks of Ralph Waldo Emerson*, ed. Joel Porte (Cambridge, MA: Harvard University Press, 1982), 123.

19. Hiram Corson, "English at Cornell University," in *English in American Universities*, ed. William Morton Payne (Boston: D. C. Heath, 1895), 64. Interestingly, Corson's emphasis on speech was renewed recently by another distinguished Cornell professor, M. H. Abrams, who published in 2012 *The Fourth Dimension of a Poem* (New York: W. W. Norton, 2012), the dimension in question being "the activity of enunciating the great variety of speech-sounds that constitute the words of a poem" (2).

20. Hiram Corson, *The Voice and Spiritual Education* (New York: Macmillan, 1914; orig. pub., 1896), 71.

21. Bliss Perry, *The Amateur Spirit* (Boston: Houghton, Mifflin, 1904), 31.

22. Albert S. Cook, "English at Yale University," in Payne, *English in American Universities*, 39. The sense of an evangelical calling for English teachers was sustained through midcentury. The onetime New Humanist Norman Foerster wrote in 1941 that criticism should think of itself as an arduous remedy for the excesses of scientism, materialism, complacency, confusion, and all that assaults the dignity of man. Freedom and order, he wrote, depend on a practice of literary criticism that takes the form of a "religious renewal, or if that is beyond our attainment, a humanistic renewal of belief in man as a rational and free animal." Foerster, "The Esthetic Judgment and the Ethical Judgment," in *The Intent of the Critic*, ed. Donald A. Stauffer (New York: Bantam Books, 1966; orig. pub., 1941), 72.

23. Robert Maynard Hutchins, *Higher Learning in America* (New Brunswick, NJ: Transaction Publishers, 2009; orig. pub., 1936), 87.

24. William K. Wimsatt and Monroe Beardsley, "The Affective Fallacy," in *The Verbal Icon: Studies in the Meaning of Poetry*, by Wimsatt, in collaboration with Beardsley (Lexington: University of Kentucky Press, 1982; orig. pub., 1954), 29.

25. John Williams, *Stoner* (New York: New York Review of Books, 2006; orig. pub., 1965). This book acquired a belated currency when the novelist Ian McEwan mentioned it approvingly on the BBC's *Today Programme*, 5 July 2013.

26. René Wellek, "American Literary Scholarship," in *Concepts of Criticism* (New Haven, CT: Yale University Press, 1963), 304.

27. Martin Wright Sampson, "English at the University of Indiana," in Payne, *English in American Universities*, 92–98.

28. Matthew Arnold, "The Function of Criticism at the Present Time" (1864), in *Culture and Anarchy and Other Writings*, ed. Stefan Collini (Cambridge: Cambridge University Press, 1993), 50. In his capacious *A History of English Criticism* (New York: Dodd, Mead, n.d.), itself only a fragment of his massive multivolume *A History of Criticism and Literary Taste in Europe* (1900–1904), George Saintsbury appropriates this post-Arnoldian view, defining criticism as "the endeavour to find, to know, to love, to recommend, not only the best, but all the good, that has been known and thought and written in the world" (522). Saintsbury provides approving documentation of the modern rejection of neoclassical rules and principles of judgment in favor of a personal responsiveness. Despite a conversational tone and a florid late Victorian manner—he both promoted and occasionally exemplified the Arnoldian "Grand Style"—he was a voice for an independent institution of criticism based on the concept of the heterocosm: "That a work of art is entitled to be judged on its own merits or demerits, and not according as its specification does or does not happen to be previously entered and approved in an official schedule—this surely cannot but seem a gain to every one not absolutely blinded by prejudice" (518).

29. Jefferson Fletcher, "The President's Address: Our Opportunity," *PMLA* 30 (1915): lii.

30. Edwin Greenlaw, preface to *Literature and Life*, ed. Edwin Greenlaw, William. H. Elson, and Christine M. Keck (Chicago: Scott, Foresman, 1922), iii.

31. Ezra Pound, "This Hulme Business," *Townsman* 2, no. 2 (1939): 15, quoted in John Paul Russo, *I. A. Richards: His Life and Work* (Baltimore, MD: Johns Hopkins University Press, 1989), 30.

32. I. A. Richards, *Science and Poetry* (London: Kegan, Paul, Trench, Trubner, 1926), 82–83; 3rd ed., revised as *Poetries and Sciences, with a Reorientation and Notes* (New York: W. W. Norton, 1970). Quotations are from the 1926 edition.

33. I. A. Richards, *Practical Criticism: A Study of Literary Judgment* (New York: Harcourt, Brace, & World, 1969; orig. pub., 1929), 322.

34. Richards was himself deeply influenced by what became known as the Newbolt Report of 1921, which had argued for the centrality of

English in the curriculum of British schools. Commissioned in 1919, the Newbolt committee, which included Sir Arthur Quiller-Couch, advanced English as an instrument for instilling national consciousness and postwar national pride, goals shared by the Redbook committee. See *The Teaching of English in England* (London: His Majesty's Stationery Office, 1921). Richards cites the report on page 313 of *Practical Criticism*.

35. Daniel Bell sees the focus on the extraordinary professor as the unfortunate fate of the general education program at Harvard, where the emphasis in subsequent years fell "not on a common course . . . but on varied treatments of a subject by an outstanding figure. Not a 'great ideas' or 'great books' course, the Harvard program, in effect, became a 'great man' course." Bell, *The Reforming of General Education: The Columbia College Experience in Its National Setting* (New York: Columbia University Press, 1966), 48.

36. The principal author of the Redbook was the classicist John H. Finley Jr., but according to Russo, Richards's "hand, distinctive tone, subject matter, and allusion may be found all across the Redbook" (*I. A. Richards: His Life and Work*, 487; see 485–90). Russo includes among Richards's contributions to the Redbook the concept of the whole man and the conceptualization of the humanities, as well as references to "the lost art of conversation," the argument that the decline of the humanities began in the sixteenth century, and a proscription against excessive reliance on history that the committee consented to include despite the dissonance this created with "heritage."

37. I. A. Richards, *Principles of Literary Criticism* (London: Routledge, 2001; orig. pub., 1924), 7–13.

38. I. A. Richards, introduction to *The Republic of Plato, a Version in Simplified English*, trans. Richards (London: Kegan Paul, Trench, Trubner, 1948), 11. Richards also produced a Basic English version of *The Republic* for the Armed Services in 1942.

39. Richards acknowledged only with some reluctance and evident vexation the role of authorial intention in understanding the literary work. In *Practical Criticism*, he goes into some depth on questions of "intention" and "subjectivity"—sufficient depth that we can see how utterly depthless his understanding of these subjects is. In his account, intention is one of the four kinds of meaning (the others being sense, feeling, and tone), although it is "plainly . . . not on all fours with the others" (176). Intention serves as a governor or regulator, creating order

among the other kinds of meaning: we understand sense, feeling, and tone when we grasp the intention that produced them. Richards seems to find this inadequate, however, and revisits the subject in an appendix, where he concedes that intention is "a more puzzling function than the others" because, while it may seem that the other three kinds of meaning "cover the uses of language" so that nothing more is needed for understanding, intention "may assist our analysis" by introducing the notion of an "unsaid" element that "controls the relation among themselves of the other three functions" (334–35). For Richards, we may summarize, intention is a logical necessity in the production and understanding of language, not a historical fact linking the poem to the poet. And yet—in the introduction to his translation of Plato's *Republic*, he comments that the irritation many readers feel in reading this text "is something Plato intended us to feel" (8).

40. R. P. Blackmur, "A Critic's Job of Work," in *Language as Gesture* (New York: Harcourt, Brace, 1952), 391; Christopher Isherwood, *Lions and Shadows: An Education in the Twenties* (Norfolk, CT: New Directions, 1947), 121–22; Walter Jackson Bate, *Criticism: The Major Texts* (New York: Harcourt, Brace, 1952), 573; Allen Tate, "Literature as Knowledge," in *On the Limits of Poetry: Selected Essays, 1928–1948* (New York: Swallow and Morrow, 1948), 43. Eliot's influence on the academic field of criticism lay not in any contribution to method or theory—other, perhaps, than the appealing astringency of his antiexpressivist pronouncements on "impersonality"—but rather in the striking assurance of his taste, his genius for comparison, and his insistence that poetry formed an ideal order that should be judged by literary standards alone. He made his contribution in a series of remarkably authoritative brief essays, including "Tradition and the Individual Talent" (1919), "The Metaphysical Poets" (1921), and "The Function of Criticism" (1923), in which he argued that criticism ought properly to focus on "the elucidation of works of art and the correction of taste"—away from the Romantics and toward the Metaphysical poets. T. S. Eliot, "The Function of Criticism," in *Selected Essays, 1917–1932* (London: Faber & Faber, 1932), 13. While Eliot and Richards were, in the 1920s, often linked, they were not in agreement: Eliot argued that poetry represented a "fusion" of thought and feeling, while Richards insisted on a sharp distinction between the emotional state of the reader and the poetic stimulus that produced that state.

41. William Empson, *The Structure of Complex Words* (Cambridge, MA: Harvard University Press, 1989; orig. pub., 1947), v, 14–15.

42. William Empson, *Seven Types of Ambiguity*, 3rd ed. (New York: New Directions, 1966; orig. pub., 1930), 11. For a careful analysis of Empson's relation to Richards, see Russo, *I. A. Richards*, 525–34.

43. The most sustained demonstrations of the accreted character of language in Empson's oeuvre can be found in the discussions of such elemental words as "honest," "fool," "sense," and "dog" in *The Structure of Complex Words*.

44. Empson's final book was *Using Biography* (Cambridge, MA: Harvard University Press, 1985). Not all the essays in this collection "use biography," but several make the case that biography is entirely and legitimately usable, and in fact inescapable. Empson's target is often what he calls "the Wimsatt Law" that declares that the author's intention is not available to the critic and should therefore not be sought. I argue later in this section that this "law" is actually far more flexible and open to an intentionalist argument—more, in this respect, Empsonian— than Empson suggests.

45. Empson to Philip Hobsbaum, 2 August 1969, cited in John Haffenden, introduction to *Argufying: Essays on Literature and Culture*, by William Empson (Iowa City: University of Iowa Press, 1987), 21.

46. One who might have been, if not a disciple, at least a devoted advocate was Christopher Norris. But when the young Norris asked the elderly Empson to contribute a comment to a book—the first— identifying and celebrating Empson's contribution to criticism, Empson, taking offense at small issues and omissions, composed instead an attack on the book and on any who might be disposed to admire it. His abrupt, ill-tempered note was duly printed as a postscript to Norris's *William Empson and the Philosophy of Literary Criticism* (London: Athlone Press, 1978), 205–6. Norris's first chapter, "Empson and Present-Day Criticism: A Chapter of Misunderstandings," tracks Empson's "increasing interest in authorial 'intention'" (27).

47. This is not to say that the American New Critics admired Empson, or he them. His activist and invasive interpretive method could not be reconciled to an approach that treated the poem as a "verbal icon" available for passive contemplation. And his insistent unraveling of poetic contradictions or ambiguities often seemed, from a New Critical perspective, a misguided effort to rationalize and reduce poetry

to prosaic argumentation or, worse, an anarchic proliferation of unrelated possibilities. Empson's open-minded practice provided a model not for New Critical orthodoxy but for the generally unstressed concessions to biography and intentions discussed later in this section.

48. Russo includes an extended if touchy and defensive account of Richards's influence on the New Critics, who, Russo argues, took all their ideas from Richards and then ungratefully "cut [him] down to their size" (*I. A. Richards*, 542; see 540–62).

49. John Crowe Ransom, *The New Criticism* (Norfolk, CT: New Directions, 1941). It should be noted that none of the critics Ransom focused on in this book—Richards, T. S. Eliot, and Ivor Winters— identified themselves as "New Critics."

50. John Crowe Ransom, "Criticism, Inc.," *Virginia Quarterly Review* 13, no. 4 (1937), reprinted in Ransom, *The World's Body* (Baton Rouge: Louisiana State University Press, 1965; orig. pub., 1938), 327–50.

51. Ransom, *World's Body*, 329 ("scientific"), 342 ("nature of the object"); John Crowe Ransom, "Wanted: An Ontological Critic," in *The New Criticism*, 279–336 ("ontological"); John Crowe Ransom, "Criticism as Pure Speculation," in Stauffer, *Intent of the Critic*, 78 ("attend to"). Ransom's call for a "scientific" criticism signals an equivocation in the position of the New Critics, many of whom denounced the secular, soulless amorality of science even while trying to fashion a practice of literary criticism that could compete with science in the professionalized scholarly world of the university.

52. As Catherine Gallagher has written, Ransom "comes up with the brilliant stroke of accusing philology of *under*specialization.... Never before had the philologists been challenged on their own professional high ground." Gallagher, "The History of Literary Criticism," in *American Academic Culture in Transformation*, ed. Thomas Bender and Carl E. Schorske (Princeton, NJ: Princeton University Press, 1997), 154.

53. Another aspect of Ransom's thought that has not mellowed into forgivability with the passing of time is his attitude toward women. The longest essay in *The World's Body*, "The Poet as Woman" (76–110), is devoted to Edna St. Vincent Millay. In general, Ransom feels that Millay's attempts to be a female poet represent a failed experiment that resulted in regrettable deficiencies. The woman poet, Ransom says, is "safer as a biological organism" than a man and therefore likely to be "indifferent to intellectuality ... moreso than a man. Miss Millay is rarely and barely very intellectual, and"—he adds, gratuitously—"I think every-

body knows it" (78). This limitation of sympathy was not Ransom's alone, but was largely shared by the entire Modernist cadre of artists and intellectuals. In fairness, however, *The World's Body* also contains a warmly appreciative review of books by Alexei Tolstoi and Rebecca West, "Contemporaneous Not Contemporary" (261–69).

54. W. K. Wimsatt and Monroe Beardsley, "The Intentional Fallacy," in *Verbal Icon*, 3.

55. Wimsatt and Beardsley, "Intentional Fallacy," 5 ("object of public knowledge"); Wimsatt and Beardsley, "Affective Fallacy," 21 ("object of specifically critical").

56. W. K. Wimsatt and Cleanth Brooks, *Literary Criticism: A Short History* (New York: Alfred A. Knopf, 1964); René Wellek and Austin Warren, *Theory of Literature* (New York: Harcourt, Brace, & World, 1956; orig. pub., 1942), 50.

57. The case for considering poetry as speech is made most suggestively by a New Critical outlier, Reuben Arthur Brower, in two essays in *The Fields of Light* (Philadelphia: Paul Dry Books, 2013; orig. pub., 1951): "The Speaking Voice" (19–30) and "The Figure of Sound" (58–74). Brower published little, but exerted an extraordinary influence through his teaching at Harvard, where his younger colleagues and course assistants included Edward Said, Neil Hertz, Richard Poirier, Paul Alpers, and Paul de Man.

58. Cleanth Brooks, "Literary Criticism: Marvell's 'Horatian Ode,'" in *Literary Criticism: Idea and Act. The English Institute, 1939–72, Selected Essays*, ed. W. K. Wimsatt (Berkeley: University of California Press, 1974), 440.

59. Cleanth Brooks, *The Well Wrought Urn: Studies in the Structure of Poetry* (San Diego, CA: Harcourt Brace Jovanovich, 1975; orig. pub., 1947).

60. Wimsatt attacked the Chicago School (R. S. Crane, Norman Maclean, Elder Olson, Richard McKeon) in *The Verbal Icon* for treating the poem as an "artificial thing" rather than, as he recommended, "a human act, physical and mental. The only 'thing,'" he said, "is the poet speaking" (50).

61. In *Theory of Literature*, Wellek and Warren list Richards among those suffering "delusions" about the power of science to explain everything: "Thus, I. A. Richards used to refer to the future triumphs of neurology as insuring the solutions of all literary problems" (16). Richards was attacked both for his antisubjective severity and for deviations from

that severity. Wimsatt flushes out a lapse into humanism in Richards's treatment of H. D. and Ella Wheeler Wilcox in *Principles of Literary Criticism*, where Richards argues that the mediocrity of these poets derives from a failure to communicate the valuable experience in the poet's mind in the first instance, and success in communicating a trite and inconsequential state of mind in the second. Wimsatt calls this "an especially mysterious instance of 'intentionalistic' interpretation" (*Verbal Icon*, 244).

62. Others associated with the New Critical camp made their own accommodations to perspectivism. Compare, for example, T. S. Eliot: "The critic . . . should endeavour to discipline his personal prejudices and cranks . . . and compose his differences with as many of his fellows as possible, in the common pursuit of true judgement" ("Function of Criticism," 25).

63. Cleanth Brooks and Robert Penn Warren, *Understanding Poetry* (New York: Holt, Rinehart, and Winston, 1938). Catherine Gallagher says this work was partially responsible for the feeling among students in the 1960s that literature as taught in the university was "a chastened, disillusioned, middle-aged response to a constantly threatening world. The relentless pessimism of the works selected for analysis in Cleanth Brooks's and Robert Penn Warren's widely-used book, *Understanding Poetry* (1938), for example . . . could give the unpleasant sensation that one was being encouraged to adopt a coping strategy of mild depression." Gallagher, "History of Literary Criticism," 163. In addition to *Understanding Poetry*, Brooks and Warren published *An Approach to Literature* (1936), *Understanding Fiction* (1943), and *Modern Rhetoric* (1949), as well as *American Literature: The Makers and the Making* (with R. W. B. Lewis, 1973). For invaluable insight into this creative collaboration, see James A. Grimshaw, ed., *Cleanth Brooks and Robert Penn Warren: A Literary Correspondence* (Columbia: University of Missouri Press, 1998).

64. This appraisal is stated as a "general belief" by Thomas W. Cutrer, in *Parnassus on the Mississippi: The "Southern Review" and the Baton Rouge Literary Community, 1935–1942* (Baton Rouge, LA: Louisiana State University Press, 1984), 186. According to another historian, "*Understanding Poetry* . . . codified many of the so-called New Critical ideas into a coherent approach to literary study. Their [Brooks and Warren's] book . . . revolutionized the teaching of literature in the universities and spawned a host of imitators who dominated English departments

well into the 1960s." Charles Bohner, "Robert Penn Warren's Life and Career," accessed 25 May 2016, http://www.english.illinois.edu/maps /poets/s_z/warren/life.htm.

65. Cleanth Brooks and Robert Penn Warren, *Understanding Poetry*, 4th ed. (New York: Holt, Rinehart, and Winston, 1976), 9, 15.

66. See Brooks and Warren, "How Poems Come About: Intention and Meaning," appendix A to *Understanding Poetry* (1976), 464–92. Like the Romantics, Brooks and Warren turn to the unconscious as the ultimate source of intention: "If the unconscious is, as Coleridge says, the genius in the man of genius, it is still far from independent of the conscious; both the conscious and the unconscious are of the same man" (475). The "unconscious" factors cited by Brooks and Warren are more formal than Freudian, and more concerned with the creation of the poem than with issues peculiar to the poet's psyche. As the poem is being written, the process of testing, judging, and experimentation eventually produces a kind of protopoem that begins to hang together in its own way, with parts relating to each other and to the whole, so that at some point a kind of formal integrity emerges that may be attributed to the poet but really belongs to the poem itself—and is in that respect "unconscious."

67. M. H. Abrams and Geoffrey Galt Harpham, *A Glossary of Literary Terms*, 10th ed. (Boston: Cengage, 2012), 184. Given the dependence of irony on intention, it may be questioned whether irony is a linguistic feature or a feature of the relationship between language and the language user.

68. Russo, *I. A. Richards*, 559. The fullest treatment of the political values and cultural criticism of the New Critics is Mark Jancovich, *The Cultural Politics of the New Criticism* (Cambridge: Cambridge University Press, 1993). Jancovich focuses on Ransom, Allen Tate, and Robert Penn Warren, arguing that while the New Criticism, especially in its early years, strongly appeared to be socially and politically reactionary, it also had "the potential to produce a radical and socially engaged criticism" (135). This potential, as Jancovich wisely concedes, was not always realized in practice.

69. A further irony is attached to the fact that much of the importance of the New Criticism derived from the centrality of English in the general education model in which the by-then-disavowed Richards had played such a central role. The primary institutional beneficiaries of his work were those who rejected him as an extremist.

70. Claude Lèvi-Strauss, *The Savage Mind* (Chicago: University of Chicago Press, 1966; orig. pub., 1962), 247.

71. For Derrida, see, for example, *Of Grammatology* (1967), trans. Gayatri Chakravorty Spivak (Baltimore, MD: Johns Hopkins University Press, 1976), 65–73, 183–84. Roland Barthes, "The Death of the Author" (1967), trans. Richard Howard, pp. 1–6, UbuWeb / UbuWeb Papers, accessed 25 May 2016, http://www.ubu.com/aspen/aspen5and6 /threeEssays.html#barthes. This translation is superior to the better-known translation that appeared in Roland Barthes, *Image Music Text*, ed. and trans. Stephen Heath (New York: Hill and Wang, 1977), 142–48. For Michel Foucault, see *The Order of Things: An Archeology of the Human Sciences* (New York: Vintage Books, 1970), 342–43, 386.

72. See Roland Barthes, "Writing and Revolution," in *Writing Degree Zero*, in *"Writing Degree Zero" [1953] and "Elements of Semiology" [1964]*, trans. Annette Lavers and Colin Smith (Boston: Beacon Press, 1968), 77–73; and *Mythologies* (1957), trans. Annette Lavers (New York: Hill and Wang, 1972), 145–48. See also Julia Kristeva, *Revolution in Poetic Language* (New York: Columbia University Press, 1984; orig. pub., 1974).

73. Walter Benjamin, "On Language as Such and on the Language of Man" (1916), in *Selected Writings*, vol. 1, *1913–1926*, ed. Marcus Bullock and Michael W. Jennings (Cambridge, MA: Belknap Press of Harvard University Press, 1996), 66; Martin Heidegger, "Language" (orig. pub., 1959, based on a lecture given in 1950), in *Poetry, Language, Thought*, trans. Albert Hofstadter (New York: Harper Colophon Books, 1971), 191; and Teodor Adorno, "On Lyric Poetry and Society," in *Notes to Literature* (1958), vol. 1, ed. Rolf Tiedemann, trans. Shierry Weber Nicholsen (New York: Columbia University Press, 1991), 43.

74. On this tendency, see Harpham, *Language Alone*, 44–57.

75. See Paul de Man, *Allegories of Reading: Figural Language in Rousseau, Nietzsche, Rilke, and Proust* (New Haven, CT: Yale University Press, 1978). "Actual language," he says in this book, "has invented the conceptual term 'man,'" (153). As Stanley Corngold has commented, de Man is "a great philosopher of the inhuman condition." Corngold, "On Paul de Man's Collaborationist Writings," in *Responses to Paul de Man's Wartime Journalism*, ed. Werner Hamacher, Neil Hertz, and Thomas Keenan (Lincoln: University of Nebraska Press, 1989), 83. For a critical account of the widespread tendency to regard language as a machine, see Roy G. Harris, *The Language Machine* (London: Duckworth, 1987).

76. See Jonathan Culler, *Structuralist Poetics: Structuralism, Linguis-*

tics, and the Study of Literature (Ithaca, NY: Cornell University Press, 1975), esp. 114–30. See also Jonathan Culler, "Beyond Interpretation," in *The Pursuit of Signs* (Ithaca, NY: Cornell University Press, 1981), 3–17; and Jonathan Culler, introduction to *Theory of the Lyric* (Cambridge, MA: Harvard University Press, 2015), 1–9.

77. Fredric Jameson, "Metacommentary" (1971), in *Situations of Theory*, vol. 1 of 2, *Ideologies of Theory: Essays 1971–1986*, Theory and History of Literature 48 (Minneapolis, MN: University of Minnesota Press, 1988), 3. Jameson's essay appeared between the publication of two books by E. D. Hirsch that were among the most authoritative statements of the argument Jameson was declaring to be discredited. Although trained at Yale under Brooks and Wimsatt, Hirsch took issue with the (reductive account of the) New Critical position on the autonomy of the text, arguing that the primary issue in literary study was meaning, to which the author's intention was the only reliable guide. See Hirsch, *Validity in Interpretation* (New Haven, CT: Yale University Press, 1967); and Hirsch, *Aims of Interpretation* (Chicago: University of Chicago Press, 1976).

78. It is difficult to substantiate any statement at this level of generalization, but for an example of an argument that exemplifies all the characterizations of advanced criticism of the 1980s in this paragraph, see Annette Kolodny, "Dancing through the Minefield: Some Observations on the Theory, Practice, and Politics of a Feminist Literary Criticism," *Feminist Studies* 6, no. 1 (Spring 1980): 1–25. Situating feminist criticism within a larger feminist movement based on the premise of a unified feminine "subculture," Kolodny proposes a reading protocol focusing not on authorial intention, which she explicitly rejects, but on the discovery of "power relations," typically, those in which "males wield various forms of influence over females." The goal of reading is not to arrive at the truth, but to contribute to "the reordering of the present and future." For this reason, Kolodny argues for a "pluralist" approach to reading and interpretation that admits the potential legitimacy even of currently unpopular or out-of-favor conclusions, such as hers (10, 20).

79. Walter Benn Michaels, *Our America: Nativism, Modernism, and Pluralism* (Durham, NC: Duke University Press, 1997).

80. Steven Knapp and Walter Benn Michaels, "Against Theory" (1982, in *Critical Inquiry*), in *Against Theory: Literary Studies and the New Pragmatism*, ed. W. J. T. Mitchell (Chicago: University of Chicago Press, 1985), 11–30. See also Steven Knapp and Walter Benn Michaels,

"Against Theory 2: Hermeneutics and Deconstruction," *Critical Inquiry* 14, no. 1 (1987): 49–68.

81. One might conclude from the argument in "Against Theory" that the authors favored an approach to literature grounded in the interpretive determination of authorial intent. This is not true. Michaels, at least, has been rejecting such an approach for many years now, arguing against any form of interpretation that engages the reader's feelings or emotions, and in favor of works of art that defy or rebuff interpretation. Such works, he argues, help us think about class exploitation, which, unlike various forms of social discrimination, is not ameliorated when people change their feelings. See Michaels, *The Shape of the Signifier* (Princeton, NJ: Princeton University Press, 2004), esp. 51–81; and Michaels, *The Beauty of a Social Problem* (Chicago: University of Chicago Press, 2016).

82. Under the extreme stress of this discovery, deconstruction itself seemed to buckle, adopting an "American" emphasis on authorial intention. In his agonized reading of the most incriminating of de Man's articles, Jacques Derrida insisted on the possibility that de Man, by criticizing "vulgar antisemitism" without mentioning any other kind, actually intended to criticize "antisemitism *itself inasmuch as* it is vulgar, always and essentially vulgar," adding, "If that is what he thought, a possibility I will never exclude, he could not say so clearly in this context" (a collaborationist publication). Jacques Derrida, "Like the Sound of the Sea Deep within a Shell: Paul de Man's War" (1988, in *Critical Inquiry*), in *Mémoires: For Paul de Man*, trans. Cecile Lindsay, Jonathan Culler, Eduardo Cadava, and Peggy Kamuf (New York: Columbia University Press, 1989): 206.

83. Stanley Fish, *Versions of Antihumanism: Milton and Others* (Cambridge: Cambridge University Press, 2012), 1.

84. Gordon Teskey, *The Poetry of John Milton* (Cambridge, MA: Harvard University Press, 2015), xiv.

85. Milton's influence was indirect and mediated by the Radical Whigs. See Bernard Bailyn, *The Ideological Origins of the American Revolution* (Cambridge, MA: Harvard University Press, 1992; orig. pub., 1967), 34, 45. In *The Hebrew Republic: Jewish Sources and the Transformation of European Political Thought* (Cambridge, MA: Harvard University Press, 2010), Eric Nelson argues persuasively that "republican exclusivism"—the notion that democratic elections are the only legiti-

mate basis for government—came from Milton, who drew it from the Bible and the Talmud.

POSTSCRIPT

1. Michael Walzer, *What It Means to Be an American: Essays on the American Experience* (New York: Marsilio, 1992), 48.

2. A list of such movements would include, very briefly, neuroaesthetics, Darwinian literary criticism, all "cognitive" approaches, "distant" reading, and all computational approaches. All of these have the effect of bending the humanistic discipline of literary study in the direction of science or social science, all marginalize the figure of the author, and none seeks to advance knowledge through the close reading or interpretation of individual works. To be sure, some advocates of these movements promise an eventual return to a more humanistic mode, but whether this return would still be feasible after the proposed excursus into deindividualization and quantification may be questioned.

Index

Lightning Source UK Ltd.
Milton Keynes UK
UKHW02f1014181117
312893UK00006B/229/P

"In this vitally important and timely new book, the celebrated critic Geoffrey Galt Harpham recovers the promise of the humanities in American higher education. He shows how interpreting texts has long been inseparable from democratic aspirations, and why English became the central humanistic discipline, the site of these aspirations, in the United States. Brilliantly conceived and beautifully written, *What Do You Think, Mr. Ramirez?* makes a powerful case for reviving a model of general education centered in the humanities."

John Stauffer, Harvard University

Geoffrey Galt Harpham's book takes its title from a telling anecdote. Harpham once met a Cuban immigrant who told him of arriving, penniless and undocumented, in the 1960s, earning a GED, and eventually making his way to a community college. In a literature course one day, the professor asked him, "Mr. Ramirez, what do *you* think?" The question, he told Harpham, changed his life: realizing that his opinion of a text had value set him on a course to becoming a distinguished professor.

That, says Harpham, was the midcentury promise of general education. A deep current of commitment and aspiration undergirded America's educational system in the postwar years, and is under extended assault today. The United States was founded, Harpham argues, on the idea that interpreting its foundational documents was the highest calling of opinion. For a brief moment at midcentury, the country turned to English teachers as the people best able to train students to thrive as interpreters—which is to say as citizens of a democracy. Tracing the roots of that belief in the humanities through American history, Harpham builds a strong case that the educational values animating the midcentury university are a resource we can, and should, draw on today.

GEOFFREY GALT HARPHAM is a senior fellow of the Kenan Institute for Ethics at Duke University and former director of the National Humanities Center. He is the author of nine books, including, most recently, *The Humanities and the Dream of America*.

The University of Chicago Press

www.press.uchicago.edu

ISBN-13: 978-0-226-48081-7
ISBN-10: 0-226-48081-X

9 780226 480817

90000

Cover photo: Lee Avison